ALFRED'S ESSENTIALS OF
JAZZ THEORY

A Complete Self-Study Course for all Musicians

■ Shelton G. Berg

FOREWORD

MUSIC IS THE MORTAR OF HUMANITY. It binds people of all backgrounds and experiences, as it poignantly expresses universal human emotions. It is an amazing and elusive complement to our existence. And yet, this spiritual art form is rooted in concepts that are easily explained in the practical realm. Music theory is the study of these concepts. The yin and yang of music results from the fact that it is created out of a limited supply of simple, theoretical formulas, and yet, any piece of music can be entirely unique.

When a musician composes or improvises, the material emanates from two creative wells. There is the "spiritual" well, which houses our emotions and experiences, and also the "technical" well, in which resides the theoretical elements that we have practiced and perfected. Music is at its best when the impetus is from the spiritual well. The technical well will be unconsciously called upon to provide the raw materials of expression. So, a study of theory is not merely a dry analysis of technical functions, but rather an exploration of how the elements can provide fuel to the creative process, an energizing activity toward the goal of meaningful music making.

WELCOME TO JAZZ—welcome to an exhilarating journey to musical freedom!—Shelly Berg

To successfully navigate this jazz theory course, you should be versed in basic music theory concepts, such as those taught in Books 1 and 2 of *Alfred's Essentials of Music Theory*. You are encouraged to play and/or sing the examples in this text, at first along with the enclosed recording, and then on your own.

BOOKS 1, 2, 3: *Alfred's Essentials of Jazz Theory* is made up of three books, 40 pages each, with each book containing six units. A unit consists of four or five pages of instructional material (including written exercises), an Ear Training page and a Review page.

COMPLETE BOOK: *Alfred's Essentials of Jazz Theory* is also available as one complete book of 120 pages that contains all the pages included in the separate books.

COMPACT DISCS: Each book in *Alfred's Essentials of Jazz Theory* is packaged with a CD, allowing students to hear the musical elements discussed, and offering students the opportunity to test their listening skills. Music examples are played by a variety of instruments.

TEACHER'S ANSWER KEY: A *Complete Book* with the answers for the exercises from the Lesson and Review pages and music for the Ear Training pages.

Alfred Publishing Co., Inc.
16320 Roscoe Blvd., Suite 100
P.O. Box 10003
Van Nuys, CA 91410-0003
alfred.com

Copyright © 2006 by Alfred Publishing Co., Inc.
All rights reserved. Printed in USA.
ISBN-10: 0-7390-4385-4
ISBN-13: 978-0-7390-4385-1

TABLE OF CONTENTS Book 1

Review of Basic Music Elements

Music is an intermingling of primary elements that include MELODY, HARMONY, and RHYTHM, and can be said to exist with the singular presence of any of the three. There are also secondary elements, chief among which are TEXTURE and FORM.

MELODY is that musical element that we sing alone. It is a succession of pitches, made memorable by contour and repetition. Melody is a linear (horizontal) musical element.

HARMONY results when two or more pitches (musical notes) are sounded simultaneously. Harmony is a vertical musical element, although it can be implied by melodic construction. The music explored in this jazz text concerns harmonies organized into CHORDS, which are consonant (pleasing) combinations of notes.

RHYTHM refers to the placement of notes in time, and their relationship to a beat (pulse). Rhythm is a linear element and is the propulsive engine of melody and harmony.

While melody, harmony and rhythm combine to give music its linear and vertical dimensions, it is TEXTURE that provides an aural dimension of "depth." Texture refers to how musical voices are combined into melodic and accompaniment components.

Among textures there is COUNTERPOINT, which is the simultaneous occurrence of two or more melodic voices. In jazz music, there typically exists a counterpoint between melody and bass.

FORM is the organization of musical statements and themes. Form is the "roadmap" of music, and it allows the listener to follow the journey.

Exercises

Track I

1 Listen to the three excerpts of CD Track 1 and describe the rhythm for each:

    a. Repeated / Varied   **b.** Driving / Calm   **c.** Syncopated (jerky) / Even

2 This excerpt has a form consisting of four musical statements. The first statement (phrase) is labeled "A" and the second is labeled "B." Label the third and fourth statements, using either the letter "A" or "C" for each.

Swing Feel & Swing Eighth Notes

The elements of music as we know them have been used in much the same way for the past four hundred years. So it is STYLE that gives any piece of music its unique imprint. Style refers to the characteristic usage of melodic, harmonic, rhythmic and textural building blocks. After all, Mozart and Dizzy Gillespie created music from virtually the same elements, yet their styles differ widely.

JAZZ is unique among Western art music styles, because it is both a composed and an improvised art. Jazz is an amalgam of elements thrown together in the "stew" of Americanism that existed at the turn of the 20th century which is why it is referred to as "America's only original musical art form." Jazz musicians developed their own harmonies, melodic gestures and rhythmic devices – even the basic subdivision of the beat is unique to jazz. Jazz is known for "blues" influences, syncopation, and most of all, swing.

SWING is an interpretation of eighth notes with a triplet subdivision, in which the first 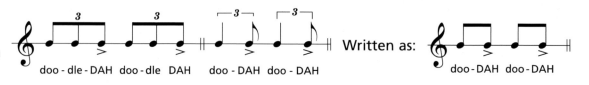 eighth note of each beat has two-thirds of that beat's value. The second eighth note, although occupying only one third of the beat, is more often accentuated and articulated.

The example below shows a melody in typical notation, followed by the notation of how it would sound when interpreted by a jazz musician. For instance, wind players typically tongue the off-beat eighth note.

* In swing feel, quarter notes are played short unless otherwise indicated.

Exercises

Track 2
1 Play CD Track 2 and chant "doodle-DAH" and then "doo-DAH" underneath the melody.

2 Rewrite the following example as it would *sound* if played in swing style:

Swing Groove

"It don't mean a thing, if it ain't got that swing!"—Duke Ellington

Another factor in achieving swing is GROOVE. Groove is a constant energy funneled into subdivision. In some way, all great performances "groove," whether Bach or Basie. The element of groove that produces swing is the concept of 2 AND 4.

In classical music in $\frac{4}{4}$ time, the agogic (natural) accent almost always falls on beats 1 and 3.

In jazz, beats 1 and 3 are where harmonic changes typically occur, but the "feel" of the music has an infectious sense of FORWARD MOMENTUM derived from an underlying stress of BEATS 2 AND 4.

As a result, jazz musicians almost always snap their fingers or clap hands on 2 and 4. Also, most drummers play the hi-hat cymbal by stepping down on the pedal on 2 and 4. Jazz teachers often recommend practicing with the metronome beats indicating 2 and 4.

ENERGY is of equal importance, because this is the element that "casts the spell" of music. Swing style will feel subtly different if the energy is happy, excited, bluesy, or agitated. Swing music grooves when energy is channeled into the triplet. So, even if eighths are played evenly, the internal voice of the soloist is thinking the underlying triplet (and usually, so is the drummer!).

Track 3
In swing feel, eighth notes are played more evenly as tempo increases. At a quarter note value of 200 bpm, eighth notes are very uniform. In addition, many contemporary jazz musicians play eighth notes evenly at moderate tempos. In these instances, swing articulation, often initiated off the beat, enhances the swing feel of even eighth notes. Conversely, "The Mickey Mouse Club Theme" and Sousa's "Washington Post" have triplet subdivisions, but they are **not** in swing feel. CD Track 3 demonstrates a more even, yet still swinging interpretation of the melody from CD Track 2.

Exercises

1 *Dig it!*—Play the "2 & 4" melody above, first without a constant energy, and then with different kinds of constant energy. What do you notice?

2 *Dig it!*—Play one of the melody examples from Lesson 2 with the metronome indicating half notes on beats 1 and 3, then on 2 and 4. You should notice that having the metronomic emphasis on beats 2 and 4 promotes a swing feeling.

Mm. ♩ = 60

1   2   3   4

Jazz Melody & Improvisation—Syncopation, Bebop Style

IMPROVISATION, or spontaneous composition, is a signature element of jazz—in fact, improvisation is such an essential ingredient of jazz performance that without it, the music really isn't jazz. The jazz language for composed melody and improvised melody is basically the same, with composed melody naturally exhibiting a greater degree of organization. This text focuses principally on the melodic language of the improviser.

A constant virtue of jazz melody is the use of SYNCOPATION, which is an off-beat (second-half of a beat) accentuation. Syncopation in 4/4 time—standard for most jazz music—occurs when: 1) an eighth note is played on the second-half of a beat followed by a rest, 2) a note of a quarter note value or longer is played on the second-half of a beat, 3) two or more notes are played on successive off-beats.

Ragtime artists, the progenitors of jazz, created the earliest "jazzy" music with what they called "ragging" march or hymn tunes, in which they syncopated some of the rhythms.

Track 4

In the 1940s, BEBOP music (originated by Charlie Parker, Dizzy Gillespie, and others) literally burst onto the jazz scene, and its impact indelibly changed jazz melody. Since then, jazz soloists have exhibited great technical virtuosity. Now, improvised jazz melody in swing feel often moves in eighth notes, triplets, and sixteenth notes. Bebop melody is unpredictable. Phrases are unpredictable in length, as is the placement of accents, which often occur off the beat, offset by the occasional on-beat. Bebop melodies also feature frequent and sudden skips and changes of direction.

Exercises

1 Re-write this melody in a "rag" style, adding syncopation:

Track 5

2 Listen to CD Track 5 as you read the following solo melody in a bebop-influenced style. What bebop characteristics do you notice?

3 Circle the instances of syncopation in the melody above (CD Track 5).

4 Write a melody in the bebop style:

Jazz Melody & Improvisation – Lick, Line and Melodic Soloing

A well conceived jazz SOLO (improvisation) balances the elements of lick, line and melodic soloing. A LICK (*motive* in classical music) is a brief melodic cell, made memorable by repetition. Early arrangements of the Count Basie Orchestra and some of Duke Ellington's tunes are based on a lick (e.g., "In a Mellow Tone"). Licks lend unity and familiarity to a melody, and often evoke a feeling of blues (see Unit 6).

A lick can be repeated over different harmonies to build tension and excitement.

A lick can also be varied to inject an element of surprise.

In jazz soloing, a LINE is a melody of one measure or longer, and moving in eighth notes or faster values. Jazz lines exhibit a spectrum, from THROUGH-COMPOSED (never repeating an idea) to ORGANIC (building on small ideas).

TENSION AND RELEASE play a vital role in the impact and emotion of music. A repeated lick, for instance, builds tension, and a sense of release is felt when the lick gives way to a more extended jazz line.

MELODIC SOLOING refers to playing phrases that sound more like a new song than a solo. These ideas move primarily in quarter notes or slower values. A melodic phrase is cohesive, with a short idea repeated and varied until it suggests the next idea. Poignant music results from this type of improvising, which is pure, spontaneous composition. This melodic solo is to the beginning of the chord progression from Billy Strayhorn's "Take the 'A' Train."

Exercises

1 *Dig It!*—As you listen to the CD, sing the melody to "Take the 'A' Train." Is it complemented by the solo melody?

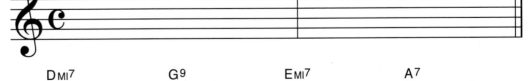

2 Compose a lick.

3 Designate the lick, line, and melodic soloing passages in the spaces provided.

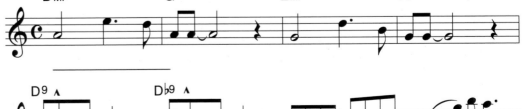

Track 10

1 You will hear 4 melodies. Indicate for each whether it is played in "swing" or "non-swing" style.

a. swing / non-swing   **b.** swing / non-swing   **c.** swing / non-swing   **d.** swing / non-swing

Track 11

2 You will hear the same melody played correctly twice, but only once with a sense of groove. Identify which performance grooves, by circling the correct answer.

a.   **b.**

Track 12

3 The recording of the following melody is altered by the usage of syncopation. Notate the melody as altered on the recording.

Track 13

4 The recorded track is a melody in the bebop style. Count the number of a) phrases, b) sudden changes of direction, c) syncopated notes, and d) unpredictable accents.

a. _____ phrases   **b.** _____ direction changes

c. _____ syncopations   **d.** _____ unpredictable accents

Track 14

5 Listen to the lick on the recording. How many times is it played before it is varied?

_____ times.

Track 15

6 Is the recorded excerpt exhibiting mostly "line" or "melodic soloing?"

Line / melodic soloing

1 This melody is notated in a standard way. Re-write it as it would sound in jazz performance.

2 This melody is notated as it would sound in jazz. Re-write it in standard notation.

3 "Rag" the following melody with syncopation.

4 "Un-rag" the melody by removing syncopation.

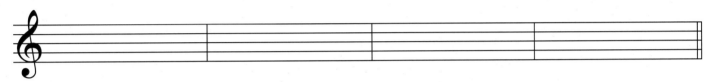

5 Bebop melodies are characterized by

_____

phrase lengths and accents.

6 Off-beat accentuation is also called

_____ .

7 _____ is a constant energy channeled into subdivision. The subdivision of swing is the

_____ .

8 Compose two variations to this lick.

9 Well-conceived jazz solos balance the elements of_____, _____,

and _____ _____ .

UNIT 2 **Lesson 6**

Major Triad, Major Scale, Consonance

Virtually everyone knows the sound of a MAJOR CHORD. It is the "-men" at the end of "Amen" in hymns. It is the sound that ends nearly any "happy" song and it is the TONIC, or "home" chord of every major key. As a review, CHORDS are constructed by stacking notes a 3rd apart and occupy every other line or every other space on a staff. A 3-note chord is called a TRIAD.

A MAJOR TRIAD can be constructed using the 1st, 3rd and 5th notes of any major scale, and we call those tones the root, third and fifth of the chord, respectively. The intervals in major triad are a Major 3rd (M3) from root to third, a minor 3rd (m3) from third to fifth, and a perfect 5th (P5) from root to fifth.

C Major Scale

The 1st and 2nd INVERSIONS of a major triad result from placing the 3rd and 5th of the chord respectively as the bottom note. By the way, when the root is on the bottom it is called ROOT POSITION.

Root position   1st inversion   2nd inversion

CONSONANCE is the occurrence of pleasing-sounding (consonant) notes throughout a melody. A consonant note is typically one that is found in the chord:

Exercises

1 Write the following major scales and triads (in root position and both inversions).

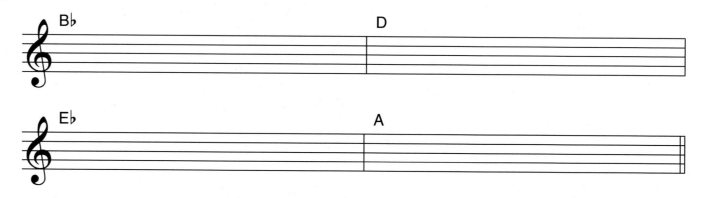

2 Circle the consonant tones in the following melody:

Major Seventh Chords (MA⁷, Δ⁷), *Chord Changes*

One of the distinctive features of the jazz language is the ubiquitous use of CHORD EXTENSIONS, such as 7ths, 9ths and beyond. Earlier musical genres used extended chords sparingly, and most often as unstable sounds, requiring resolution into triads. In jazz, chords with extensions are often considered to be consonant. They are staple harmonies that contribute to the exotic richness of jazz music.

The MAJOR SEVENTH CHORD adds the 7th note of the scale above the major triad. Since chords are a result of stacking 3rds, the chord 7th is the next 3rd in the chain, in this case a M3 above the fifth of the chord (also the interval of M7 above the root). Adding a 7th to a chord has a profound effect on the sound, which can be described as mellower, more emotional, or more exotic.

Major seventh chords have three inversions.

Root position   1st inversion   2nd inversion   3rd inversion

In jazz vernacular, the CHANGES are the chords of the song. The "game" of being an improviser is to create a line that lands on a consonant tone each time the chord changes. So each new chord is referred to as a chord change, or CHANGE.

Exercises

1 Construct the indicated scales and MA⁷ chords and their inversions.

D♭MA⁷

EMA⁷

Track 17

2 *Dig it!*—CD Track 17 begins with an F major triad played by the pianist over a bass line and swing drum feel. After a few bars, the seventh is added to the chord. You can hear how much richer the sound becomes, and this is the richness of jazz! In what bar is the seventh added to the chord? _____

Track 18

3 Notice how the melody below "makes the changes."
Circle the chord tones and label each syncopated note with an "S."

UNIT 2 **Lesson 8**

Tonic Function, Scalar Melody, Passing & Neighboring Tones

Jazz musicians love to play STANDARDS – great songs from a lexicon of music created roughly between the 1920s and 1960s. Standard song forms are brief (usually 32 bars in length) and were often composed for Broadway musicals, or film. The harmonic language of jazz was codified in the standards, created by such composers as George Gershwin, Irving Berlin, Hoagy Carmichael, Harold Arlen and Cole Porter.

A chord built on the tonic (first) note of the scale is the TONIC CHORD, or ONE CHORD. Roman numerals are used to symbolize chords, so the symbol I MA7 is used for this "home" chord. Virtually all jazz standards in major keys end on the I MA7 chord (e.g., songs in the key of Bb major end on a BbMA7 chord).

For tonic chords, jazz musicians typically use the TONIC SCALE (major scale) to fill in other notes for melody or improvisation. Any SCALAR MELODY emphasizing the chord tones on most of the beats will be effectively consonant and will *make the changes*. Melody notes which are not part of the chord are called NON-HARMONIC TONES.

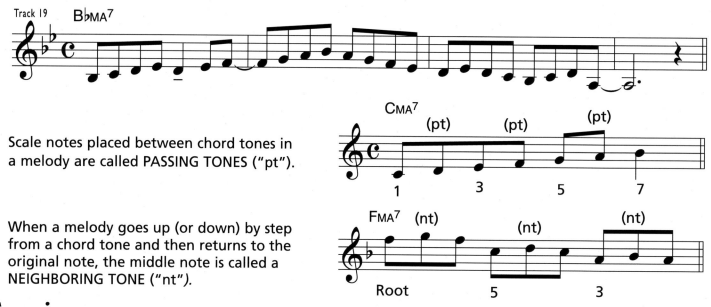

Scale notes placed between chord tones in a melody are called PASSING TONES ("pt").

When a melody goes up (or down) by step from a chord tone and then returns to the original note, the middle note is called a NEIGHBORING TONE ("nt").

Exercises

1 For the 4-bar melody above, circle and label the passing tones (pt) and neighboring tones (nt).

2 Compose a jazz melody to the tonic MA7 chord using chord tones, the tonic scale, and characteristic devices. Indicate the chord symbol above the staff.

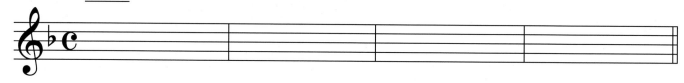

3 Analyze the following melody: label the chord tones, identify and circle passing and neighboring tones. Label syncopated notes (S), and also the beginnings of each phrase (phrase 1, phrase 2, etc.).

Dissonant 4th and Resolution

Beware the DISSONANT FOURTH! Except for one note, every note of the major scale sounds reasonably consonant over tonic harmony, because these pitches can be explained as chord tones or extensions. The offending, DISSONANT (non-consonant) tone is the fourth note of the scale. In fact, the note a perfect 4th (P4) above any major chord is very dissonant. When a melody emphasizes the dissonant 4th the result is extremely tense, and so the note must RESOLVE (release) by step—usually into the 3rd of the chord, 1/2 step below (CD Track 20). Skipping both into and out of the P4 above a major chord is not possible, because that is arpeggiating the wrong chord!

Each 4th above is used as an APPOGGIATURA, which is a dissonant note on a strong beat.
An appoggiatura (appog.) must be RESOLVED by stepwise motion into a chord tone (usually downward). As you can hear, the use of appoggiaturas is a wonderfully expressive device in music.

Exercises

1 *Dig It!*—Go back to CD Track 17, which features an FMA7 chord. Play the dissonant fourth along with the track. Next, play the 4th and resolve the dissonance by moving down a 1/2 step to the 3rd of the chord. You just experienced the power of appoggiatura and resolution!

2 Label each dissonant 4th (appog.) and circle each. Draw an arrow between each 4th and 3rd to show the resolution.

3 Compose jazz melodies to the following major seventh chords using 4th appoggiaturas and other characteristic devices. Can you use other notes as appoggiaturas?

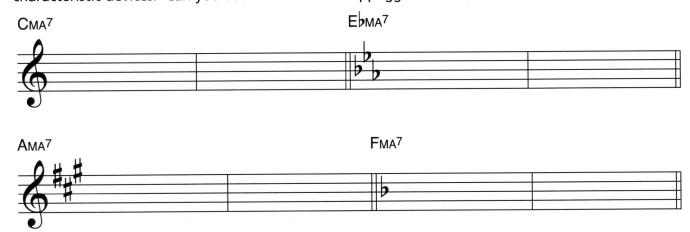

UNIT 2 Ear Training for Lessons 6–9

Track 21

1 Listen to the F major triad in root position and 1st inversion.
Write whether each chord you hear is in root position or 1st inversion.

a. _____

b. _____

c. _____

d. _____

Track 22

2 You will hear four major triads, followed by one of the notes in the triad.
For each example, indicate if the note is root, 3rd or 5th of the chord.

a. _____

b. _____

c. _____

d. _____

Track 23

3 Listen to the B♭ major triad and B♭MA7 chord.
Write whether each chord you hear is a major triad or MA7 chord.

a. _____

b. _____

c. _____

d. _____

Track 24

4 Listen to the GMA7 chord in root position, 1st, 2nd and 3rd inversion.
Circle the correct answer for each subsequent chord you hear.

a. root position / 1st inversion

b. root position / 2nd inversion

c. root position / 3rd inversion

d. root position / 3rd inversion

Track 25

5 For each melody you hear, write if it is primarily scalar or arpeggiated.

a. scalar / arpeggiated

b. scalar / arpeggiated

c. scalar / arpeggiated

d. scalar / arpeggiated

Track 26

6 For each melody you hear, write if it contains an appoggiatura 4th.

a. yes / no   b. yes / no   c. yes / no   d. yes / no

Review of Lessons 6–9 UNIT 2

1 In 3rd inversion, the _____ of the chord is on the bottom.

2 Identify the following major triads and indicate root position or which inversion each is in.

Root Position _____ _____ _____ _____

3 Each chord in jazz is referred to as a _____ .

4 Notate the indicated MA7 chords in root position and all three inversions.

GMA7   EbMA7   AMA7   DbMA7

5 An _____ is a dissonant note which resolves by step into a chord tone.

6 The most dissonant note over a tonic major chord is the _____ note of the major scale.

7 Jazz musicians love to play the _____ songs, which were composed throughout the early to middle twentieth century.

8 Analyze this jazz melody by circling and identifying the chord tones and labeling appoggiaturas (appog.), passing tones (pt) and neighboring tones (nt), and syncopated notes (s). Also indicate the start of each phrase.

9 Compose melodies to the following major seventh chords, using the language studied so far.

FMA7

DMA7

CMA7

EbMA7

Subdominant Major Seventh Chords (IVMA7, IVΔ7)

As you know, chords are stacked 3rds, or "every other note" of a scale. Harmony in keys comes from creating chords over the various SCALE TONES (also called SCALE DEGREES). A chord built on the second note of the scale is the "ii" chord, over the third degree results in the "iii" chord, and so on. These are called the DIATONIC CHORDS (diatonic means "of the scale"). The diatonic chords have functions in the music. For instance, as you know, TONIC FUNCTION indicates the "home" chord of the key.

In every major key, the chord constructed of the 4th degree is also a Major 7th chord! This degree is called SUBDOMINANT and so the chord is the SUBDOMINANT SEVENTH CHORD (IVMA7). Here are the diatonic seventh chords in the key of G major, highlighting the two major seventh chords, IMA7 and IVMA7.

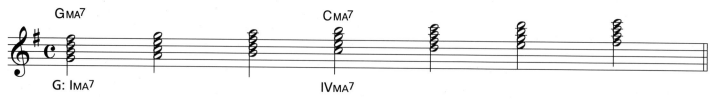

Track 27

Take note that chord tones are referenced from the chord root and not from the key the chord is functioning in. So, although the IVMA7 chord is constructed of the 4th, 6th, 1st and 3rd notes of the scale, we still refer to its tones as root, third, fifth, and seventh of the chord.

The subdominant chord is used in at least 75% of jazz standards! SUBDOMINANT FUNCTION creates a feeling in the harmony that the music has gone to a temporary new home. But, since it is a diatonic chord, the IVMA7 chord progresses seamlessly back to

IMA7, as you hear in CD Track 27, which alternates between tonic and subdominant MA7 chords in the key of C major in two-bar increments. (Note: a set of chord changes is also called a CHORD PROGRESSION.)

Exercises

1 Notate the IVMA7 chords in root position and all three inversions for the indicated major keys. Write each chord symbol above the staff.

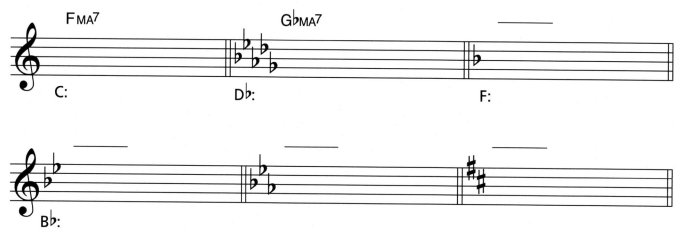

2 For each note of the IVMA7 chord, write a note of the IMA7 that is a diatonic step away, or closer.

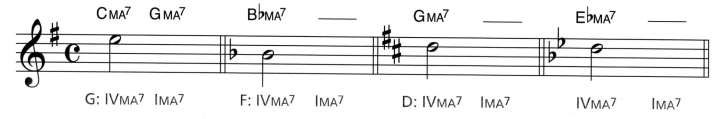

Voice Leading Tonic & Subdominant Major Seventh Chords

The IMA7 and IVMA7 chords have two COMMON TONES: scale degrees 1 and 3 of the key are root and 3rd of the IMA7, and also 5th and 7th of the IVMA7.

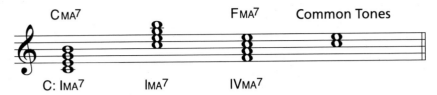

If you play the IMA7 and IVMA7 chords successively in root position, every note skips up a 4th (or down a 5th), resulting in an awkward sound. The effect would be worse if four instruments, each playing a chord tone of the tonic chord, skipped up a 4th.

Proper and musical VOICE LEADING is achieved by placing one of the chords in inversion, so that each note of the first chord moves little or not at all into the next. The smoothest connection retains the common tones between the two chords. So, a IMA7 chord in root position smoothly leads to a IVMA7 in 2nd inversion.

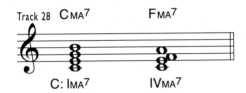

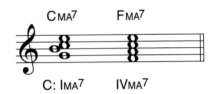

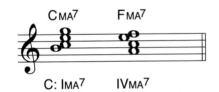

The 1st inversion IMA7 chord leads to a 3rd inversion IVMA7 chord.

The second inversion IMA7 connects to root position IVMA7.

And the 3rd inversion IMA7 connects to 1st inversion IVMA7.

CD Track 28 plays all of these progressions.

Exercises

1 *Dig It!*—Listen to this melody to hear the sound of smooth voice leading. Write in the chord symbols.

Track 29

2 For each IMA7 chord, notate the IVMA7 chord in that key, using inversion as necessary to achieve smooth voice leading. Indicate the chord symbols above the staff, and the chord inversions below the staff.

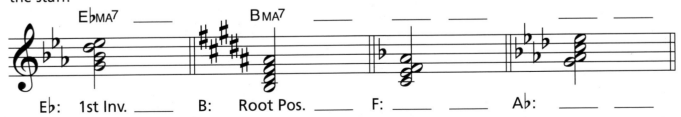

3 Compose a characteristic melody to the following progression, using proper voice leading.

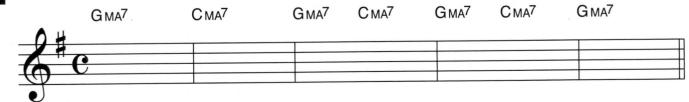

UNIT 3 — Lesson 12

Modes, Lydian Scale

There has been ample confusion in jazz about the modes. In the medieval period, DIATONIC CHURCH MODES were used as the basis for MODAL compositions. In jazz we use the church mode *names* as a convenient way to refer to the scales we practice, even though standard songs are in *keys,* not modes.

Each MODE is a way of playing the major scale, starting and ending on one particular note. So, there are 7 modes of the major scale. The names of the consecutive diatonic church modes, beginning with the actual tonic major scale are *Ionian, Dorian, Phrygian, Lydian, Mixolydian, Aeolian,* and *Locrian.* A major scale starting and ending on degree 2 is called Dorian, etc.

C Major (Ionian) Scale   2nd Mode — D Dorian Scale   3rd Mode — E Phrygian Scale

The tonic scale is effective for creating melodies to IMA⁷ and IVMA⁷ chords, because the chord tones for both are within the scale. In fact, the tones of every diatonic chord are in the tonic scale, which is why musicians should practice the modes in eighth notes, from the root of each chord. Doing this places a chord tone on each beat.

The tonic scale in the fourth mode (from root to root of the IVMA⁷ chord) sounds like a major scale with a raised 4th degree. So, a C major scale from F-F sounds like an F major scale with raised 4. This mode is called LYDIAN, and the raised fourth note is the LYDIAN FOURTH.

F Lydian Scale (Major, from 4-4)

C:

In jazz, the Lydian (raised) 4th is consonant to any major chord, as opposed to the dissonant P4 above the root. So, jazz musicians typically use the Lydian 4th in improvising and composing to the IMA⁷ chord.

C Lydian Scale (Major, raised 4)

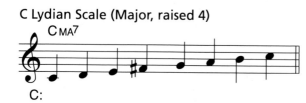

C:

Exercises

Track 30

1 Listen to this jazz melody to IMA⁷ and IVMA⁷ chords which emphasizes chord tones, and employs the Lydian scales for both. Circle and identify chord tones (R, 3, 5, 7,) and draw a square around each Lydian 4th.

2 For each major key, write a Lydian scale in the fourth mode.

G Lydian

3 Alter each major scale to become Lydian.

4 Compose a characteristic jazz melody to this progression, employing Lydian sounds.

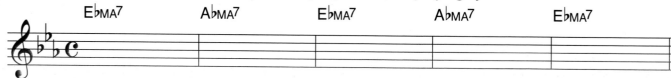

Hierarchy of 3rds and 7ths

Jazz is a contrapuntal music, which is to say that simultaneous melody and bass lines function together to obviate the harmony. Most often, each chord change begins with the bass line establishing the root, so the melody must clarify the chord in some other way. The two chord tones which "lock in" the sound of the chord against its root are the 3rd and 7th, and we place these notes at the top of the jazz melody hierarchy.

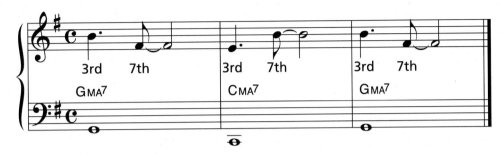

3rds and 7ths are at the top of the hierarchy because 5ths and chord extension 9ths (discussed in Unit 4), are the same for several different types of chords and are thus, far less effective in defining the harmony. As you study chord types, you'll find that $C_{MA}9$, $C_{MI}9$, and $C9$ all share the same 5th and 9th.

Jazz musicians must gain an "automatic" knowledge of 3rds and 7ths. The art of "making the changes" involves improvising a line (scalar, arpeggiated, or otherwise) which lands on the defining chord tone (3rd or 7th) just as the chord changes. If you analyze composed music from Bach, to Brahms, to Charlie Parker you find the same principle applies!

Exercises

Track 31

1 Listen to this melody to $MA7$ chords, in which the 3rd and/or 7th of each chord clarifies the chord change against the root. Circle and identify chord 3rds and 7ths. Also analyze the use of other jazz melody devices, such as syncopation, licks, phrases, sudden direction shifts, etc.

2 Compose a jazz melody to this progression, emphasizing the 3rd and/or 7th as each chord changes. Use accidentals as needed!

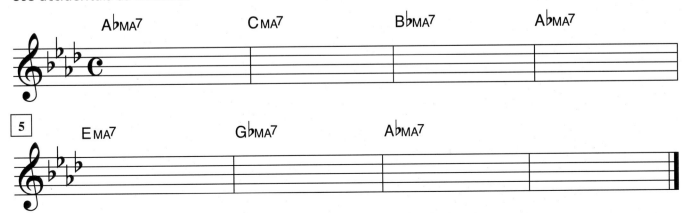

Track 32

1 Listen to the IMA⁷ followed by the IVMA⁷.
Write whether the chord in each example is a IMA⁷ or a IVMA⁷.

a. _____   b. _____

c. _____   d. _____

Track 33

2 Listen to the IMA⁷ arpeggio in root position followed by the IVMA⁷ arpeggio in 2nd inversion.
You will hear four examples of IMA⁷ followed by IVMA⁷.
For each, write which position/inversion each chord is in.

a. IMA⁷ _____   IVMA⁷ _____   b. IMA⁷ _____   IVMA⁷ _____

c. IMA⁷ _____   IVMA⁷ _____   d. IMA⁷ _____   IVMA⁷ _____

Track 34

3 Listen to the major scale followed by the Lydian scale. You will hear four scales.
Write whether each is major or Lydian.

a. _____   b. _____

c. _____   d. _____

Track 35

4 Listen to the 3rd and 7th of the MA⁷ chord. You will hear four MA⁷ chords.
After each is played a 3rd or 7th will follow. Circle the correct answer for the chord tone you hear.

a. 3rd / 7th   b. 3rd / 7th   c. 3rd / 7th   d. 3rd / 7th

Track 36

5 Listen to the melody. One of the notations below is correct.
Circle A or B to indicate the correct melody :

a.   b.

Track 37

6 Listen to the following progression of IMA⁷ and IVMA⁷ chords (bass plays the root for each
and each chord lasts for one measure), write the progression.

_____ _____ _____ _____ _____ _____ _____

1 The two major seventh chords found in a major key are _____ and _____ .

2 When chords are connected smoothly, it is referred to as proper _____

_____

3 Jazz standard songs are in modes.   True / False.

4 There are ____ modes of the major scale. The fourth mode is called _____ , and sounds like a major scale with the _____ note raised ½ step.

5 The most important notes for "making the changes" are the _____ and

_____ of a chord.

6 Notate the IVMA7 chord in the following keys, in root position and all three inversions.

GMA7   _____   _____

D: Bb: A:

7 For each IMA7 chord, notate the IVMA7 in that key, using smooth voice leading.

FMA7   ____   ____   ____   ____   ____

F: 3rd Inv. ____   C: 2nd Inv. ____   Eb: ____   D: ____

8 For each IVMA7 chord, notate the IMA7 in that key, using smooth voice leading.

CMA7   ____ ____ ____ ____ ____ ____ ____

G: 2nd Inv. ____   Ab: 3rd Inv. ____   F: ____ ____   Db: ____ ____

9 Notate the Lydian scales for the IV chords below.

BbMA7   GbMA7   DMA7

F: Db: A:

10 Compose a characteristic jazz solo melody to the following progression, using Lydian sounds, and 3rd and 7th emphasis.

FMA7   CMA7   FMA7   CMA7   FMA7   CMA7

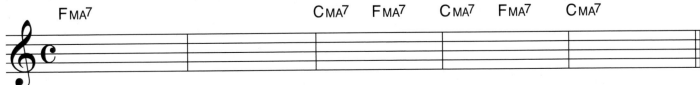

Major 9th Chords (MA9, Δ9)

Jazz composers and soloists freely add ninth extensions to most chords. Adding a 9th to a MA7 chord results in a MAJOR NINTH CHORD. A 9th can be understood as the second note of a scale, repeated in the next octave.

C Major Scale

A note is called a 9th, and not a 2nd, because chords are stacked thirds, and the 9th is the next third over the chord 7th. The 9th of a MA9 chord is a major 9th (M9) above the root (a whole step, up an octave), and the proper symbol for the chord is MA9

Ninths can be considered consonant in jazz, and they add richness to the harmony.

Major ninth chords can be arpeggiated in 4-note groupings (in four inversions) omitting the root. Since jazz bass players

almost always play the root, these ROOTLESS ARPEGGIOS are more interesting and complex. In jazz, 9th chords and 7th chords are interchangeable.

Ninths can also be heard as appoggiaturas, resolving down to the chord root.

Exercises

1 *Dig it!*—Using CD Track 27, play the rootless CMA9 and FMA9 arpeggios from 3rd to 9th, lingering on each 9th to experience its consonance. Next, play the 9ths as appoggiaturas, and resolve downward to the chord roots. The chords change every two measures.

2 Construct the following IMA9 chords in all four rootless inversions.

3 Construct the following IVMA9 chords in all four rootless inversions.

4 Circle the chord 9ths and indicate whether each is consonant (C) or an appoggiatura (appog).

Major 6/9 Chords ($^6\!/_9$)

Interchangeable with MA7 or MA9 chords is the MAJOR 6/9 CHORD, which is designated as $^6\!/_9$ (e.g.: C$^6\!/_9$, F$^6\!/_9$ etc.). The $^6\!/_9$ chord is much the same as a MA9 chord, only with the chord 7th replaced by the 6th note of the scale (a Major 6th above the root).

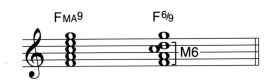

Like MA9 chords, $^6\!/_9$ chords are typically arpeggiated without the root (which will be supplied by the bass player in jazz performance).

3 5 6 9 5 6 9 3 6 9 3 5 9 3 5 6

This sound of the $^6\!/_9$ chord is more stable than that of a major 7th chord, because the interval of a M6 above the root is more consonant than the M7. Compositionally, major $^6\!/_9$ chords should be used when the melody features the chord root. A major 7th in the harmony actually clashes with the root a ½ step away, while the 6th of the chord is harmonious against it. So, for example, the first two bars of "On Green Dolphin Street" or the first measure of "L-O-V-E" would best be harmonized by major $^6\!/_9$ chords. The following melody should employ a $^6\!/_9$ chord:

Track 39   C$^6\!/_9$

Exercises

Track 39

1 *Dig it!*—Play the melody above on the piano with your right hand, and a MA7 chord in root position in your left hand. Can you hear the 7th clashing against the root in the melody? Compare that to the sound of the melody using the $^6\!/_9$ chord.

2 Construct each $^6\!/_9$ chord, followed by the rootless arpeggios, in all four inversions.

Bb$^6\!/_9$ Db$^6\!/_9$ G$^6\!/_9$

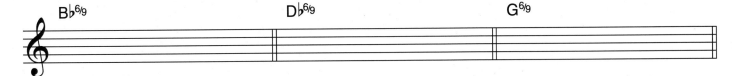

3 For this melody, indicate whether each chord should be $^6\!/_9$ or MA9.

Major Pentatonic Scale (Pentatonic)

PENTATONIC means "five notes," so any scale of five notes can be called pentatonic. In jazz music, the scale referred to as pentatonic is actually a MAJOR PENTATONIC SCALE, which is analogous to notes 1, 2, 3, 5, and 6 of the major scale. These are exactly the notes found in the $^6/9$ chord!

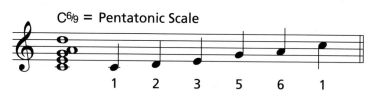

Composed only of chord tones, the pentatonic scale is entirely consonant, and very useful for the corresponding MA^9 and $^6/9$ chords. There is no dissonant 4th in the pentatonic scale, so it is a great tool for both composition and improvisation. Some hymn tunes, such as "Amazing Grace" and "Swing Low, Sweet Chariot" (which have their basis in earlier Celtic music), are entirely pentatonic.

Although not named, there are modes of the pentatonic scale, and improvisers often take four-note groupings from the PENTATONIC MODES to use as MELODIC CELLS.

Exercises

1 Construct the indicated pentatonic scales.

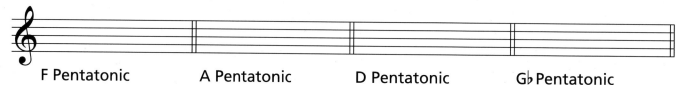

F Pentatonic   A Pentatonic   D Pentatonic   G♭ Pentatonic

2 Notate the 4-note melodic cells from the modes of the pentatonic scales above.

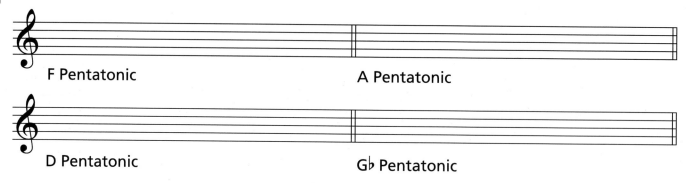

F Pentatonic   A Pentatonic

D Pentatonic   G♭ Pentatonic

3 Compose a characteristic jazz solo melody, using pentatonic scales.

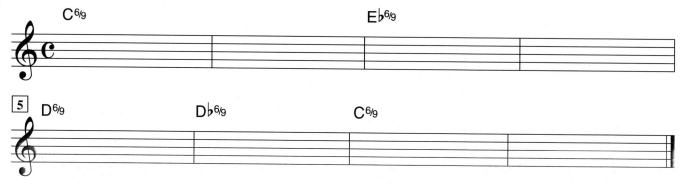

Jazz Language – Grace Notes, Scoops & Turns

So far, this text has dealt with global aspects of jazz melody. GRACE NOTES, SCOOPS and TURNS represent more specific components of the jazz language.

Because jazz musicians value emotional impact over pristine clarity and perfection of line, GRACE NOTES are a frequent melodic embellishment. A grace note is an emphatic sound, which can add "heart" or "bluesyness" to the ensuing tone.

Grace notes can be diatonic...	or chromatic....(i.e., a 1/2 step away, even if that tone is non-diatonic).	or a few consecutive tones can "grace" a melody note.
		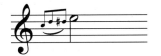

A SCOOP into a note creates the same effect as using grace notes. "Scooping" is executed by beginning a note slightly flat, and sliding up to the pitch. Scoops are notated with the symbol (⤴).

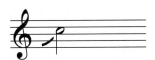

A TURN (mordent) is an embellishing melodic device, involving a tone quickly going to its neighbor (usually above) and back. The rhythm of a turn is typically an eighth-note triplet figure, or an eighth note followed by two sixteenths, or four sixteenth notes.

Turns can be written out or indicated with the symbol ∿. Often turns are followed with eighth-note movement by step or third in the opposite direction.

Turns have been around for hundreds of years, and are used liberally in jazz melody, especially in a bebop context. The hot bop styles of trumpeter, Lee Morgan and pianist, Oscar Peterson are characterized by the regular use of melodic turns.

Conversely, a stark characteristic of Miles Davis's "cool" playing was the eschewing of turns.

Exercises

1 Add grace notes, scoops, and turns to this melody.

Track 42

1 Listen to the MA7 arpeggio (r–7) and the MA9 arpeggio (3–9).
Circle whether each arpeggio is MA7 or MA9.

        a. MA7 / MA9   **b.** MA7 / MA9

        c. MA7 / MA9   **d.** MA7 / MA9

Track 43

2 Listen to the rootless MA9 arpeggio in all four inversions.
Write which note is on the bottom of each arpeggio you hear.

        a. _____ on bottom   **b.** _____ on bottom

        c. _____ on bottom   **d.** _____ on bottom

Track 44

3 Listen to the MA9 arpeggio and the 6/9 arpeggio (3–9).
Circle whether each arpeggio is MA9 or 6/9.

        a. MA9 / 6/9   **b.** MA9 / 6/9

        c. MA9 / 6/9   **d.** MA9 / 6/9

Track 45

4 Is this melody accompanied by a MA9 chord or a 6/9 chord?

                MA9   6/9

Track 46

5 Listen to the major scale from 1–5 and the pentatonic scale.
Circle whether each scale you hear is major (1–5) or pentatonic.

        a. major / pentatonic   **b.** major / pentatonic

        c. major / pentatonic   **d.** major / pentatonic

Track 47

6 Listen to the melodic cells from the 1st (root on bottom), 3rd (3rd on bottom),
and 4th (5th above root on bottom) modes of the pentatonic scale.
Circle whether each example is the 1st, 3rd, or 4th mode cell.

        a. 1st / 3rd / 4th   **b.** 1st / 3rd / 4th

        c. 1st / 3rd / 4th   **d.** 1st / 3rd / 4th

Track 48

7 Listen to the melody and count the number of jazz turns.

                _____ turns.

1   Jazz musicians typically arpeggiate 9th chords without playing the _____.

2   _____ means five notes.

3   Sliding into a note from below is called a _____.

4   A pentatonic scale is just another way of playing a ⁶⁄₉ chord.   True   /   False

5   Another name for turn is _____.

6   Write the MA⁹ chords vertically (not arpeggiated) in all four rootless positions.

C MA⁹   E MA⁹   B♭ MA⁹   F MA⁹

7   Notate the ⁶⁄₉ chords in rootless fashion (3rd on bottom), followed by the corresponding pentatonic scale.

E♭⁶⁄₉   G⁶⁄₉   D♭⁶⁄₉   B⁶⁄₉

8   Write the 4-note melodic cells from the modes of each of these pentatonic scales.

A Pentatonic   F♯ Pentatonic

E♭ Pentatonic   D Pentatonic

9   Compose a characteristic jazz solo melody, using pentatonic scales, grace notes and turns.

F⁶⁄₉   E♭⁶⁄₉

5   B♭ MA⁹   F MA⁹

Dominant 7th and 9th Chords (7, 9)

To understand the importance of DOMINANT SEVENTH CHORDS in music, sing a major scale from "do" to "ti." That overwhelming desire you feel to add the ensuing "do" is the tendency created by the existence of the dominant 7th chord. Dominant 7th chords are even more important in jazz because they can imply a sense of blues not found in earlier music. Advanced musicians find that dominant seventh chords offer a tapestry of melodic note choice, which is more varied than that of any other chord-type in jazz. The dominant chord is a favorite of jazz musicians for the richness of melodic options it invites.

DOMINANT 7TH AND DOMINANT 9TH CHORDS are analogous to major 7th and 9th chords, only with the chord seventh flatted a 1/2 step. The chord symbol for a dominant 7th or 9th chord is simply the number 7 or 9 (e.g.: C^7, F^9, etc.).

Root pos.   1st inv.   2nd inv.   3rd inv.

So, a dominant 7th chord contains a major triad and the interval of a *minor* 7th from root to seventh.

Track 49

The 1/2 step difference between major 7th and dominant 7th chords may seem insignificant, but in the way the chords *sound*, the difference is quite profound. CD Track 49 alternates between $E\flat_{MA}^7$ and $E\flat^7$ chords. The sound of the dominant 7th chord is more intense.

As is the case with MA^9 chords, the ninth of a dominant 9th chord is a major ninth above the root. Of course, the dominant 9th chord can be written and played in four, rootless inversions.

Rootless Inversions

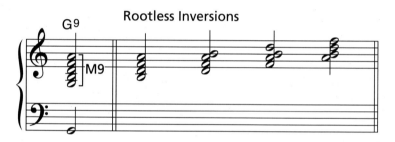

Exercises

1 Construct the indicated dominant 7th chords in root position and the three inversions.

2 Construct the indicated dominant 9th chords in four rootless inversions.

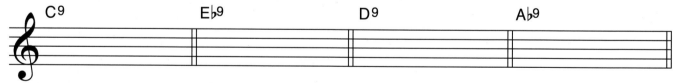

3 These MA^7 and MA^9 chords are in various inversions. For each, alter the chord so that it is a dominant 7th or 9th chord, and write in each chord symbol.

Dominant Function

The fifth degree of a major scale is called the DOMINANT PITCH, and a dominant 7th chord naturally results over that note. So, in major keys, we know the *quality* of the V^7 chord will always be dominant 7th . . .

. . . and it is understood that the V^9 chord in any major key is always a dominant 9th chord.

Notice that the V^7 chord contains major scale tones 5, 7, 2, and 4, consecutively (although we still refer to these tones as root, 3rd, 5th, and 7th of the chord).

DOMINANT FUNCTION: In music of the past several hundred years, V^7 chords have had a crucial role, because they don't merely progress, but rather "resolve" to tonic chords. The sound of V^7 feels like a musical tension, with a strong "tendency" to resolve to I.

Track 50
Dig it!—CD Track 50 alternates V^7 and IMA^7 chords in the key of B♭ major. Can you feel a *pull* between these chords?

The resolution of V^7 to I is called a CADENCE (authentic cadence in classical music), and the cadence is how virtually all jazz standards (and classical pieces, for that matter) end. Listening to CD Track 50, you notice how "final" it sounds each time V^7 progresses to the tonic chord.

Exercises

1 For each major key below, construct the V^7 chord in root position and all three inversions, and indicate the chord symbol.

2 For each major key below, construct the V^9 chord in all four rootless positions, and indicate the chord symbol.

3 For each major key, indicate the chord symbols for the V^7 to IMA^7 cadence.

D♭: V^7 ____ IMA^7 ____   E♭: V^7 ____ IMA^7 ____   F♯: V^7 ____ IMA^7 ____   A♭: V^7 ____ IMA^7 ____

Lesson 20

Resolution of V7 Chords, Tendency Tones and Tritone

As mentioned in Lesson 18, the 3rd of the V7 chord, which is the seventh scale degree, pulls towards the root of the tonic chord (7–8).

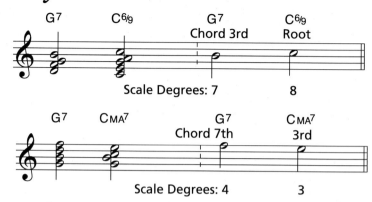

Also, the chord 7th, (which is the fourth scale degree) has a strong tendency to resolve down by diatonic step into the 3rd of the tonic chord (4-3).

Track 51

The 3rd and 7th of V7 chords are called TENDENCY TONES, because of their need to resolve. CD Track 51 performs the tendency tone resolutions (7-8, 4-3) over the V7-Ima7 progression. Listening to the track, you feel the satisfaction of tension and release with the tendency tones.

Dig It!—The interval between the 3rd and 7th of a dominant chord is a tritone (in other words A4 or d5). The tritone interval resolves either inward or outward, depending on which note is placed on top.

The 9th of a V9 chord is also a tendency tone, which resolves down by step into the 5th of the tonic chord.

Exercises

Track 52

1 Listen to this melody to hear the tendency-tone resolutions of V7–I. Find each tendency tone and draw an arrow from it to the resolving note. Write the chord-tone names of both notes.

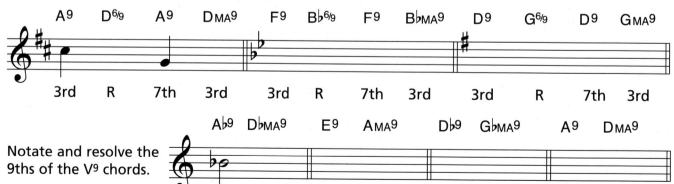

2 For each V7–I progression, write and resolve the tendency tones, chord 3rd and chord 7th.

3 Notate and resolve the 9ths of the V9 chords.

4 For each major key, notate and resolve the tritone from V7–I.

V⁷– Iᴍᴀ⁷ *Common Tones and Voice Leading*

There are two common tones between the V⁷ and Iᴍᴀ⁷ chords. Most significantly, the 3rd of V⁷ is the same note as the 7th of Iᴍᴀ⁷!

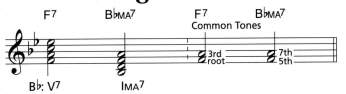

In jazz, the 7th of a tonic chord is consonant. So rather than resolving the chord 3rd of V⁷, jazz musicians often hold it as a common tone to the most expressive note of the Iᴍᴀ⁷ chord.

Still, the resolution of the 7th of the V⁷ chord into the 3rd of the Iᴍᴀ⁷ chord is more significant.

In creating both melodies and harmonic accompaniments, jazz musicians use inversions for smooth voice leading between the V⁷ and Iᴍᴀ⁷ chords.

Rootless inversions of the V⁹ chord also smoothly connect to Iᴍᴀ⁹.

Exercises

1 *Dig It!*—This melody "makes the changes," with common tones, resolution, and voice leading. Notice the compelling sense of tension-and-release and musical emphasis. Label the tendency tones and the notes they resolve to, and draw straight lines to show the common tone connection from V⁷ to Iᴍᴀ⁷.

2 For each V⁷ and V⁹ chord, notate the closest inversion of a rootless Iᴍᴀ⁹. Draw straight lines between the common tones.

3 Compose a melody featuring tendency tones, resolution, common tone, and proper voice leading.

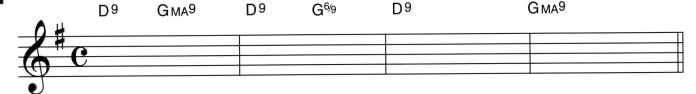

UNIT 5 **Lesson 22**

Dominant Scale (Mixolydian), Bebop Dominant Scale

As mentioned in Unit 3, all diatonic chords can use the scale from the tonic as a means for having other melody notes between the chord tones. So a G^7 chord, functioning as V^7 in C major, uses a C major scale from G to G. The major scale, when played in the fifth mode, sounds like a normal major scale, only with the seventh note flatted, and its church mode name is MIXOLYDIAN. When played in eighth notes, the ascending major scale from 5–5 (Mixolydian) places chord tones of the V^7 on each beat, thus "making the change."

Jazz composers and soloists love the BEBOP DOMINANT SCALE, which is a descending major scale with *both* the major seventh and the flatted seventh. This scale, played in eighth notes, also places all the chord tones of the dominant seventh chord on the beats.

WHAT IS A SCALE? In jazz, a scale can be defined as "chord tones and notes in between." This is why both the major scale and major with raised 4 (Lydian) sound great for MA^7 chords, and both the Mixolydian and bebop dominant scales are effective for dominant chords.

Here is a melody that makes the changes using both the Mixolydian and bebop dominant scales .

Exercises

1 For the jazz melody above, circle and label usage of the dominant and bebop dominant scales (note: the entire scale might not be used).

2 For each chord, write the dominant (Mixolydian) scale.

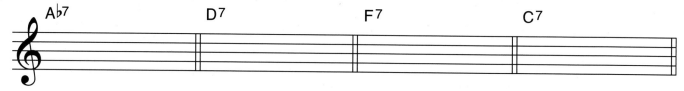

3 In each major key, write the bebop dominant scale for the V^7 chord, and write the chord symbol above the staff.

Track 57

1 Listen to the MA^7 chord and the dominant 7th chord.
Indicate whether each chord is MA^7 or dominant 7th (V^7).

    a. MA^7 / V7   **b.** MA^7 / V7

    c. MA^7 / V7   **d.** MA^7 / V7

Track 58

2 Listen to V^9 and IMA^9. Write whether each progression is V^9-IMA^9, or IMA^9-V^9.

    a. _____   **b.** _____

    c. _____   **d.** _____

Track 59

3 Listen to the tendency tone resolution of V^7-IMA^7; 7th (to 3rd) and the
common tone (3rd to 7th). Indicate which connection each melody uses.

    a. 7–3 / 3–7   **b.** 7–3 / 3–7

    c. 7–3 / 3–7   **d.** 7–3 / 3–7

Track 60

4 Listen to 7th resolving to 3rd and 9th resolving to 5th as V^7 progresses to IMA^7.
Indicate which resolution you hear.

    a. 7–3 / 9–5   **b.** 7–3 / 9–5

    c. 7–3 / 9–5   **d.** 7–3 / 9–5

Track 61

5 Listen to the major scale and the dominant (Mixolydian) scale.
Indicate whether each melody uses major or Mixolydian.

    a. major / Mixolydian   **b.** major / Mixolydian

    c. major / Mixolydian   **d.** major / Mixolydian

Track 62

6 Listen to the descending dominant and bebop dominant scales.
Indicate whether each melody uses dominant (Mixolydian) or bebop dominant.

    a. Mixolydian / bebop   **b.** Mixolydian / bebop

    c. Mixolydian / bebop   **d.** Mixolydian / bebop

1 A dominant 7th chord is like MA⁷ with the _____ note flatted, and naturally occurs over the _____ note of the major scale.

2 The V⁷-I progression is called a _____ .

3 Notes which require resolutions are called _____ _____ .

4 The fifth mode of the major scale is called _____ .

5 Bebop dominant is a descending major scale with two _____ .

6 For each major key, write a V⁷ chord, a V⁹ arpeggio (rootless) and the dominant scale.

7 For each V⁷ or V⁹ chord, write the best inversion of (rootless) IMA⁹ for smooth voice leading.

8 For each chord, write the bebop dominant scale.

9 Analyze the melody, indicating scales, arpeggios, resolution, common tone, non-harmonic tones and other characteristic jazz devices.

"Bluesy" Dominant Chords

Blues music presents a true departure from the harmonies of classical music, because in a blues context dominant 7th chords can be stable. For instance, flatting the seventh of the IMA7 chord results in a dominant 7th chord which is a "bluesy" tonic (I7 instead of IMA7).

G: I7

Bluesy subdominant chords with a dominant quality are also found in jazz.

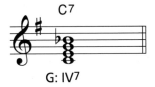

G: IV7

Here is a melody to the dominant I9 and IV9 chords (interchangeable with dominant 7th chords).

Track 64

How do you know whether a dominant 7th chord is functioning as V7 or as a bluesy tonic? You can tell by what happens next, because V7 chords are associated with the tonics they resolve to. For instance, a G7 chord progressing to CMA7 definitely is functioning as V7! CD Track 64 has the progression I7 – IV7 – V7 – IMA7, with each chord lasting two measures. You can hear the difference between the "bluesy" I7 and IV7 chords and the tension-and-release of V7 resolving to IMA7.

Exercises

1 *Dig It!*—Play the melody above. You should notice that the 7ths of the dominant I and IV chords don't feel like tendency tones, but rather as stable, bluesy sounds.

2 For each major key, notate the I7 and IV7 chords.

3 For each I7 chord, write the IV7 chord using inversion (if necessary) to create smooth voice leading.

4 Compose a melody to this progression, using a lick to unify the I7 and IV7 chords.

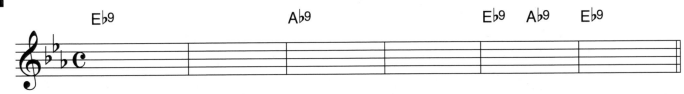

Blue Notes

Blue notes are a unique and important feature in the language of jazz. They are pitches that can be played in a key without "making the changes," creating a profound tension that must be resolved into chord tones.

The blue notes are the flatted 3rd, 5th, and 7th pitches of a key **or** chord, and are typically used over dominant 7th harmonies. Here are the blue notes in the key of F, and their usage over the I7, IV7 and V7 chords.

Next, blue notes are separately constructed over bluesy tonic and subdominant chords. The subdominant chord seems more like a tonic when it has its own blue notes.

*enharmonically spelled as ♯4

In our musical system the blue notes cannot be precisely notated, because they fall somewhere in the "cracks" between the actual pitches. Genuine performance of blue notes is predicated on an intensity of feeling in the "gut" of the performer.

Blue notes are ideal for usage in repeated licks, creating and escalating tension, followed by a release into a strong chord tone.

Exercises

1 *Dig It!*—As you listen to and play the excerpt above, concentrate on the intense feeling of the blue notes and also the feeling of resolution into the diatonic 3rd (tension/release).

2 For each major key, write the 3 blue notes.

3 For each major key, write the blue notes to the I7, IV7 and V7 chords.

4 Compose a lick-based melody to the progression, using the blue notes of the key.

5 Compose a lick-based melody to the progression, using separate blue notes for each chord.

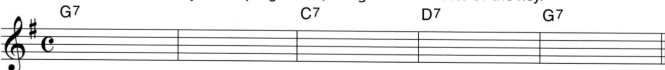

12-Bar Blues Progression, Blues Scale

The 12-BAR BLUES is the most often played chord progression in jazz. There are thousands of 12-bar blues tunes. Blues has its roots in "field hollers" from American slavery. The basic 12-bar blues contains the I⁷, IV⁷ and V⁷ chords, in three, 4-bar phrases.

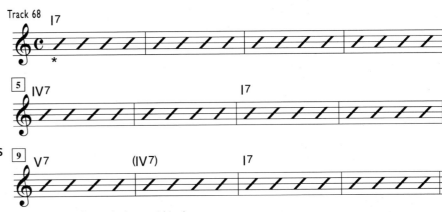

* The slashes indicate the beats within the measure.

The first phrase of the blues (measures 1-4) establishes tonic. The second (mm. 4-8) uses IV⁷ as a secondary area and then returns to tonic. The final phrase (mm. 9–12) is a cadence.

Without the parenthetical IV⁷ chord in measure 10 above, there is a V⁷-I authentic cadence. The IV⁷–I progression is called a PLAGAL CADENCE, which is the church ("amen") cadence.

Blues melodies can be in CALL-AND-RESPONSE form, also reminiscent of field hollers. The first phrase (call), is mimicked in the second (response). The third phrase is a summation. Once through a progression is called a CHORUS, so this is a one-chorus melody.

Jazz musicians have developed a BLUES SCALE which contains the 3 blue notes of the key, and also scale degrees 4 and 5.

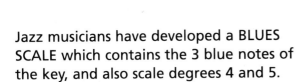

The blues scale is played in simple, repetitive licks, using a few of the tones in order.

Because blue notes are dissonant, it is effective to resolve blues scale licks into chord tones.

Exercises

1 Compose a chorus to the 12-bar blues, based on a lick and using call-and-response form.

2 Compose a chorus to the 12-bar blues, using few or no blue notes, and clearly "making the changes."

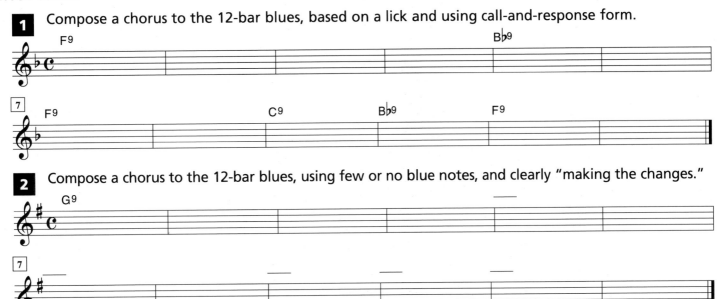

Track 71

1 Listen to the I7 and IV7 chords. Indicate whether each chord is I7 or IV7.

        a. I7 / IV7   **b.** I7 / IV7

        c. I7 / IV7   **d.** I7 / IV7

Track 72

2 Listen to the blue notes ♭3, ♭5, ♭7. Indicate which blue note you are hearing.

        a. ♭3 / ♭5 / ♭7   **b.** ♭3 / ♭5 / ♭7

        c. ♭3 / ♭5 / ♭7   **d.** ♭3 / ♭5 / ♭7

Track 73

3 For each melody, indicate whether the blue notes are in the key, or of each chord.

        a. in the key / each chord   **b.** in the key / each chord

        c. in the key / each chord   **d.** in the key / each chord

Track 74

4 Listen to the I7, IV7, and V7 chords.
Write down the progression you hear (each chord lasts 2 bars).

_____ _____ _____ _____ _____ _____ _____ .

Track 75

5 Listen to the F blues scale. Write down the notes in the order you hear them.

F Blues Scale

Track 76

6 Listen to the V7-I7 authentic cadence and IV7-I7 plagal cadence.
Write whether each cadence is authentic or plagal.

        a. authentic / plagal   **b.** authentic / plagal

        c. authentic / plagal   **d.** authentic / plagal

Track 77

7 Listen to a blues lick which resolves to the 3rd of the chord.
Write whether each phrase resolves into the chord 3rd.

        a. yes / no   **b.** yes / no

        c. yes / no   **d.** yes / no

1 When the 7th of IMA7 is flatted, the resulting chord is a _____ .

This same alteration is also typical for the _____ chord in a key.

2 Dominant-quality I7 and IV chords are unstable.　True / False.

3 The blue notes are the flatted _____, _____ and _____ of a chord or _____ .

4 Blue notes and the blues scale are best suited for lick / line / melody (circle one).

5 The 12-bar blues is based on the ____, ____ , and ____, chords, and is organized into _____ phrases.

6 Blues melodies are often in a _____-and-_____ form.

7 Blue notes "make the changes."　True / False.

8 Above the staves, write out the basic 12-bar blues progression in the key of B♭.
Next, notate the rootless dominant ninth chords, using inversions for smooth voice leading.

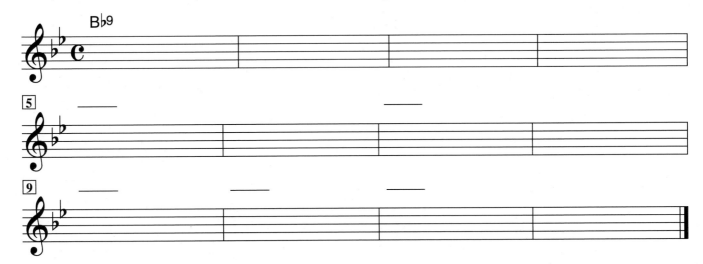

9 Write out the blue notes for each key, followed by the blues scale.

10 Write a bluesy lick for the I7 chord, and transpose or alter it for IV7 and V7.

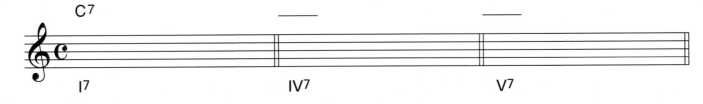

GLOSSARY & INDEX OF TERMS & SYMBOLS

Includes all the terms and symbols used in Book 1 and the page on which they are first introduced.

APPOGGIATURA: a dissonant note on a strong beat that resolves, usually downward, by stepwise motion into a chord tone (p. 13).

BEBOP: a virtuosic jazz style with unpredictable melodic phrase lengths and accentuation, with sudden skips and changes of direction (p. 6).

BEBOP DOMINANT SCALE: a major scale with an added flatted seventh; see also Mixolydian (p. 32).

BLUE NOTES: ♭3, ♭5 and ♭7 of a key or chord typically used over dominant harmonies (p. 36).

BLUES: expressive style that evolved from the "field hollers" from American slavery (p. 37).

BLUES PROGRESSION: the 12-bar blues contains the I7, IV7 and V7 chords arranged in three, 4-bar phrases (p. 37).

BLUES SCALE: contains the 3 blue notes of the key and scale degrees 4 and 5; best suited for simple and repetitive licks (p. 37).

BLUESY: playing with an intensity in the "gut" (p. 36).

BLUESY DOMINANT 7TH CHORDS: dominant chords that are built on the tonic (I7) or subdominant (IV7), and are considered stable in jazz (p. 35).

CADENCE: resolution of V7 to I (authentic cadence in classical music) (p. 29).

CHANGES: chords of the song; each new chord is called a "change" (p. 11).

CHORD(S): consonant combinations of notes (p. 3).

CHORD EXTENSIONS: 3rds that extend beyond a triad, such as 7th, 9th, 11th, 13th and so on (p. 11).

CHORD PROGRESSION: A set of chord changes (p. 16).

CHORUS: one time through a chord progression (p. 37).

COMMON TONES: shared notes between two chords (p. 17).

CONSONANCE: pleasing-sounding notes in a chord or melody (p. 10).

CONSONANT: pleasing sounding (p. 3).

COUNTERPOINT: simultaneous occurrence of two or more melodic voices. In jazz, it typically exists between melody and bass (p. 3).

DIATONIC: of the scale (p. 16).

DISSONANT: non-pleasing (p. 13).

DISSONANT 4TH: non-pleasing P4 above any major chord, unless resolved into the 3rd of a major chord, as in an appoggiatura (p. 13).

DOMINANT FUNCTION: the sound of V7 feels like a musical tension, with a strong "tendency" to resolve to I (p. 29).

DOMINANT SEVENTH CHORD: contains a major triad and the interval of a minor 7th from root to 7th (p. 28).

DOMINANT NINTH CHORD: a dominant 7th chord with an added major ninth above the root (p. 28).

FORM: organization of musical statements and themes; the "roadmap" of music (p. 3).

FORWARD MOTION: underlying stress of beats 2 & 4 (p. 5).

GRACE NOTE: emphatic diatonic or chromatic melodic embellishment (p. 25).

GROOVE: Constant energy funneled into subdivision (p. 5).

HARMONY: results when two or more pitches are sounded simultaneously (p. 3).

IMPROVISATION: spontaneous composition (p. 6).

IMPROVISE: to create spontaneously (p. 6).

INVERSION: The notes of a chord are rearranged and a tone other than the root is the bottom note of the chord (p. 10).

1ST INVERSION: The notes of a chord are rearranged so the 3rd is the bottom note (p. 10).

1st inversion

2ND INVERSION: The notes of a chord are rearranged so the 5th is the bottom note (p. 10).

2nd inversion

3RD INVERSION: The notes of a seventh chord are rearranged so the 7th is the bottom note of the chord (p. 11).

3rd inversion

LICK: a brief melodic cell (motive), made memorable by repetition (p. 7).

LINE: a melody of one measure or longer, moving in eighth-notes or faster values (p. 7).

LYDIAN: church mode name for the 4th mode; in jazz, the tonic scale played from the 4th note to the 4th note (p. 18).

LYDIAN FOURTH: raised 4th note of the Lydian mode (p. 18).

MAJOR NINTH: scale degree 2 of a major scale, one octave higher (p. 22).

MAJOR NINTH CHORD: a major seventh chord with an added major ninth interval above the root (p. 22).

MAJOR SEVENTH: the interval between the root and the seventh degree of a major scale (p. 11).

MAJOR SEVENTH CHORD: a 4-note chord consisting of a root, Major 3rd, perfect 5th and Major 7th (p. 11).

MAJOR 6/9 CHORD: similar to the MA9 chord, only with the chord 7th replaced by the 6th note of the scale (a M6 above the root) (p. 23).

MAJOR TRIAD: Triad consisting of a root, major 3rd and perfect 5th (p. 10).

MELODIC SOLOING: playing a phrase, or phrases that sound like a new song, rather than a solo; spontaneous composition (p. 7).

MELODY: a linear succession of pitches, made memorable by contour and repetition (p. 3).

MIXOLYDIAN: a major scale played in the fifth mode (p. 32).

MODE: a way of playing the major scale, starting and ending on one particular note of the scale. There are 7 modes of the major scale: Ionian, Dorian, Phrygian, Lydian, Mixolydian, Aeolian, and Locrian (p. 18).

MORDENT: see Turn (p. 25).

NEIGHBORING TONE: when a melody goes up (or down) by step from a chord tone and then returns to the original note, the middle note is called a neighboring tone (p. 12).

NON-HARMONIC TONE: a melody note that is not part of the chord (p. 12).

ORGANIC: building on small ideas (p. 7).

PASSING TONES: Scale notes placed between chord tones in a melody (p. 12).

PENTATONIC: five notes (p. 24).

PENTATONIC MAJOR SCALE: scale degrees 1, 2, 3, 5, and 6 of the major scale (p. 24).

PENTATONIC MODES: four-note groupings from the pentatonic major scale, used as melodic cells (p. 24).

PITCH: a musical note (p. 3).

PLAGAL CADENCE: resolution of IV7 to I (p. 37).

RAGGING: syncopating the rhythms of a melody (p. 6).

RHYTHM: the placement of notes in time, and their relationship to a beat; the propulsive engine of melody and harmony (p. 3).

ROOT: first note of a scale or chord (p. 10).

ROOT POSITION: a chord is in root position when the root is on the bottom (p. 10).

ROOTLESS ARPEGGIOS: arpeggiation of chords with the root omitted, since in jazz, the bass typically plays the root (p. 22).

SCALAR MELODY: follows the scale and emphasizes chord tones (p. 12).

SCALE DEGREE: a note of a scale (p. 16).

SCOOP: ✓ beginning a note slightly flat and sliding up to the pitch (p. 25).

SOLO: improvisation (p. 7).

STANDARDS: songs composed for Broadway and motion pictures between the 1920s and the 1960s (p. 12).

SUBDOMINANT: the 4th scale degree (p. 16).

SUBDOMINANT MAJOR SEVENTH CHORD: a 4-note chord naturally occurring over the 4th degree of a major scale (p. 16).

SWING: an interpretation of eighth notes with a triplet subdivision in which the first eighth-note of each beat receives 2/3 of that beat's value and the second eighth-note, although only occupying 1/3 of the beat, is more often accentuated and articulated (p. 4).

SYNCOPATION: off-beat accentuation by placing a quarter note off the beat or skipping into an off-beat note (p. 6).

TENDENCY TONES: notes requiring resolution, for instance, 3rd and 7th chord tones of a V7 chord (p. 30).

TENSION AND RELEASE: a dissonant note that resolves into a consonant note (such as an appoggiatura), or a repeated lick that builds tension and releases into a melodic line (p. 7).

TEXTURE: aural depth that results when musical voices are combined into melodic and accompaniment components (p. 3).

THROUGH-COMPOSED: never repeating an idea (p. 7).

TONIC: naming note of a key (p. 10).

TONIC FUNCTION: "home" or root chord of a key (p.12).

TONIC SCALE: the major scale of any major key (p. 12).

TRIAD: a 3-note chord (p. 10).

TRITONE: interval between the 3rd and 7th of a dominant chord (an augmented 4th/diminished 5th) (p. 30).

TURN: (mordent) an embellishing melodic device involving a tone quickly going to its neighbor (usually above) and back (p. 25).

2 & 4: emphasis of beats 2 & 4 gives swing music its infectious sense of forward momentum (p. 5).

VOICE LEADING: achieved by placing one of two chords in inversion, so that each note of the first chord moves little or not at all into the next. The smoothest connection retains the common tones between the two chords (p. 17).

ALFRED'S ESSENTIALS OF
JAZZ THEORY

Lessons ▪ Ear Training ▪ Workbook

BOOK 2

Pages 41–80 ▪ Lessons 26–50

TABLE OF CONTENTS Book 2

Counterpoint—Bass and Melody

COUNTERPOINT is the simultaneous occurrence of two or more musical voices. The beauty of counterpoint lies in the interest created by the voices and the harmony that arises from them. Counterpoint between melody and bass has been an organizing principal of Western music for hundreds of years. In jazz, the bass voice establishes the harmony, which the melody clarifies and augments with "color" tones, such as 3rds and 7ths.

The joyful, forward momentum of swing music is due in large part to walking bass lines. WALKING BASS is a continual, quarter-note bass motion in which, more often than not, the chord root is on the downbeat of each measure. These lines typically are played in a register more than an octave below middle C, creating a polar counterpoint to the melody. String and electric basses have a range down to (at least) the E almost three octaves below middle C. (Note that bass sounds an octave lower than written.)

Track 2 demonstrates that walking bass is always played very legato; otherwise the feeling of swing is lost. Beats 1 and 3 are the *functional* beats, and are more apt to feature the chord root, 3rd, or 5th. Beats 2 and 4 are the *energy* beats. By energizing beats 2 and 4, and playing passing tones and other less structural pitches on these beats, the bass creates an energetic tendency to resolve to the next functional beat.

A TWO FEEL is created when the bass plays either half notes in each bar, or a dotted quarter, eighth-note pattern. This causes the music to feel in a 2-beat meter (cut time, $\frac{2}{2}$), as opposed to $\frac{4}{4}$. The bass plays almost exclusively an alternation of root and fifth.

Exercises

1 Analyze these walking bass lines by circling and identifying the chord tones. Label any passing (p.t.) or neighboring (n.t.) tones as well.

2 Compose a jazz melody to the bass line above. Remember that 3rds and 7ths (and even 9ths) complete the "picture" of counterpoint.

3 Compose a two-feel bass line to the progression.

Walking Bass Lines

The most important things a bass line can do are: 1) reinforce the groove and momentum of swing, and 2) make the chord changes clear. The first element is a matter of performance (as discussed in Lesson 26), while the second is one of construction.

The two simplest ways for a walking bass to establish the chord progression are:

by playing roots and fifths. . .

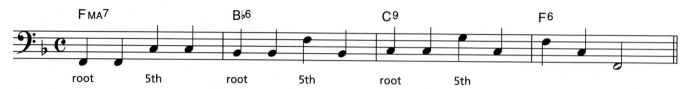

or by arpeggiating the chords.

Passing and neighboring tones are also effective for walking bass construction. Typically, these tones are employed on the weak beats (2 and 4), and lead to structural (chord) tones on the strong beats (1 and 3).

One of the most appealing devices for walking bass lines is the usage of CHROMATIC APPROACH TONES (leading tones), which are notes a ½ step below or above the next chord tone. As with other non-harmonic tones, approach tones most often occur on the weak beats.

Exercises

1 Analyze this walking bass line by circling and identifying the chord tones. Label any passing (p.t.), neighboring (n.t.), or chromatic approach tones (a.t.).

2 Compose a walking bass line to this progression.

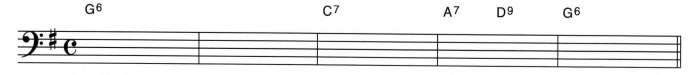

Walking Bass Lines in the Circle of Fifths, Two-Note Voicings

You know that the V7–I progression establishes a key. In Lesson 33 you will learn about the pervasive ii–V ("two-five") progression in jazz. Both are "circle-of-fifth" progressions, in which the bass moves by a perfect fifth interval from one chord to the next. Even the progression from I to IV is in the circle of fifths. Since these progressions are ubiquitous in jazz, standardized walking bass patterns have emerged.

The most common bass line for circle-of-fifth progressions is an ascending scale from one chord root to the next, using both major and minor third degrees. A variation on this line drops a 7th from the root.

The simplest bass line for the circle-of-fifth progression is a descending scale from one root to the next.

The combination of walking bass and melody creates a CONTRAPUNTAL TEXTURE (one using counterpoint). When ACCOMPANIMENT is added to the texture, such as one or more instruments playing chords, the texture is enhanced. Accompanimental chords can be played by a keyboard or guitar, or two or more instruments simultaneously sounding notes. These arrangements of chords are called voicings.

Simple, yet effective, TWO-NOTE VOICINGS are achieved by sounding just the chord 3rd and 7th, assuming the bass voice plays the root. These notes sound best in the "comping" range (see Lesson 29), which is approximately a sixth, either side of middle C.

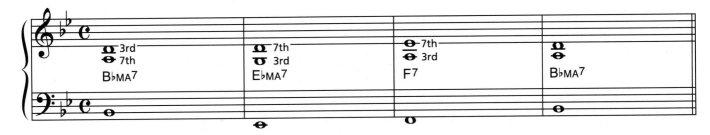

Exercises

1 Compose a walking bass line to the melody and chord progression, employing typical, circle-of-fifth construction.

2 Notate two-note voicings, in the comping range, to the following chords:

UNIT 7 **Lesson 29**

Comping & Comp Rhythms, Voice Leading

COMPING is a rhythmic accompaniment of chords, generally played by keyboard or guitar. Comping is the "glue" between the counterpoint of melody and bass, and can add to the tension and release in the music. Comping is reactive and interactive, like a listener in a conversation who says, "Mm-hmm," "Go on," or "Really!?" Comping is effective, as long as the music retains its clarity. If a comping instrument plays too loudly, or too often, the chords will clutter and obscure the beauty of the counterpoint.

COMP RHYTHMS are essential to the sense of groove. Voicings played on the occasional off-beat contribute to the propulsion of swing, and can be in short or long note values.

Jazz musicians often employ comp rhythms where chords are sounded one-and-a-half beats apart, e.g., beats "one" and the "and-of-two"; the "and-of-one" and "three", etc., in either long or short durations. So, just this one rhythmic device gives rise to 20 different comping figures! Chords played off a beat anticipate the next beat; so a chord played on the "and-of-four" anticipates the next measure.

VOICE LEADING refers to chord voicings moving smoothly from one chord to the next. You know that when chords progress by a fifth (V–I, I–IV), the 7th of the first chord *resolves* down by a ½ step into the 3rd of the next, and, the 3rd of the first chord is a common tone with the 7th of the next. Applying these principles will result in appealing voice leading.

Even when chords are not moving by fifth, voice leading should be as smooth as possible. The decision of whether the 3rd or 7th is on the bottom is determined by two factors: 1) placing the chord in the comping range, and 2) creating smooth voice leading.

Exercises

1 Use smooth voice leading to connect two-note voicings in the circle of fifths.

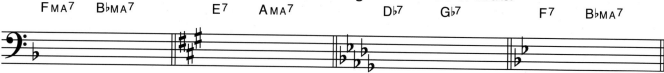

2 Create a comping texture using two-note voicings and a walking bass line.

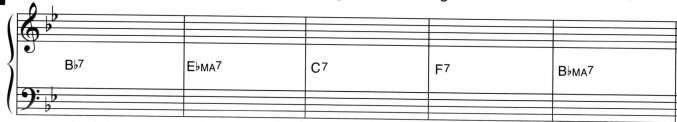

Brazilian Bass Lines & Comping Patterns

Jazz music and swing feel developed together, and they are permanently intertwined. Other forms of popular music have incorporated jazz elements, and have also been subsumed into jazz. For example, Brazilian *bossa nova* and *samba* rhythms are very popular among jazz musicians and composers. The two grooves are almost identical, with bossa being in ($\frac{4}{4}$), while samba is faster and feels in cut time ($\frac{2}{2}$).

The prevalent Brazilian comping pattern is referred to as PARTITO ALTO, and is played by guitar and/or piano. In a traditional jazz group, the drummer will sometimes play all or part of the partito alto pattern using a cross stick on the snare drum.

Track 10

In Brazil, the samba drum sounds prominently in the middle of the measure, and an authentic Brazilian bass figure does the same, alternating root and 5th.

Track 11 C6

The Americanized version of bossa or samba bass uses a dotted quarter and eighth rhythm.

Track 12 C MA7

The partito alto has four permutations, including the one you learned above. The figure is two bars long, and can begin on either downbeat, or in the middle of either bar.

Track 13   Beginning meas. 2   Beginning middle meas. 1   Beginning middle meas. 2

Track 13 has a rhythm section playing each of the four partitio alto figures in eight-measure phrases. The bass may play the authentic figure you learned, or incorporate elements of the partito alto rhythm.

Exercises

1 Find a Brazilian jazz recording and analyze the rhythm. Is the bass playing Brazilian or American style? How many permutations of partito alto are used? Are other comping patterns incorporated?

2 For this chord progression, write a bossa bass line and also two-note voicings, in the comping range, employing partito alto rhythms.

EbMA7	AbMA7	F7	Bb7	EbMA7

UNIT 7 Ear Training for Lessons 26–30

Track 14

1 Listen to the walking bass line and fill in the missing notes below.

Track 15

2 Listen to the bass note and two-note voicing with the 3rd on the bottom. Next, listen to the same chord, inverted to place the 7th on the bottom. You will hear four additional chords. For each, indicate whether the 3rd or 7th is on the bottom of the voicing.

    a. 3rd / 7th   **b.** 3rd / 7th   **c.** 3rd / 7th   **d.** 3rd / 7th

Track 16

3 Listen to the bass note, followed by two-note voicings of MA7 and Dominant 7th. For the following four-chord voicings, indicate whether each is MA7 or 7.

    a. MA7 / 7   **b.** MA7 / 7   **c.** MA7 / 7   **d.** MA7 / 7

Track 17

4 Listen to this rhythm section with piano comping and indicate which example below correctly notates the comp rhythms.

Track 18

5 Listen to this rhythm section with piano comping and write the number of times that the comp rhythm is two chords one-and-a-half beats apart.

_____ comp rhythms one-and-a-half beats apart.

Track 19

6 Listen to the partito alto, and then the same rhythm beginning on the second measure. For each example, indicate whether the partito alto begins in the first or second measure.

    a. measure 1 / measure 2   **b.** measure 1 / measure 2   **c.** measure 1 / measure 2

1 The simultaneous occurrence of two or more melodic voices is called _____,

which often exists between melody and _____ in jazz.

2 _____ _____ is constructed of legato quarter notes in a range approximately two octaves below middle C.

3 When a jazz bass line seems to be in $\frac{2}{2}$ time, this is called a _____ feel.

4 Bass lines are made more colorful with _____ tones and _____ _____ tones.

5 A two-note _____ is constructed of the chord 3rd and 7th.

6 _____ is a rhythmic accompaniment by piano or guitar, and relies on smooth

_____ _____.

7 In Brazilian music the _____ is in $\frac{4}{4}$ time, while the _____ is in $\frac{2}{2}$ (cut) time.

8 Brazilian bass lines typically alternate between _____ and _____, while the comping

pattern is known as _____ _____.

9 Notate a walking bass line using passing and approach tones, and also characteristic circle-of-fifth construction.

GMA7   CMA7   A7   D9   GMA7

10 Write two-note, voicings in a partito alto rhythm, employing smooth voice leading, and a samba bass line to the following progression:

FMA7   G7   B♭MA7   C7   FMA7

11 Write a walking bass line and voicings to the progression, employing characteristic comp rhythms.

B♭MA7   C7   E♭7   F7   B♭MA7

UNIT 8 **Lesson 31**

Minor 7th and 9th Chords (MI⁷, MI⁹) & Inversions

When music is in a minor key there is a melancholy result. In jazz, however, the minor seventh chord is also the hopeful sound that propels the changes towards a major tonic.

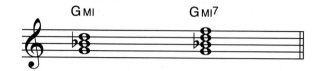

A MINOR TRIAD is analogous to a major triad with the 3rd flatted a ½ step. This lowered 3rd accounts for the somber sound associated with minor. A MINOR SEVENTH CHORD is a minor triad with a minor 7th (m7) interval above the root, and is indicated by the chord symbol "MI7" (sometimes min7, m7 or –7).

It is striking how similar major seventh, dominant seventh and minor seventh chords are to each other, especially when you consider how different their sounds are. Flat the 7th of a MA7 chord and a dominant seventh chord results. A MI7 chord simply results from lowering the 3rd of a dominant seventh chord.

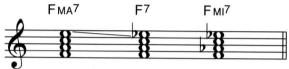

A MINOR NINTH CHORD is a MI7 chord with an added note a major 9th above the root. What's more, dominant 7, MI7, and MA7 chords all share the same ninth. In fact these three chords, built on a single root will share the same root, 5th, and 9th! This is precisely why 3rds and 7ths of chords are so important, because these tones establish chord *quality*.

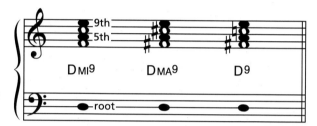

Minor seventh chords, of course, can be arranged in root position and in three inversions, while MI9 chords can be practiced in four, rootless inversions. For jazz musicians, these rudimental inversions should be second nature.

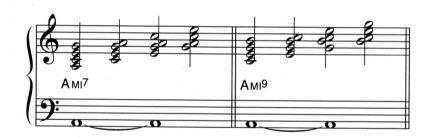

Exercises

1 Construct the indicated MI7 chords in root position and all three inversions.

2 Construct the indicated MI9 chords in all four rootless inversions.

3 Below are MA7, MA9, and also dominant 7th and 9th chords in various positions. Alter each chord to be a MI7 or MI9, and indicate the chord symbol.

Supertonic Function—ii*MI*⁷ and ii*MI*⁹ *Chords*

You already know that constructing seventh chords above the tonic and subdominant notes (scale degrees 1 and 4) of major keys results in major seventh chords. Similarly, the chord constructed over the fifth degree is always a dominant seventh. Well, the diatonic chords over the 2nd, 3rd and 6th scale degrees are all minor seventh chords!

The SUPERTONIC SEVENTH CHORD (ii*MI*⁷ or ii*MI*⁹) is constructed with major scale degrees 2, 4, 6, and 8 (1). This chord is of great importance to jazz musicians because of its fifth relationship with V⁷ (see Unit 8, Lesson 33). Remember that chord tones are always referred to as root, 3rd, 5th and 7th, regardless of what scale degrees they represent.

Track 20

Track 20 begins by alternating between I*MA*⁷ and ii*MI*⁷ chords in the key of E-flat major. Notice that, in this context, the minor seventh chord does not sound sad, but rather hopeful or perhaps, more mellow than the *MA*⁷ sound. Subsequently, the recording alternates between ii*MI*⁷ and V⁷ in that same key. You will notice a sense of tendency and resolution between these two chords.

When the major scale is played in eighth notes from scale degrees 2 to 2, all the tones of the supertonic seventh chord are on the beat, so the chord change is clearly established. This second mode of major is referred to as the DORIAN scale, and is practiced by jazz musicians over supertonic harmony. Notice that dorian sounds analogous to natural minor, but with the sixth note raised.

Exercises

1 Construct the ii*MI*⁷ and rootless ii*MI*⁹ chords in the indicated major keys.
Also notate the dorian scales for each key.

2 For the ii*MI*⁷ and ii*MI*⁹ chords below, label all chord tones—root (r), 3rd, 5th, 7th, and 9th.

UNIT 8 **Lesson 33**

Resolution of iiMI⁷ to V⁷

You learned in Book 1, Lesson 20 that the V⁷ chord *resolves* to the tonic chord (I) because when chord roots are a fifth apart the tendency for resolution naturally occurs. You may have studied the circle of fifths in classical theory, which is a sequential chain of all the chords with their roots a fifth apart. The ii chord is, after V⁷, the next removed from tonic in the circle of fifths.

Because of the circle of fifths, there is a strong tendency for resolution between iiMI⁷ and V⁷. Just like V⁷–IMA⁷, the 7th of iiMI⁷ is a tendency tone, which pulls downward by diatonic step into the 3rd of V⁷ (scale degrees 8–7), and the 3rd of the ii chord is a common tone to the 7th of the V⁷.

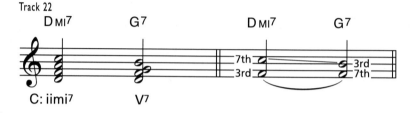

Analogous to V⁷–I is the fact that the 9th of the ii chord is another tendency tone, which resolves down by step to the 5th of V⁷.

The iiMI⁷ chord has two common tones with V⁷, and three with V⁹! So, appealing melodies can be made with use of the common tones and resolution between ii and V⁷.

Track 20

Dig It!—Because the 7th of the iiMI⁷ chord is scale degree 8, a resolution of iiMI⁷–V⁷ is essentially "do–ti." Listen to the iiMI⁷–V⁷ progression in the second half of Track 20. Play "do" (E-flat—the 7th) for the iiMI⁷ chord, and resolve it to "ti" (D—the 3rd) for the V⁷ chord. These two pitches create the wonderful feeling of tension and release in the progression.

Exercises

1 Complete the indicated iiMI⁷ and rootless iiMI⁹ chords, followed by the V⁷ or V⁹ indicated. Use smooth voice leading. Draw straight lines to connect the common tones and arrows showing the resolutions.

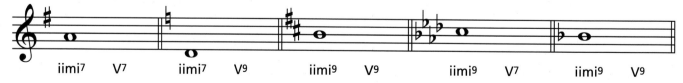

2 Compose melodies to these ii-V progressions, using appropriate jazz language and making use of common tones and resolution.

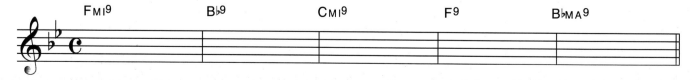

The ii–V–I Turnaround Progression

Track 25 The circle-of-fifth "pull" of iiMI7 to V7 to IMA7 is how keys are established in jazz music. The iiMI7–V7–IMA7 progression is called THE TURNAROUND PROGRESSION, because the resolving tendencies of these chords "turn" the music back to tonic. Amazingly, approximately 75% of the chords in the standard jazz repertoire are ii–V or ii–V–I progressions! A ii–V sequence, without tonic, is enough to imply the key, and is also quite typical. Track 25 features the ii–V and ii–V–I turnaround in the key of F major.

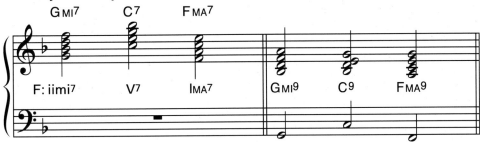

The 3rd of the ii chord is also the 7th of V7, and the 7th of the ii resolves down by a ½ step to the 3rd of V7. This is exactly how chord tones move in the V7–I progression. As a rule, there is this *swapping* of 3rds and 7ths in the circle of fifths.

The common tones and resolutions in the turnaround progression allow jazz musicians to smoothly arpeggiate between the chords.

Exercises

1 For each major key, indicate the chord symbols above the staff for iiMI7–V7–IMA7 and notate the chords, using inversion to create smooth voice leadings. Draw a line from each chord 3rd to the common tone 7th, and an arrow from 7ths to 3rds.

2 For each major key, indicate the chord symbols for iiMI9–V9–IMA9 and notate the chords (rootless), using smooth voice leading. Draw a straight line from each chord 3rd to the common tone 7th, and an arrow from 7ths to 3rds.

3 Compose a melody to the ii–V–I turnarounds, using appropriate jazz solo language and clear resolutions.

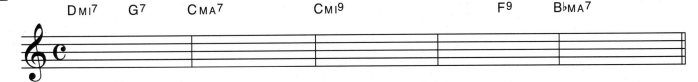

UNIT 8 Ear Training for Lessons 31–34

Track 27

1 Listen to the bass note, followed by two-note voicings of MA7 and MI7.
For the following four-chord voicings, indicate whether each is MA7 or MI7.

    a. MA7 / MI7   **b.** MA7 / MI7   **c.** MA7 / MI7   **d.** MA7 / MI7

Track 28

2 Listen to the sound of the MI7 chord, and then the MI9 chord.
Indicate whether each subsequent chord you hear is MI7 or MI9.

    a. MI7 / MI9   **b.** MI7 / MI9   **c.** MI7 / MI9   **d.** MI7 / MI9

Track 29

3 Listen to the MA9, dominant 9, and MI9 chords. Indicate the quality of each subsequent chord you hear.

    a. MA9 / 9 / MI9   **b.** MA9 / 9 / MI9   **c.** MA9 / 9 / MI9   **d.** MA9 / 9 / MI9

Track 30

4 Listen to the major scale and the Dorian scale.
Indicate whether each subsequent scale is major or Dorian.

    a. major / Dorian   **b.** major / Dorian   **c.** major / Dorian   **d.** major / Dorian

Track 31

5 You will hear an eight-measure phrase played by the rhythm section.
Indicate whether the chord for each bar is IMA9 or iiMI9.

    IMA9 | _____ | _____ | _____ | _____ | _____ | _____ | _____ ||

Track 32

6 Listen to the 7th of iiMI7 resolving to the 3rd of V7, then the 9th of iiMI9 resolving to the 5th of V9.
Write whether each resolution you hear is 7–3 or 9–5. You will hear each resolution TWICE.

    a. 7–3 / 9–5   **b.** 7–3 / 9–5   **c.** 7–3 / 9–5   **d.** 7–3 / 9–5

Track 33

7 Listen to smooth arpeggiation of iiMI7–V7, then iiMI9–V9.
Identify each example as indicated.

    a. iiMI7–V7 / iiMI9–V9   **b.** iiMI7–V7 / iiMI9–V9

    c. iiMI7–V7 / iiMI9–V9   **d.** iiMI7–V7 / iiMI9–V9

1 The common tones of a dominant 9, MA9, and MI9 chord sharing the same root are

_____, _____, and _____.

2 In major keys, there are diatonic minor 7th chords on scale degrees

_____, _____, and _____.

3 The second mode of the major scale is called _____, which sounds like a natural minor

scale with the _____ note raised.

4 The _____ _____ _____ is a sequential chain of chords with roots a descending fifth apart.

5 The _____ of the iiMI7 chord resolves down by a ½ step to the _____ of V7, while the _____ of the

iiMI7 chord is a common tone to the _____ of V7.

6 ii–V–I is called a _____ progression.

7 Alter the following MA7 and dominant 7th and 9th chords into MI7 and MI9 chords,
indicating the new chord symbols above.

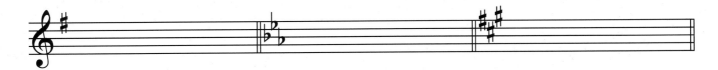

8 For each major key, notate the iiMI9 chord in all four, rootless inversions,
followed by the major scale in the second (Dorian) mode.

9 For each iiMI7–V7–IMA7 progression, notate 3rds and 7ths, showing the "swapping" that occurs.

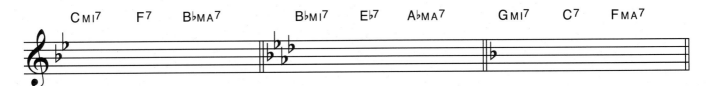

Jazz Language—Combined Scale/Arpeggio & "The ii-V Lick"

Consonance is the overriding factor in compelling melody. Since melody implies, and is constructed over chord changes, the chord tones must be primary. Using a scale in a melody without regard to the chord may not be consonant. Scalar melodies must emphasize the chord.

COMBINED SCALE/ARPEGGIO is a melodic fragment which is largely scalar, but also skips between successive chord tones. The example below shows combined scale/arpeggio for a iiMI7 chord, but these melodic figures are applicable to any type of harmony.

There is a scale/arpeggio figure so prevalent to jazz that it bears the name THE ii–V LICK:

Notice that the 7th to 3rd resolution of ii–V is present in the ii–V lick, although in the example above it occurs early. The ii–V lick can be moved one beat later, placing the resolution on the proper downbeat.

Another permutation finds the ii–V lick extended up to the chord ninth, and resolving by descending scale into the V7.

Exercises

1 Use combined scale/arpeggio in creating a melody to this progression:

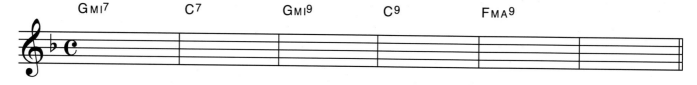

2 Create melodies to these ii–V progressions, using various versions of the ii–V lick.

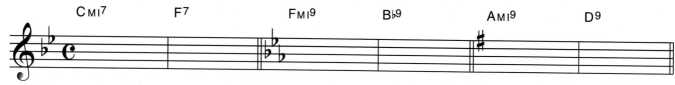

Jazz Language—Triplet Arpeggio & "The Bebop Dominant Lick"

A language is distinguished, in part, by phrases associated with it. We hold together sentences with phrases like, "in other words," "as a matter of fact," and so on. The triplet arpeggio similarly propels the language of a jazz musician. Typically, a TRIPLET ARPEGGIO begins off the beat, a ½ step below the root or 3rd of a chord, and then arpeggiates up the chord with a triplet rhythm.

Descending triplet arpeggio figures occur, but these typically begin on the 7th or 9th of a chord.

A variation of the triplet arpeggio uses 16th notes to encompass a wider range.

In Book 1, Lesson 22 you learned that the bebop dominant scale is an important part of the jazz language for dominant 7th harmony. This descending scale is based on the major scale but begins with two ½ steps. The BEBOP DOMINANT LICK (and its variations) uses the first three notes of the bebop dominant scale, followed by a skip up to the chord 9th, and then another skip down to the 6th and then 5th of the chord. The bebop dominant lick often follows the ii-V lick, and any melody which makes use of the signature first three notes of bebop dominant scale is referred to as a bebop dominant idea.

Exercises

1 For each chord, construct a triplet arpeggio figure, striving for variety.

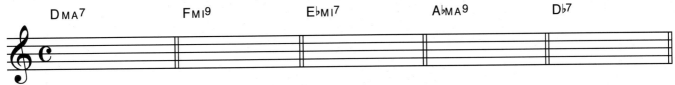

2 For each chord, notate the bebop dominant lick.

3 Compose a melody to the progression, using triplet arpeggio, the ii-V lick, and bebop dominant.

Dominant 13th Chords (13) & ii–V–I Voicings

When a scale is followed to its second octave, the tones gain a value of seven (scale degree 2 becomes 9, degree 3 becomes 10, and so on). By that formula, scale degree 6 becomes 13 in the second octave. The 13th also results by continuing to stack 3rds above the root.

The DOMINANT 13th CHORD is important in jazz, and is the same as a dominant 9th chord with a 13th added. (The 11th, which is the same as a 4th, is not consonant and so is not used.) A dominant 13th chord is called simply "13" (e.g., G13, Bb13, etc). A tone is called a 6th when it replaces a 7th, as in the 6/9 chord. When a chord has both a 6th and a 7th, the 6th is now called a 13th.

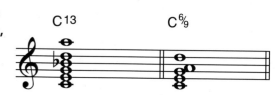

Track 40
Dig it!—Track 40 features a rhythm section playing dominant harmony. Every two measures the chord voicing switches from V9 to V13. The 13th chord is so much more colorful that jazz musicians don't consider the V9 to be very *hip* in comparison.

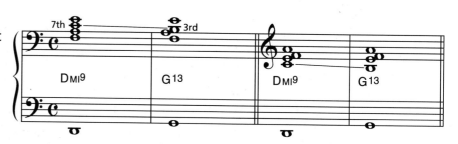

You know that when iiMI7 progresses to V9, only one note changes (the 7th of the iiMI7 resolves to the 3rd of V). The other tones of the iiMI7 are common to V9. When iiMI9 resolves, the same principle applies, and the result is a V13 (the 9th of iiMI9 is the 13th of V13). For iiMI9–V13 voicings, simply place the 3rd or 7th of iiMI9 on the bottom and add the remaining, consecutive chord tones. To get to V13, resolve the 7th of the ii and leave the other notes as common tones.

When V13 voicings connect to IMA9, an opposite procedure is used. The note that moved from ii–V (7 to 3) now is a common tone to I (3–7), and *all* the other notes of V13 are tendency tones and must move down by diatonic step into the IMA9 chord. So, 13ths are also tendency tones, and resolve to 9ths in the circle of fifths.

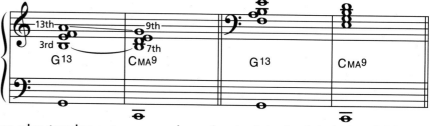

Exercises

1 For each major key, construct four-note voicings in the comping range for iiMI9–V13–IMA9, where either the 3rd or the 7th of the ii chord is on the bottom of the voicing.

FMI9 Bb13 EbMA9

2 For each major key, construct three-note voicings in the comping range for iiMI9–V13–IMA9, where the 3rd of the ii chord is on the bottom of the voicing (hint: omit the 5th of iiMI9).

Passing Minor Major 7th Chord (MI(MA7)) & Progression

Music thrives on tension and release. Fulfilled and thwarted expectations are used alternatively to spark interest and convey emotion. The MINOR MAJOR 7th CHORD is a minor triad with the 7th raised a ½ step. The PASSING MINOR MAJOR 7th PROGRESSION consists of the chords ii–iiMI(MA7)–iiMI7–V7, and uses this raised 7th sound as an unexpected pleasure, which pulls towards the "expected" iiMI7 and increases the fulfillment of the resolution to V7.

Track 41

The iiMI(MA7) is called a PASSING CHORD, because the raised 7th is a passing tone that is not consonant for iiMI7 harmony, but that is precisely why the chord is expressive. In Track 41 you'll notice that the addition of the MI(MA7) chord *delays* the timing of V7 by two beats.

Melodies based on the passing iiMI(MA7) idiom often rely on repeated figures (motives), in which the only notes that change are the ones that highlight the idiom. These figures are typically based on arpeggio, which make the progression very clear.

Conversely, it is possible to form melodies in which the passing iiMI(MA7) idiom is more subtle.

Exercises

1 For each major key, notate the ii, iiMI(MA7), iiMI7, and V9 chords, as in the first example of this lesson.

2 Compose melodies to these ii-V-I progressions, using the passing MI(MA7) idiom based on a repeated figure.

3 Compose melodies to these ii-V-I progressions, using the passing MI(MA7) idiom in a more subtle way.

Track 44

1 For each of the following four examples you will hear a chord followed by a combined scale/arpeggio to that chord. Circle the notation that is correct.

a.
E MI7

b.
A♭MA7

c.
F MA7

d.
B MI9

Track 45

2 The recorded excerpts feature the ii-V lick. For each, indicate whether the 7th of the ii resolves to the 3rd of V early (before the chord changes), on time (as the chord changes), or late.

a. early / on time / late   **b.** early / on time / late

c. early / on time / late   **d.** early / on time / late

Track 46

3 Count the number of triplet arpeggios in the recorded melody.

_____ triplet arpeggios

Track 47

4 Indicate how many bebop dominant ideas you hear. Then, from those how many contain the exact bebop dominant lick?

_____ bebop dominant ideas   _____ bebop dominant licks

Track 48

5 You will hear the progression iiMI9–V13–IMA9, first with the 3rd of ii-mi9 on the bottom, then with 7th of iimi9 on the bottom. Indicate whether each iiMI9–V13–IMA9 progression begins with 3rd or 7th on bottom.

a. 3rd / 7th   **b.** 3rd / 7th   **c.** 3rd / 7th   **d.** 3rd / 7th

Track 49

6 You will hear the ii-V progression with four different two-note melodies in random order. These are resolution 7–3 and 9–5 and common tone 3–7 and 9–13. For each melody you hear (a, b, c, d), circle which of those connections it represents. You will hear each example TWICE.

a. 7–3 / 9–5 / 3–7 / 9–13   **b.** 7–3 / 9–5 / 3–7 / 9–13

c. 7–3 / 9–5 / 3–7 / 9–13   **d.** 7–3 / 9–5 / 3–7 / 9–13

Track 50

7 For each melody using the passing MI(MA7), indicate whether a repeated figure, or a more subtle melody is used.

a. repeated / subtle   **b.** repeated / subtle   **c.** repeated / subtle

1 A scalar melody that skips between successive chord tones is called _____ _____/_____,

and a favored figure using that device is the _____ _____ lick.

2 Fill in the blanks and circle correct answers:

A _____ arpeggio begins:

on / off the beat,

a half step / whole step below a chord tone,

and then uses a _____ rhythm to arpeggiate the chord.

3 Any melody to dominant harmony, beginning on the root and descending two consecutive ½ steps

can be called a _____ _____ figure.

4 When a chord contains both the 6th and 7th, the 6th is more properly referred to as _____.

5 When the 7th of iiMI9 is resolved, and the other voices stay stationary, the resulting chord is

_____.

6 Supertonic chords sometimes are used with passing _____ tones, to add tension and tendency.

7 Compose a melody to the progression using combined scale/arpeggio and versions of the ii-V lick.

EMI7   A7   DMI9   G9   CMA9

8 Compose a melody to the progression using triplet arpeggio and bebop dominant ideas.

G7   B7   C7   AMI9   D9   GMA9

9 For the progression below, write three-note voicings (in the comping range) in appropriate comp
rhythms. On the upper staff, compose a jazz solo melody. Incorporate a passing MI(MA7) into your melody.

AbMA9   GMI9   C13   FMI9   Bb13   EbMA9

Tonicisation of the IV Chord

In Lesson 34 it was noted that about 75% of the chords in standard jazz songs are in ii–V–I idioms. Quite simply, jazz standards almost always begin in the home key and tonicise other key areas with ii–Vs. Preceding any major or minor chord with its own V^7, or ii and V chords, TONICISES it (makes it sound like its own key center).

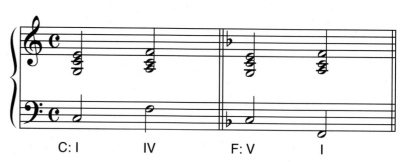

C: I   IV   F: V   I

In major keys, the most likely chord to be tonicised is the IV chord (IV_{MA}^7). The bass motion from I to IV is a descending perfect fifth, just like V–I. So, for instance, the I–IV progression in C major is identical to the V–I progression in F major:

By simply altering the I_{MA}^7 to a dominant quality (lowering the 7th a ½ step), it becomes the V^7 chord *of* IV (e.g., C^7 is V^7 in F major). IV now sounds like a transitory tonic, and therefore has been *tonicised*.

Note: In classical music theory, a chord altered to serve this function is called a secondary dominant. I^7 would be called "V^7 of IV" and indicated with the symbol V^7/IV.

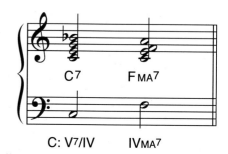

C: V^7/IV IV_{MA}^7

Examining the keys of C and F major, you find that only one note is different: a B♮ in C major and a B♭ in F major. In fact, B♭ was the resulting, *new* note when we altered the C_{MA}^7 chord shown above. So in major keys, the flat 7th degree is the note that establishes the tonicization of the IV chord. Flat 7 is the 7th of the I^7 chord, and it resolves to the 3rd of IV_{MA}^7, as is the case for any V^7–I progression.

Exercises

1 Alter each tonic chord to become a dominant 7th (or 9th) of IV and write the chord symbols.

2 For each major key, notate a V^7/IV in root position and a rootless V^9/IV with the 3rd on the bottom.

3 For each major key, write the 7th of I^7 (V^7/IV) and resolve it to the 3rd of IV_{MA}^7. Write the chord symbols.

The ii–V Turnaround to IV

In early jazz music (up to around 1930) V⁷–I alone was often used to establish tonalities. As the music evolved and matured, ii chords became a staple sound. So, from the bebop period on, a fully tonicised IV is usually preceded by both its ii and V chords and called the TURNAROUND TO IV. Let's return to the key of C major to examine that progression.

- We know that in C major, FMA⁷ is IV, and an altered I chord (C7) is V⁷/IV.

- We also know that in the key of F major, GMI⁷ is ii.

- In C major, G⁷ is V, so we must alter that chord to a MI⁷ quality to realize the iiMI⁷ of IV.

- The complete turnaround to IV is vMI⁷–I⁷–IVMA⁷.

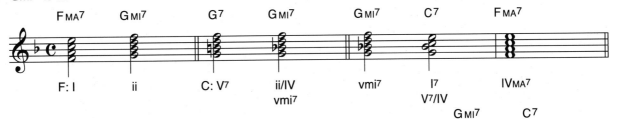

Remember that vMI⁷ is functioning as the ii chord to IV (ii/IV), and so its 7th resolves to the 3rd of the next chord, V⁷/IV (I⁷).

Dig it!—The great thing about tonicising IV is that it takes the music, tonally, to a temporary new home, a needed harmonic variety. And yet, since IV is diatonic to the key, it is never abrupt when the music returns to tonic.

After a turnaround to IV the music can return to IMA⁷. . .

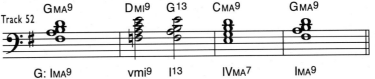

or the next chord might be ii, since IVMA⁷ is entirely contained in iiMI⁹!

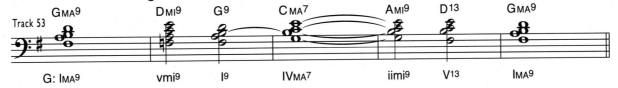

The turnaround to IV is found in a large cross section of jazz standards, including "Just Friends," "There Will Never Be Another You," "Take the 'A' Train," "My Romance," "Misty" and so on.

Exercises

1 Alter the following V⁷ (or V⁹) chords to become ii of IV (ii/IV, vmi).

2 Indicate the chord symbols for the turnaround progression to IV in the following major keys.

3 For each major key, notate the chord symbols for a turnaround to IV.
Then, write and resolve each chord 7th to the following chord 3rd.

Melody for the Turnaround to IV

Beethoven's "Eroica" Symphony begins with arpeggiation of the tonic triad altered in the fifth measure to V⁷/IV. A critic described this opening as a hero riding into battle. In the fifth measure, the hero pauses to think of the woman he left behind! Why this description? When a progression tonicises IV, a flat is temporarily added, or a sharp deleted. The result is that the music becomes warmer or darker.

The flat 7th is more than just a harmonic note. It is the expressive note in melodies that establishes the darker feeling of a turnaround to IV.

Bebop dominant ideas are very important to jazz melody in the turnaround to IV because they "tease" the listener with the major 7th before sounding the darker flat 7.

The ii–V lick is also a frequent component of melody for the turnaround to IV.

The turnaround to IV progression is a "borrowed" ii–V–I progression. For instance, in the key of C major, we are borrowing ii–V–I from F major. So naturally, the principals of voicing and voice leading you have learned for ii–V–I progressions will apply.

Exercises

1 Compose a melody to the progression using bebop dominant and resolution in the turnaround to IV.

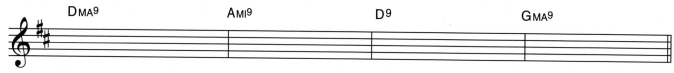

2 For the following keys, indicate the chord symbols for the vmi⁷–I⁷–IVma⁷ turnaround progression. On the staves, notate two-note voicings in the comping range.

3 For the following keys, indicate the chord symbols for the vmi⁹–I¹³–IVma⁹ turnaround progression. On the following staff, notate four-note voicings in the comping range.

II Dominant Seventh Chords (II⁷)

After ii–V–I and the turnaround to IV, the next most common idiom in jazz harmony uses the II DOMINANT SEVENTH CHORD, a dominant chord built on ii. This chord is found in countless standards, including, "Take the 'A' Train," "There Will Never Be Another You," "Just Friends," "The Girl from Ipanema" and so on. Since the diatonic ii seventh chord is a minor 7th, simply raising the chord 3rd a ½ step results in a dominant II⁷.

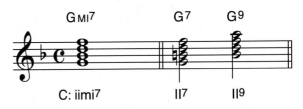

The II⁷ chord is actually a secondary dominant, the V⁷ of V (V⁷/V). For instance, in the key of C major, Dmi⁷ is ii and G⁷ is V. But, in the key of G, D⁷ is V!

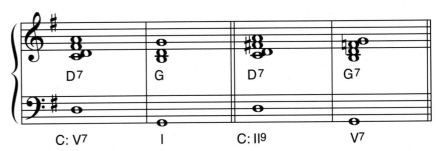

Sometimes, II⁷ chords resolve to V, with the usual treatment of tendency tones. Notice, though, that the 3rd of II⁷ isn't a common tone to the 7th of V⁷, but rather is enharmonically a ½ step away.

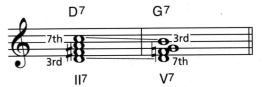

While it is true that II⁷ chords move to V in some jazz tunes, more often they simply progress (or regress) to the diatonic iimi⁷. In this usage, the II⁷ chord is sort of "hanging around" and waiting for the iimi⁷–V–I cadence. The raised 3rd of II⁷ is a hopeful sound in melodies, and produces a pleasing sense of resolution into the natural 3rd of the following iimi⁷.

Exercises

1 For each major key, write a II⁷ chord in root position and also a rootless II⁹. Indicate chord symbols above the staff.

2 Resolve each II⁷ voicing into the indicated V chord. Label the 7th of II⁷ and draw an arrow to the 3rd of V. Draw a jagged line between the 3rd of II⁷ and the enharmonically different 7th of V⁷.

3 Compose a melody to the progression using resolution, jazz language, and highlighting the 3rds of both the II⁷ and iimi⁷ chords.

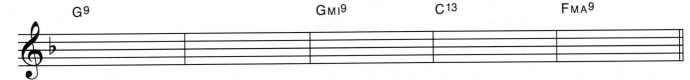

UNIT 10 Lesson 43

II⁹⁽♯¹¹⁾ *Chords, Lydian Dominant Scale, I Augmented Chord Extension (I+)*

As mentioned in the previous lesson, the II⁷ chord sometimes resolves to V, but more often *dissolves* into the diatonic iiMI⁷. In the latter context, II⁷ isn't functioning as a secondary V⁷, but rather as a more stable sound. Jazz musicians typically extend this chord to a ♯11th, adding to its uniqueness in the progression, and call it the II⁹⁽♯¹¹⁾ CHORD.

Since ♯11 is the same note as ♯4, there is an inherent Lydian nature to the II⁹⁽♯¹¹⁾ chord. (You learned about the Lydian fourth in Book 1, Lesson 12.) A LYDIAN DOMINANT SCALE is the Mixolydian scale used for dominant harmony, altered by raising the 4th degree by a ½ step.

When a II⁷ melody features the ♯11, as it usually does, a sense of resolution is achieved by moving to the 5th of the ensuing iiMI⁷ chord.

The most effective melodies for II⁹⁽♯¹¹⁾ employ the I AUGMENTED CHORD (I+). The I+ chord is a tonic triad with the 5th raised chromatically. Notice that the I+ chord can also be explained as 7, 9 and ♯11 of II⁷! In fact, adding the major 7th (I+⁽ᴹᴬ⁷⁾) gives you the 13th of II⁷ (II¹³⁽♯¹¹⁾). So, any melody figure to IMA⁷ can be repeated, raising the 5th for II⁹⁽♯¹¹⁾.

The easiest way to create voicings for a II⁹⁽♯¹¹⁾ is to replace the chord 5th with the ♯11 (♯4) ½ step below.

Exercises

1 For each indicated II⁹⁽♯¹¹⁾, write the Lydian dominant scale and a rootless voicing in the comping range. In each case, circle the ♯11 (♯4) in the scale.

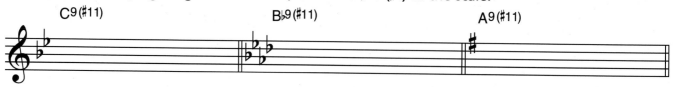

2 Compose a melody to the progression using I+ as extensions to II⁹⁽♯¹¹⁾ and achieving a sense of resolution into the iiMI⁷.

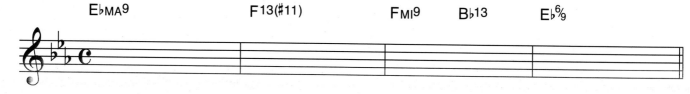

Track 61

1 You will hear I_{MA}^9–IV_{MA}^9 followed by I^9–IV_{MA}^9.
For each example, write whether the first chord is I_{MA}^9 or I^9.

    a. I_{MA}^9 / I^9 **b.** I_{MA}^9 / I^9 **c.** I_{MA}^9 / I^9 **d.** I_{MA}^9 / I^9

Track 62

2 Listen to the melody with rhythm section.
Indicate in which measure the turnaround to IV begins.

    Measure ____.

Track 63

3 Listen to the demonstrated II^7, ii_{MI}^7, and V^7 chords.
Indicate whether each following progression uses II^7, ii_{MI}^7, or both.

    a. II^7 / ii_{MI}^7 / both   **b.** II^7 / ii_{MI}^7 / both   **c.** II^7 / ii_{MI}^7/ both   **d.** II^7 / ii_{MI}^7 / both

Track 64

4 You will first hear a II^9 chord and a $II^{9(\#11)}$ chord.
Listen to the four chords following and indicate whether each chord you hear is II^9 or $II^{9(\#11)}$.

    a. II^9 / $II^{9(\#11)}$ **b.** II^9 / $II^{9(\#11)}$ **c.** II^9 / $II^{9(\#11)}$ **d.** II^9 / $II^{9(\#11)}$

Track 65

5 Listen to the demonstrated dominant scale (Mixolydian) and the Lydian dominant scale.
For the four scales following, circle whether each scale is Mixolydian or Lydian dominant.

    a. Mixolydian / Lydian dominant   **b.** Mixolydian / Lydian dominant

    c. Mixolydian / Lydian dominant   **d.** Mixolydian / Lydian dominant

Track 66

6 Transcribe the remaining notes of the melody you hear.

1 A chord is _____ by preceding it with its own ii and V.

2 Lowering the 7th of the _____ chord creates a dominant of IVma7.

3 The complete turnaround to IV involves the chords _____, _____, and _____.

4 The turnaround to IV is seldom used in jazz standards.   **True / False.**

5 Most often the II7 chord progresses to _____. It is typical to alter the II7 by adding ____.

6 II9(#11) melodies can use the _____ _____ scale.

Also a _____ chord is really the upper extensions of II9(#11).

7 Compose a melody to the progression using resolution and characteristic melody devices for the turnaround to IV. On the bass staff, write two-note voicings, in the comping range.

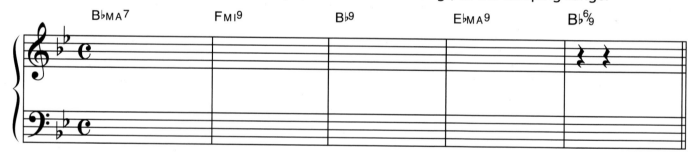

8 In the key of C major compose a melody to the progression II7–V7–Ima9, where we hear the 3rd of II7 moving chromatically into the 7th of V7, and also the 7th of V7 resolving into the 3rd of Ima9. Indicate the chord symbols above the staff.

9 Compose a melody to the progression using Lydian dominant and also the I+ extension for II9(#11).

Diminished 7th Chords (°7) & Diminished Scales

The DIMINISHED 7TH CHORD is one of the more fascinating and exotic sounds in music. It is mysterious and unstable, and in a jazz context, quite beautiful. Constructed of three minor thirds stacked on top of each other, it is indicated by the symbol °7 (also dim7). The chord is *symmetrical*, because no matter what note you put on the bottom, it is still the same arrangement of minor 3rds.

Notice that C#°7, E°7, G°7, and A#°7 are all the same chord! Consequently, there are only three different diminished 7th chords. Here are the two others.

The DIMINISHED SCALE contains all the notes of the diminished seventh chord, and is an alternation of whole and ½ steps. This scale is also known as OCTATONIC.

Because of the symmetry of diminished 7th chords, there are likewise only three diminished scales. To clarify, if you begin the C-sharp diminished scale (above) on E, G or Bb, you have E, G and Bb diminished scales, alternating whole and ½ steps. On the contrary, a C major scale, starting on E is certainly *not* an E major scale! Here are the other two diminished (octatonic) scales.

Notes 1, 3, 5, and 7 of the diminished scale are the tones of the °7 chord.
Notice that tones 2, 4, 6, and 8 combine to form a different °7 chord.

Exercises

1 Construct the indicated diminished seventh (°7) chords.

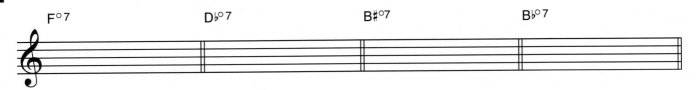

2 Construct the indicated diminished (octatonic) scales.

U N I T   11   **Lesson 45**

The vii°7 Chord, #iv°7 Chord, Diminished 7th Melody

In classical music, the diminished 7th chord functions as a dominant, just like V7. To clarify, a triad built on the 7th degree of a major scale is diminished, although a chromatic note is needed to form a diminished seventh chord (°7), and the diminished chord has three common tones to V7. So in classical music (and sometimes in jazz) THE vii°7 CHORD is a dominant function chord.

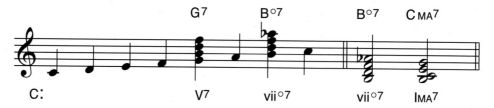

Often in jazz music, diminished seventh chords are NONFUNCTIONAL CHORDS, or embellishing sounds between two functional chords of a progression. Typically they connect chords with bass notes one step apart. THE #iv°7 CHORD is used in this manner in the progression IV6–#iv°7–IMA7/V (tonic chord with the 5th in the bass). Note: the IV6–#iv°7–IMA7/V idiom is found in "I Got Rhythm," "Paper Moon," and some versions of the 12-bar blues.

Ironically, the notes of the diminished chord are not very expressive for jazz melody, but rather sound old fashioned. The other notes of the diminished scale (2, 4, 6, 8) form the "juicy" notes. Jazz musicians often use the symmetry of diminished to fashion sequential motives, emphasizing these expressive notes, whole and ½ steps on either side of each chord tone. A melodic SEQUENCE repeats itself exactly, transposed by some interval. In the case of diminished, the sequence is by minor 3rd interval, as you would guess!

Track 70 C#°7

Track 71

Dig it!—Track 71 has a rhythm section playing a C#°7 chord. Try playing (or singing) the notes of the chord. Now, play the other notes of the diminished scale, resolving each one up ½ step, or down 1 step. Hear the difference?

Exercises

1 For the indicated major keys, indicate the chord symbols for IV6–#iv°7–IMA7/V and write four-note voicings in the comping range, with smooth voice leading.

2 For each °7 chord, construct a sequential melody.

The Turnback Progression & The VI⁷ Chord

It is common to find phrases in jazz tunes ending with two measures of the tonic chord. In cases where the next phrase also begins on the IMA⁷, jazz musicians frequently employ a turnback progression to provide harmonic variety. A TURNBACK is the chords I–VI⁷–iiMI⁷–V⁷, with each chord usually lasting two beats. And of course in jazz music, chordal extensions are encouraged!

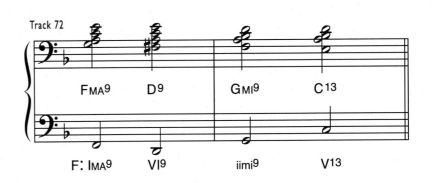

You know that ii–V creates a pull towards IMA⁷. Similarly, a dominant VI chord pulls to ii, because VI precedes ii in the circle of fifths.

In major keys, the diatonic sixth chord is minor (vi), but in the turnback the 3rd is raised chromatically to make VI a dominant 7th. VI⁷ (or VI⁹) then, is the secondary dominant of ii (V⁷/ii). As you see below, D⁷ to GMI is V–I in the key of G minor, but those same chords are V⁷/ii to ii in F major.

The VI⁷ chord provides a colorful new note for melody and soloing, because the 3rd of that chord is a ½ step above tonic in the key.

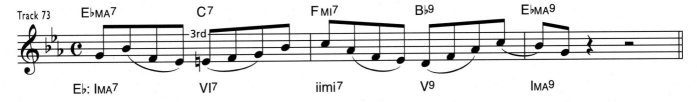

Exercises

1 For the indicated major keys, indicate the chord symbols for the turnback progression and notate keyboard voicings on the staff.

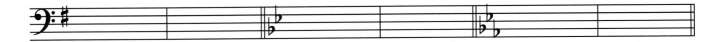

2 Construct jazz solo melodies to the turnback progressions emphasizing the 3rd of VI7 and jazz language you have learned so far.

AABA Standard Song Form—"Take the 'A' Train" Progression

Nearly a century of great jazz performance has been poured into a group of tunes (mostly in 32 bars) called "standards." At least half of these STANDARD SONGS are in AABA FORM, consisting of four, eight-bar phrases. The 'A' phrases are nearly identical in melody and harmony, while the 'B' phrase, or BRIDGE, is contrasting in both. Take a look at the harmonic progression to Billy Strayhorn's, "Take the 'A' Train:"

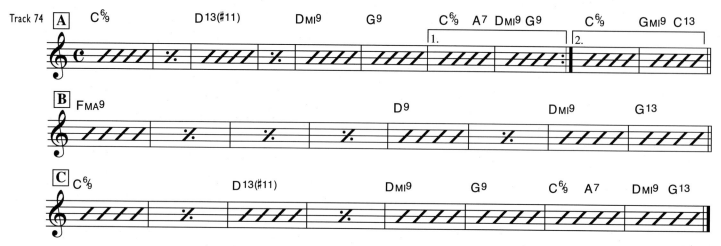

You can see that the 'A' phrases are almost identical, beginning with IMA7 and then II7 (Strayhorn's melody features #11). As expected, II7 goes to iiMI7, which begins the inevitable ii–V–I turnaround. The first 'A' has an optional turnback to I (1st ending). The end of the second 'A' has a turnaround to IV, which begins the bridge (2nd ending). The final 'A' also has an optional turnback.

The Bridge ('B') provides contrast. Beginning on IVMA7, it creates a feeling that the music has gone to a new destination. The II7 signals that ii and V are on the way, so that the 'A' theme can return. This is a great example of how AABA standards are constructed.

Here is a solo to the "Take the 'A' Train" progression.

Exercise

1 Analyze the solo above, identifying characteristic jazz melodic devices, scales, resolutions, chord extensions, etc.

Track 76

1 Listen to the dominant 9th chord voicing and the diminished 7th chord.
Write whether each chord is dominant 9th or diminished.

a. Dom 9 / °7   **b.** Dom 9 / °7   **c.** Dom 9 / °7   **d.** Dom 9 / °7

Track 77

2 Listen to the diminished scale and the Lydian dominant scale.
Indicate whether each melody uses diminished or Lydian dominant.

a. diminished / Lydian dominant   **b.** diminished / Lydian dominant

c. diminished / Lydian dominant   **d.** diminished / Lydian dominant

Track 78

3 Listen to the progression, IV6–#iv°7–IMA7/V, demonstrated first. In the ensuing progression,
at what bar does the IV–#iv°7–I/V progression begin?

Measure _____.

Track 79

4 Listen to the melody to a °7 chord, which employs both the diminished chord tones and the
expressive, other notes of the scale. How many of the expressive notes are used?

_____ expressive notes.

Track 80

5 Listen to the IMA9 and VI7 chords, the concurrent, two-note melody is the tonic note moving up ½
step to the 3rd of VI7. For each of the turnback melodies you hear next, indicate whether the 3rd
of VI7 is used.

a. yes / no   **b.** yes / no   **c.** yes / no   **d.** yes / no

Track 81

6 Listen to the solo over the first half of the progression to "Take the 'A' Train."
Indicate whether each of these melodic devices is employed.

7–3 resolution:	**yes / no**
Combined scale/arpeggio:	**yes / no**
The ii–V lick:	**yes / no**
Triplet arpeggio:	**yes / no**
Bebop dominant:	**yes / no**
Minor +7:	**yes / no**
Lydian dominant:	**yes / no**
I+ extension:	**yes / no**
3rd of the VI7 chord:	**yes / no**

UNIT 11 Review of Lessons 44–47

1 The diminished 7th chord (°7) is _____ _____ intervals stacked on each other.
The chord is _____ because any of its notes could be the root.

2 The diminished or _____ scale is an alternation of _____ and _____ _____.

3 Diminished 7th chords (°7) in jazz are typically used to connect bass notes _____ apart.

4 Notes 1, 3, 5, and 7 of the diminished scale are the most expressive tones. **True / False**.

5 A _____ line features repetition of a melody, transposed by some interval.

6 The chords IMA7–VI7–iiMI7–V7 form a _____ progression.

7 The _____ is the 'B' section of an _____ form.

8 In the key of G major compose a melody to the progression II7–V7–IMA9, where we hear the 3rd of II7 moving chromatically into the 7th of V7, and also the 7th of V7 resolving into the 3rd of IMA9. Indicate the chord symbols above the staff.

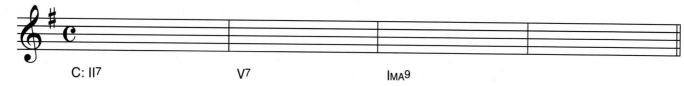

C: II7   V7   IMA9

9 Compose a melody to the first four bars of the "Take the 'A' Train" progression, using the I+ extension for II9(#11). Write the chord symbols above the staff.

10 Compose a melody to the last four bars of the bridge of the "Take the 'A' Train" progression, using Lydian dominant for II9(#11). Write the chord symbols above the staff.

Jazz Language—Chromatic Leading & Passing Tones, Bebop Scales

Melodic chromaticism plays an important role in jazz melody. Chromatic notes which are not in the chord are used to great effect, because they create tension and tendency. A chord tone feels more satisfying when it arrives after chromatic embellishment. Classical musicians refer to these non-harmonic tones as *decorative chromaticism*.

A decorative LEADING TONE (l.t.) is a note a ½ step below a chord tone.
Jazz melody often skips into chromatic leading tones

A good definition of "scale" is *chord tones and notes in between*. The scale below, entirely chord tones and leading tones, is actually "hipper" than the diatonic one.

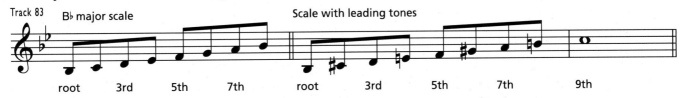

Jazz musicians love to approach a chord tone from a step above, and then move by descending ½ steps into a CHROMATIC PASSING TONE and then the chord tone.

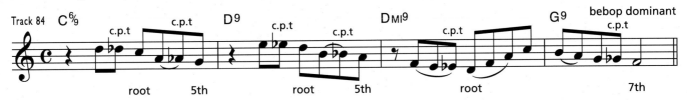

The bebop dominant scale is a result of this idea, approaching the chord 7th from a step above. So, it is possible to invent other bebop scales, by inserting a leading tone between chord tones.

Exercises

1 Analyze this melody by circling chromatic leading and passing tones, and labeling bebop scales. Do you notice how each decorative chromatic note *points* to the ensuing chord tone?

2 For each chord below, construct a bebop scale.

Jazz Language—Auxiliary "Enclosure" Tones

There is one melodic gesture that sums up the language of the bebop era more than any other, and that is the use of multiple auxiliary, or enclosure tones. When a melody moves from a chord tone to a note a ½ or whole step away and back, the middle (decorative) note is called an auxiliary tone (also neighbor tone).

ENCLOSURE TONES are two or more auxiliary tones on both sides of the chord tone, sounded prior to the chord tone.

Most often, jazz musicians employ enclosure tones around the root, 3rd or 5th of a chord, but any chord tone can be embellished in this fashion. Here are a variety of enclosure tone figures around a chord root.

Track 86

The note a ½ step away from a chord tone is always a viable enclosure tone, whether or not that note is consonant. A note one whole step away from a chord tone, which is outside of the consonant scale or key will not make a suitable enclosure tone. In that case, the dissonant note can be used, but it must move chromatically into the chord tone.

Bebop jazz melody often skips from one chord tone to enclosures of the next, even if the chord is going to change. This device provides the angularity that is a signature element of bebop style.

Track 87

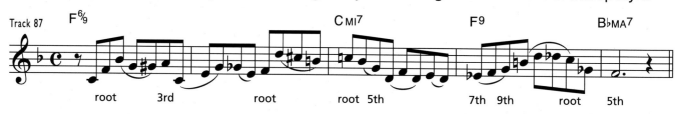

root   3rd   root   root 5th   7th 9th   root   5th

Exercises

1 For the melody above, circle the enclosure tones.

2 Compose a melody using only chord tones and enclosure tones.

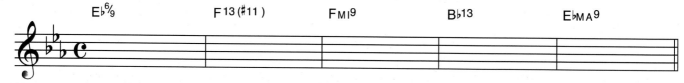

The Jazz Blues Progression, Finding the Chromatics

You learned a simple 12-bar blues progression in Book 1, Lesson 25. Now you have the tools to understand the blues as performed by more proficient jazz musicians. Here is the jazz blues progression in the key of F major (parenthetical chords are optional):

Notice that measure 4 can be a turnaround (ii–V) to the IV chord in measure 5. In measure 6, a ♯iv°7 chord creates a pull towards the return of I7 in measure 7. Likewise, the VI7 chord in measure 8 is V7 of the ii chord, which begins the last four measures. Finally a turnback is used in the last two measures, to repeat for more choruses.

Here is a solo melody to the jazz blues progression.

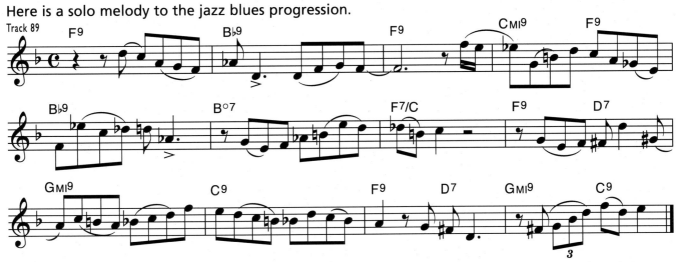

Jazz musicians know that chord tones (especially 3rds and 7ths), which are not in the key of the song, are very colorful and important to melody. Emphasizing those notes might be called FINDING THE CHROMATICS. In the solo above: the 7th of the IV chord is emphasized in measure 2, because it is a ½ step away from the 3rd of I7; the flat 7th of the key enables the turnaround to IV in measure 4; the iv°7 has a chromatic root and 7th; the 3rd of VI7 is a ½ step above the tonic.

Exercises

1 *Dig it!*—When a musician finds the chromatics, you can hear the changes in the melody alone. In the solo above, locate and circle the chord tones that are chromatic to the key, then try playing the solo alone. Do you hear the progression?

2 Optional: on your own music manuscript paper, compose a solo to the jazz blues progression in E-flat major. Indicate the chord symbols above the staff.

UNIT 12   Ear Training for Lessons 48–50

Track 90

1 In this jazz melody, how many chromatic leading tones are used?
How many enclosure tone figures are used?

_____ chromatic leading tones   _____ enclosure tone figures

Track 91

2 For this jazz melody, how many chord tones are approached chromatically from a step above?

_____ chromatic approaches from above

Track 92

3 Listen to the bebop dominant and bebop major scales.
Indicate whether each scale is bebop dominant or bebop major.

     a. bebop dominant / bebop major   **b.** bebop dominant / bebop major

     c. bebop dominant / bebop major   **d.** bebop dominant / bebop major

Track 93

4 Listen to these bebop major and bebop minor scales.
Indicate whether each scale is bebop major or bebop minor.

     a. bebop major / bebop minor   **b.** bebop major / bebop minor

     c. bebop major / bebop minor   **d.** bebop major / bebop minor

Track 94

5 Listen to the solo to the 12-bar blues, which is written below.
Add accidentals so that the notation is correct.

1 Chromatic _____ tones and _____ tones add tension and tendency to a melody.

2 A scale can be defined as _____ tones and _____ in between.

3 Major, minor, and dominant chords can all have bebop scales.   **True / False**

4 _____ tones help create the angularity of bebop melody.

5 The important chromatic (non-diatonic) tones in the 12-bar blues are the 7th of _____

in measure 4, and the _____ of VI⁷ in measure 9.

6 Write bebop scales to these chords:

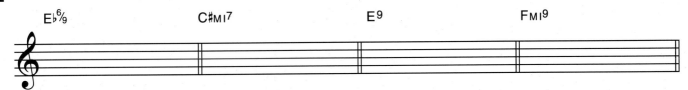

7 Analyze this melody. Circle and identify instances of decorative chromaticism. Label bebop
scales and any other scalar devices. Label resolutions and prominent functionally chromatic tones.

8 Compose a melody to the 12-bar jazz blues using leading tones, enclosure tones, bebop scales,
and emphasizing important non-diatonic notes. Write the chord symbols above the staff.

GLOSSARY & INDEX OF TERMS & SYMBOLS

Includes all the terms and symbols used in Book 2 and the page on which they are first introduced.

AABA SONG FORM: 32-bar song with four, 8-bar phrases where the "A" phrases are nearly identical while the "B" phrase (bridge) is contrasting (p. 72).

ACCOMPANIMENT: an enhancement of melody through texture, such as one or more instruments playing chords (p. 45).

ACCOMPANIMENTAL CHORDS: played by a keyboard or guitar, or two or more instruments simultaneously sounding notes (voicings) (p. 45).

AUXILIARY TONE: when a melody moves from a chord tone to a note a ½ or whole step away, and back, the middle note is an auxiliary tone (p. 76).

THE BEBOP DOMINANT LICK: first three notes of the bebop dominant scale, followed by a skip up to the chord 9th, another skip down to the 6th, and then the 5th of the chord (p. 57).

BRIDGE: "B" section of an AABA song form (p. 72).

CHROMATIC LEADING TONE: decorative note a ½ step below a chord tone (p. 75).

CHROMATIC PASSING TONE: decorative note a ½ step from a chord tone, used to fill in a melodic whole step. (p. 75).

CIRCLE OF FIFTHS: bass movement of a P5 interval from one chord to the next (p. 45).

COMBINED SCALE/ARPEGGIO: melodic fragment which is largely scalar, but also skips between successive chord tones (p. 56).

COMPING: rhythmic accompaniment of chords, adding tension and release in the music (p. 46).

COMPING RANGE: a range of approximately a sixth on either side of middle C (p. 45).

CONTRAPUNTAL TEXTURE: aural depth created by counterpoint, such as the combination of walking bass and melody (p. 45).

COUNTERPOINT: simultaneous occurrence of two or more musical voices (p. 43).

DIMINISHED SEVENTH CHORD (°7): symmetrical chord constructed of three minor thirds (p. 69).

DIMINISHED SCALE: an 8-note scale that contains all the notes of the diminished seventh chord and an alternation of whole and ½ steps (also known as octatonic) (p. 69).

DOMINANT 13TH CHORD: a dominant 9th chord with an added interval of a major 13th above the root (p. 58).

DORIAN SCALE: major scale played from scale degrees 2 to 2, particularly useful when played over supertonic harmony (p. 51).

ENCLOSURE TONE: 2 or more auxiliary tones on both sides of a chord tone, sounded prior to the chord tone (p. 76).

FINDING THE CHROMATICS: emphasizing chord 3rds and 7ths that are not in the key of a song (p. 77).

JAZZ BLUES PROGRESSION: a variation on the standard 12-bar blues, popular with jazz musicians (p. 77).

LEADING TONE: a chromatic leading tone a ½ step away from the chord tone (p. 75).

LYDIAN DOMINANT SCALE: Mixolydian scale, altered by raising the 4th degree by a ½ step (p. 66).

MINOR MAJOR 7 CHORD: a minor triad with the 7th raised a ½ step (p. 59).

MINOR TRIAD: a 3-note chord consisting of a root, minor 3rd and perfect 5th (p. 50).

MINOR SEVENTH: the interval between the root and seventh degree of a natural minor scale (p. 50).

MINOR SEVENTH CHORD: a 4-note chord with root, minor 3rd, perfect 5th and minor 7th (p. 50).

MINOR NINTH CHORD: a minor seventh chord with an added major 9th above the root. If bass is playing, omit the root (p. 50).

NONFUNCTIONAL CHORDS: embellishing chords typically used to connect two chords with bass notes one step apart, e.g. IV6–#IV°7–IMA7/V (p. 70).

OCTATONIC: see diminished scale (p. 69).

ONE AUGMENTED CHORD (I+): tonic triad with the 5th raised chromatically (p. 66).

PARTITO ALTO: prevalent Brazilian comping pattern and permutations heard in bossa nova and samba (p. 47).

PASSING CHORD: chord with a non-diatonic passing note that adds expressiveness (p. 59).

RESOLUTION: result of a chord (or note) that is musically compelled to go to the next chord (or note); when chord roots are a fifth apart the tendency for resolution naturally occurs (p. 52).

SEQUENCE: melodic motive that repeats itself exactly, transposed by a selected interval (p. 70).

SEVEN DIMINISHED SEVENTH CHORD (vii°7): diatonic triad built on the 7th degree of a major scale with a chromatically lowered 7th (p. 70).

SHARP 4 DIMINISHED SEVENTH CHORD (#IV°7): embellishing chord commonly used in the progression IV6–#IV°7–IMA7/V (p. 70).

SHARP 11 (#11): chord extension a sharp 11 above the chord root (same note as #4), often added to II7 (p. 66).

SIX DOMINANT SEVENTH CHORD (VI7): A secondary dominant of ii; a dominant seventh chord built on the 6th degree of a major scale used in the turnback progression (p. 71).

SUPERTONIC SEVENTH CHORD: a minor seventh chord constructed with major scale degrees 2, 4, 6 and 8 (1) (p. 51).

TONICISATION: making a temporary or new key center by preceding any major or minor chord with its own V7, or ii and V chords, particularly common in major keys with the IV chord (p. 62).

TRIPLET ARPEGGIO: an arpeggio that begins off the beat a ½ step below the root or 3rd of a chord, then arpeggiates up the chord with a triplet rhythm (p. 57).

TURNAROUND: ii-V progression that "turns" the music back to a tonic (p. 53).

TURNAROUND TO IV: tonicisation of the IV chord that takes the music, tonally, to a temporary new home by preceding the IV chord with its own ii-V (p. 63).

TURNBACK: chord progression I–VI7–iiMI7–V7, with each chord usually lasting two beats (p. 71).

II DOMINANT SEVENTH CHORD (II7): a dominant chord built on scale degree ii (p. 65).

II DOMINANT NINTH CHORD (II9(#11)): a II7 chord with extensions M9 and #11 (p. 66).

TWO FEEL: created when bass plays two half notes in each bar of 4/4 (or a dotted quarter, eighth-note pattern), causing the music to feel in a two-beat meter (cut time, 2/2) (p. 43).

ii–V: ("two–five") chord progression consisting of a minor chord built on scale degree 2, followed by a dominant seventh chord built on scale degree 5 (p. 52).

THE ii–V LICK: scale/arpeggio figure prevalent in jazz featuring 7th to 3rd resolution of ii-V (p. 56).

TWO-NOTE VOICING: chord arrangement sounding just a chord 3rd and 7th in the comping range, assuming the bass plays the root (p. 45).

VOICINGS: arrangements of chords with two or more chord tones, particularly chord 3rds and 7ths (p. 45).

WALKING BASS: continual quarter note bass motion in which, more often than not, the chord root is on the downbeat of each measure (p. 43).

ALFRED'S ESSENTIALS OF
JAZZ THEORY

Lessons ■ Ear Training ■ Workbook

BOOK 3

Pages 81–120 ■ Lessons 51–75

TABLE OF CONTENTS
Book 3

Jazz Language—Melodic Soloing & Melodic Sequence

If music is compared to painting, then melody represents the finest and most detailed brush strokes, and melodic devices are the paint colors. As introduced in Book 1, Lesson 5, MELODIC SOLOING (MOTIVIC SOLOING) is basing musical phrases on simple ideas, which are repeated and varied. It is actually composing a new melody to the chord structure. Using this device, a soloist may think of the original motive as a thought or emotion: repetition deepens or intensifies the emotion, while variation expands on it. Because the ideas are simple in melodic soloing, individual notes take on heightened significance. The example below demonstrates melodic soloing to the beginning of the "Take the 'A' Train" chord progression. Notice how the repetition is not exact, but altered to reflect the new color of the second chord.

Playing is said to be "organic" when the variation of a motive becomes the seed for the next variation.

MELODIC SEQUENCE is the repetition of an idea transposed by some interval. An idea may be sequenced once, or several consecutive times. An ascending sequence can be successively more soaring or thrilling…

…while a descending sequence can make a melody more somber or introspective.
Track 3 demonstrates both an ascending and descending melodic sequence.

Exercises

1 Continue the melody in the motivic style, using repetition and variation.

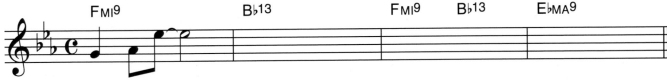

2 Continue the melody using sequence.

Afro-Cuban Jazz: Clave & Tumbau

Thanks to trumpeter Dizzy Gillespie, a great jazz ambassador, Afro-Cuban influences were introduced into jazz in the 1940s when Gillespie traveled to Cuba and incorporated the vitality of the repetitive Cuban rhythms into the jazz mainstream.

The Afro-Cuban rhythms used in jazz are based on a figure called CLAVE (KLAH-vay), which is a two-measure rhythmic pattern, alternating two or three notes per bar. These figures can be clapped or played on *claves*, which are a pair of hardwood sticks struck together. There are variations of the rhythm pattern, but the two basic claves are either 3–2 CLAVE ("three-two clave"):

Or the opposite, 2–3 CLAVE:

Notice that when three notes are played in a measure, they occur on beat 1, the "and" of 2, and on beat 4. This clave is accentuated by another pattern, the tumbau (TOOM-bow). The TUMBAU rhythm, played on a bass drum and also by the bass player, features notes on the "and" of 2, and on beat 4.

In the tumbau, beat 1 is not accentuated at all, and often, beat 4 feels more like the downbeat. As a result of the lack of an accented beat 1, Afro-Cuban music feels very "circular" as the pattern endlessly repeats.

Bass lines based on tumbau feature chord roots and 5ths almost exclusively. They may or may not have a note on the downbeat of a bar, and the note on beat 4 may be tied into the next measure. Track 4 demonstrates the clave rhythms described above and then adds a tumbau bass line.

Track 4   F MA7

Exercises

1 Find a recording of an Afro-Cuban jazz song. Listen and determine if the clave is 2–3 or 3–2. Practice clapping along with the clave.

2 Compose a bass line to the progression below, based on tumbau.

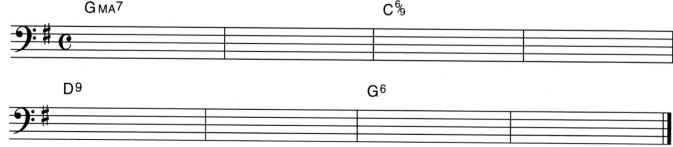

Afro-Cuban Jazz: Cascara & Montuno

You've probably noticed that Afro-Cuban rhythms are nuanced and are more effectively learned aurally than visually. The cascara rhythm is no exception. CASCARA (KHAS-kah-rah), or paila, is an Afro-Cuban rhythmic figure played in a two-measure pattern, which is based on, and embellishes the clave. Cascara is named for playing on the "shell" or side of a drum, but it is also played at times on the bell of a cymbal, cowbell, or with a rim knock on a snare drum.

Track 5

Notice that the cascara has notes on beats 2 and 3 in one measure, and accentuates the "and" of 2 and beat 4 in the other, just the same as clave. So, the cascara should always be played in sync with the clave.

clavè

cascara

In Afro-Cuban jazz, pianists employ identifiable and repetitive comping patterns called montunos. A MONTUNO is a triadic and highly syncopated comping figure, often played in octaves, or two octaves apart. Some Afro-Cuban tunes repeat a ii–V progression, and in these instances the montuno often features common tones and the 7–3 resolution.

Track 6   G MI7   C9   G MI7   C9

Another ii–V montuno uses the passing minor major 7th idiom (MI(MA7)).

Track 7   A MI   A MI(MA7)   A MI7   D9

A montuno to a single chord can emphasize two chord tones a step apart (often with a passing tone in between), such as 6th and 7th, 5th and 6th, etc. There are dozens of effective montuno patterns.

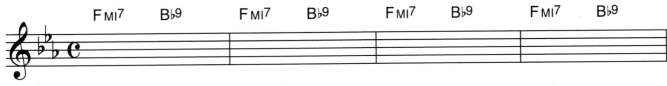

Track 8   C6   F MA7

Exercises

1 Compose a montuno to the ii–V progression.

F MI7   Bb9   F MI7   Bb9   F MI7   Bb9   F MI7   Bb9

2 Compose a montuno to the Major 7th chord.

G MA7

Drop-Two Voicings

You have learned that four-note voicings arise out of consecutive chord tones and usually omit the root. Chord arrangements with consecutive tones are called CLOSED VOICINGS, and you know that proper *voice leading* results from using common tones and resolutions.

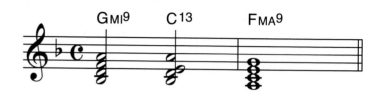

DROP-TWO VOICINGS are derived directly from four-note, closed voicings. For a drop-two voicing, simply take the second note from the top of a closed voicing, and drop it one octave. The new, drop-two sound, is more open, or spacious than that of the closed voicing. Pianists use two hands for drop-two voicings, and drop-two voicings are effective when arranging for wind and string instruments.

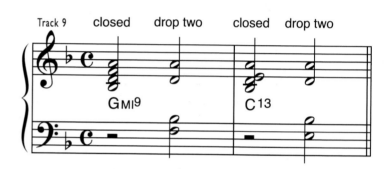

A drop-two voicing may also be achieved using an opposite procedure, which you might call "fly-two." In this instance, the second note from the bottom is raised one octave.

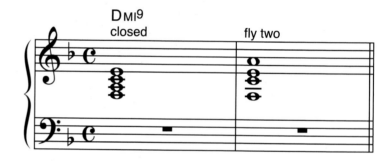

The principles of using common tones and resolution for smooth voice leading apply to drop-two chords.

Exercises

1 Convert the chords to drop-two or fly-two voicings as indicated.

2 Notate drop-two voicings for the progression, using smooth voicing leading.

Minor 11th Chords (MI¹¹) & Sus Chords (SUS, ⁷SUS)

As discussed in Book 1, Lesson 9, the note a perfect 4th (P4) above the root of any major triad is very dissonant. When the 4th is used in a melody to major or dominant chords, it creates tension, and must be resolved by step (usually downward).

Conversely, the P4 above the root of a minor triad is consonant and stable in jazz, and is known by its name up one octave, the 11th. A MINOR 11TH CHORD (MI¹¹) is a MI⁷ chord with an added 11th. Voicings of the MI¹¹ may omit the chord 5th, and may or may not include a 9th.

A MI¹¹ chord functions the same as other minor chords in jazz, but may also serve as a modal tonic. In the 1960s MODAL JAZZ tunes, based on a mode rather than a key, came into fashion. The notes of the MI¹¹ chord are in both the Dorian and Aeolian scales, so the chord is a mainstay of modal jazz. A modal jazz tune may stay on one chord for a long duration; for example, Miles Davis's hit, "So What."

A chord that functions similarly to a MI¹¹ chord is the SUS CHORD (SUS or ⁷SUS). A sus chord replaces the chord 3rd with a 4th. Just as in jazz, classical composers of the 17th through 19th centuries considered the 4th dissonant, and called it a *suspension*, because it was suspended just above the 3rd. So, *sus* is jazz shorthand for *suspended*. Sus chords tend to use the 5th in the voicing, and the root also can be used. ⁷SUS chords have a minor 7th above the root.

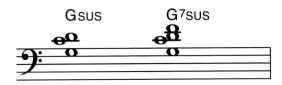

Dig it!—The ⁷SUS chord may be arranged entirely in perfect 4ths, and modal jazz tunes and solos often favor the 4th interval. A chord arranged in perfect 4ths is called QUARTAL HARMONY.

Exercises

1 Write voicings to the MI¹¹ and ⁷SUS chords, in closed spacing in the comping range.

2 Write a melody to the ⁷SUS chord, emphasizing 4ths.

E⁷SUS

3 What scale is used in the second example of this lesson? _____

UNIT 13 Ear Training for Lessons 51–55

Track 12

1 You will hear four melodies.
For each, answer if the melody is motivic.

  a. yes / no   **b.** yes / no   **c.** yes / no   **d.** yes / no

Track 13

2 You will hear four melodies.
For each, indicate if the melody is sequential.

  a. yes / no   **b.** yes / no   **c.** yes / no   **d.** yes / no

Track 14

3 You will hear four sequential melodies.
For each, write if the melody is sequenced up or down.

  a. up / down   **b.** up / down   **c.** up / down   **d.** up / down

Track 15

4 For each excerpt, indicate if the clave is 2–3 or 3–2.

  a. 2–3 / 3–2   **b.** 2–3 / 3–2   **c.** 2–3 / 3–2   **d.** 2–3 / 3–2

Track 16

5 Write whether each montuno is to a ii–V, major chord, or minor chord.

  a. ii–V / MA / MI   **b.** ii–V / MA / MI   **c.** ii–V / MA / MI   **d.** ii–V / MA / MI

Track 17

6 You will hear a closed voicing, then a drop-two voicing.
Write whether each following chord is closed or drop-two.

  a. closed / drop-two   **b.** closed / drop-two   **c.** closed / drop-two   **d.** closed / drop-two

Track 18

7 Listen to the MI7 chord and the 7SUS.
Write whether each following chord is MI7 or 7SUS.

  a. MI^7 / ^{7}SUS   **b.** MI^7 / ^{7}SUS   **c.** MI^7 / ^{7}SUS   **d.** MI^7 / ^{7}SUS

1 The repetition of a melodic idea, transposed by an interval is called _____.

2 When three notes of clave are in one measure they fall on beat ____, the "and" of ____, and ____.

3 In Afro-Cuban music, a bass/bass drum figure on the "and" of 2, and 4 is called _____.

4 The Cascara pattern is based on clave.   **True / False**

5 _____ is a highly syncopated Afro-Cuban piano pattern.

6 Convert the closed voicings into drop-two (or fly-two), staying close to the comping range.

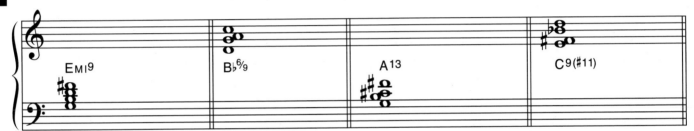

EMI9   Bb6⁄9   A13   C9(#11)

7 Write drop-two voicings for the indicated chords.

C13   GMI9   Bb9   BMA9

8 Write chord symbols for these rootless voicings. Hint: each has a 3rd or 7th on the bottom.

9 Write voicings for the indicated chords, in closed spacing in the comping range.

A7SUS   EbMI11   BbMI11   Db7SUS

Minor Tonic Chord (iMI(MA⁷), iMI⁶/⁹), Jazz Minor Scale

In jazz music, as in all other Western musical genres, sad or somber pieces are in minor keys. (For a review of minor keys see *Essentials of Music Theory, Book 3*) In classical music, a minor triad functions as the tonic chord. Jazz, on the other hand, features chord extensions of at least a 7th. Adding a diatonic 7th to the imi triad creates a minor seventh chord, a sound we associate with ii not tonic. So, jazz musicians chromatically raise the diatonic 7th to create a stable, tonic sound.

The raised 7th degree, which is from the melodic-minor scale, results in a minor major 7th chord,

Another minor tonic is the MINOR 6/9 CHORD (MI⁶/⁹), using the raised 6th degree of melodic minor.

Dig it!—The sound of both minor tonics (iMI(MA⁷) and iMI⁶/⁹) are stable in jazz and the altered notes are the interesting, "juicy" notes that give the music its distinctive character.

Obviously, jazz musicians use the ascending melodic-minor scale to create melody to minor tonics. When the scale descends, the alterations remain, rather than reverting to the natural minor, and this is called the JAZZ MINOR SCALE.

Exercises

1 Notate the indicated rootless MI⁹(MA⁷) chords in all four positions.

2 Notate the indicated rootless MI6/9 chords on the treble staff,
and then notate a drop-two voicing for each.

3 For each minor key, notate the jazz minor scale in ascending and descending direction.

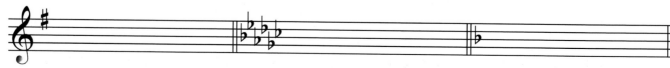

Minor ii–V Turnaround, Half-Diminished Chord (ø7) & V7(♭9) Chord

Keys are established by ii–V and ii–V–I turnaround progressions, and minor keys are no exception.
The MINOR ii–V–i TURNAROUND uses the chords iiø7–V7(♭9) –iMI(MA7) (or iMI6/9).
The diatonic ii7 chord in a minor key is the same as a minor 7th chord with the chord 5th flatted.
This chord is called a HALF-DIMINISHED CHORD (ø7) or MINOR SEVEN FLAT FIVE CHORD (MI7(♭5)).

The diatonic 9th of ii in a minor key is a minor 9th
above the root and is not a consonant note. So
when a 9th is added to a half-diminished chord, it
is typically a major 9th above the root (iiø7(MA9)).

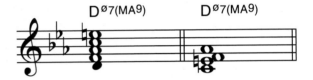

As with MI7 chords, the 11th over ø7 harmony
is consonant and can be included.

Just as with minor keys in classical music, V7 chords in jazz are altered
by raising the chord 3rd, in order to have dominant 7th quality.

The diatonic 9th above V7 in minor keys is a minor 9th
above the chord root. This note is great for V7 chords,
and the resulting chord is called FIVE SEVEN FLAT NINE
(V7(♭9)). The chord tones from 3rd to ♭9th of a V7(♭9)
chord are a diminished 7th chord.

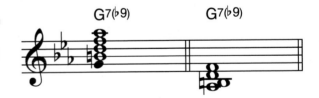

Exercises

1 Notate iiø7 and V7(♭9), in root position in the indicated keys, and write the chord symbols above the staff.

2 Write the indicated ø7 and 7(♭9) chords, in closed spacing in the comping range.

    Cø7   Aø7(MA9)   E♭7(♭9)   F♯7(♭9)

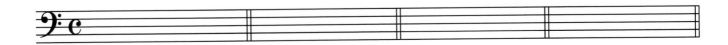

Resolutions and Voice Leading

The ii⌀7, V7(♭9) and tonic minor chords (iMI(MA7) or iMI⁶/₉) in jazz each have a unique color, quite different from their counterparts in major keys. Yet, the resolutions in the ii–V–i minor turnaround are

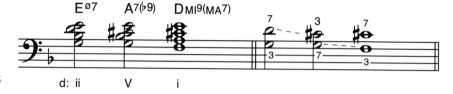

exactly the same as those in major. In other words, the ii–V–i minor turnaround is a circle-of-fifths progression. So, chord 7ths are tendency tones seeking resolution downward into 3rds, and each 3rd is a common tone to the next chord 7th.

It also holds true that 9ths resolve downward into 5ths, which are common tones to ensuing 9ths.

Dig it!—Tension and release is an important element in the drama of music, and it is the reason that melodies sound so good when tendency tones are used and resolved. When a tendency tone is a whole step above the resolving note, extra tension and release is achieved by passing through the chromatic half step, as with the natural 9th of ii⌀7 going to the 5th of V7(♭9) below.

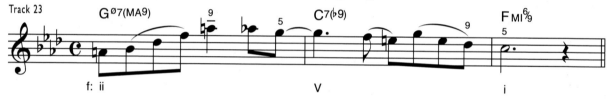

Closed and drop-two voicings for ii⌀7–V7–i in minor are constructed as expected, using tendency tones and common tones for smooth voice leading. But, the root *is* a permissible note in a ⌀7 voicing, because it creates tension with the chord 5th, a tritone away.

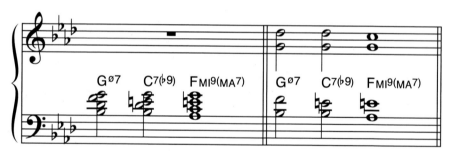

Exercises

1 Compose melodies to the minor turnaround progressions, using tendency tones and resolution for tension and release.

2 Construct drop-two voicings to the indicated ii–V–i progressions. Indicate the chord symbols; draw arrows to show resolving tones, and straight lines for common tones.

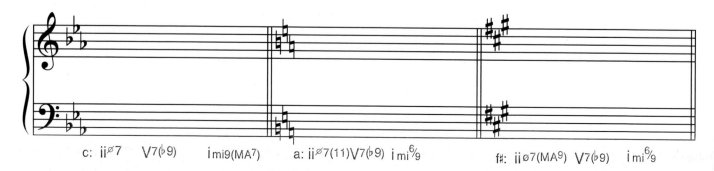

Jazz Language—Scales for the Half-diminished Chord (ø7)

Jazz musicians practice scales as a tool for instrument mastery, and also as "raw material" for melodic ideas. There are two typical scales for ø7 melody.

One is the SECOND MODE OF NATURAL MINOR. For instance, since Bø7 is iiø7 in A minor, that chord uses an A natural minor scale, from B to B.

The other scale for ø7 is achieved by raising the second note of the scale shown above. The second note of any scale is the chord 9th, and in this case the raised second degree is the chord's major 9th, which is more consonant.

Dig it!—CD Track 24 has a rhythm section playing Aø7 harmony. Try both ø7 scales and listen for the subtle difference between them.

Melodies that use the natural minor scale for iiø7 stay in a somber tone because the second scale degree is also the 3rd of the minor tonic chord.

The raised 2nd of the altered natural minor scale allows for more emphatic or, perhaps, hopeful melodies. That note resolves downward into the natural 3rd degree of the key.

Exercises

1 For each minor key, indicate the chord symbol for iiø7 and construct both scales.

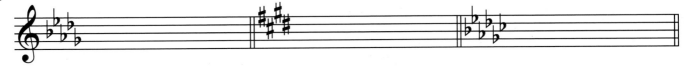

2 Write a melody using tones from the natural minor scale for iiø7.

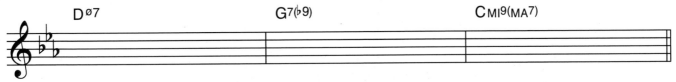

3 Write a melody using the tones from the altered natural minor scale for iiø7.

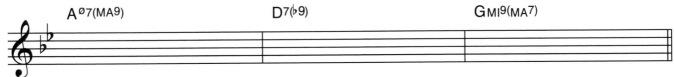

Jazz Language—Harmonic-Minor Scale & Lick for V7(♭9)

A very effective and often-used scale for V7(♭9) is the 5TH MODE OF HARMONIC MINOR (in other words, harmonic minor of the tonic).

A unique feature of harmonic minor is the augmented second contained within it. These two notes happen to be the 3rd and ♭9th of the V7(♭9) chord, so just playing the scale brings the chord alive.

The harmonic-minor scale is often played in descending order, and is very consonant when started on a beat, beginning with the 3rd, 5th, 7th, or ♭9th of the chord.

The HARMONIC-MINOR LICK is based on the harmonic-minor scale, and skips from the 3rd up to the ♭9th of V7(♭9), and then moves down the scale, resolving 7–3 into the tonic. This line is equally effective whether used over just the V7(♭9) harmony, or both the ii∅7 and V7(♭9).

The harmonic-minor lick works just as well with a descending skip from the 3rd to ♭9th.

A variation of the lick arpeggiates from the 3rd to ♭9th, and then resolves directly into the 5th of tonic.

Melodic ideas based on harmonic minor are very important for dominant harmony in jazz, and you will hear endless examples on great jazz recordings from all eras.

Exercises

1 For each V7(♭9), add the key signature and write the descending harmonic-minor scale of tonic from the indicated chord tone.

2 For each V7(♭9)–i progression, use a different harmonic-minor lick in composing a melody.

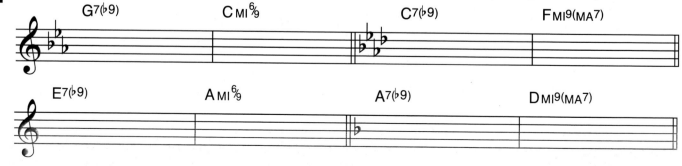

Track 31

1 You will hear a MI^9 chord and then a MI^9(MA^7) chord.
Indicate whether each subsequent chord is MI^9 or MI^9(MA^7).

   a. MI^9 / MI^9(MA^7)   **b.** MI^9 / MI^9(MA^7)   **c.** MI^9 / MI^9(MA^7)   **d.** MI^9 / MI^9(MA^7)

Track 32

2 You will hear a natural-minor scale and then a melodic-minor scale.
Indicate whether each subsequent scale is natural or melodic minor.

   a. natural / melodic   **b.** natural / melodic   **c.** natural / melodic   **d.** natural / melodic

Track 33

3 You will hear a MI^7 chord and then a $^\varnothing{}^7$ chord.
Indicate whether each subsequent chord is MI^7 or $^\varnothing{}^7$

   a. MI^7 / $^\varnothing{}^7$ **b.** MI^7 / $^\varnothing{}^7$ **c.** MI^7 / $^\varnothing{}^7$ **d.** MI^7 / $^\varnothing{}^7$

Track 34

4 You will hear a V^9 chord and then a V$7^{(\flat 9)}$ chord.
Indicate whether each subsequent chord is V^9 or V$7^{(\flat 9)}$.

   a. V^9 / V$7^{(\flat 9)}$ **b.** V^9 / V$7^{(\flat 9)}$ **c.** V^9 / V$7^{(\flat 9)}$ **d.** V^9 / V$7^{(\flat 9)}$

Track 35

5 You will hear iiMI^9–V^{13} and then a ii$^{\varnothing 7}$–V$7^{(\flat 9)}$.
Indicate whether each subsequent progressions is iiMI^9–V^{13} or ii$^{\varnothing 7}$–V$7^{(\flat 9)}$.

   a. iiMI^9–V^{13} / ii$^{\varnothing 7}$–V$7^{(\flat 9)}$ **b.** iiMI^9–V^{13} / ii$^{\varnothing 7}$–V$7^{(\flat 9)}$

   c. iiMI^9–V^{13} / ii$^{\varnothing 7}$–V$7^{(\flat 9)}$ **d.** iiMI^9–V^{13} / ii$^{\varnothing 7}$–V$7^{(\flat 9)}$

Track 36

6 Listen to the ii$^{\varnothing 7}$ with the natural-minor scale of tonic and then the altered natural minor
(with the 2nd note raised). Write whether each of the following scales is natural or altered.

   a. natural / altered   **b.** natural / altered   **c.** natural / altered   **d.** natural / altered

Track 37

7 You will hear four melodies to ii$^{\varnothing 7}$–V$7^{(\flat 9)}$–iMI$^{6/9}$ using ideas based on the harmonic-minor lick.
For each, indicate whether 7th resolves to 3rd, or $\flat$9th resolves to 5th, when V^7 goes to tonic.

   a. 7–3 / $\flat$9–5   **b.** 7–3 / $\flat$9–5   **c.** 7–3 / $\flat$9–5   **d.** 7–3 / $\flat$9–5

UNIT 14 Review of Lessons 56–60

1 The tonic chord for minor keys is MI7 or MI9. **True / False**

2 The jazz minor scale uses the ascending form of _____ minor in both directions.

3 The ii chord for minor is _____ and the V7 chord is _____.

4 The natural minor scale of tonic, which is used for iiø7 chords, can be altered by raising the _____ scale degree over the root of iiø7.

5 For each minor key, write rootless iMI9(MA7) and iMI6/9 chords with the 3rd on the bottom. Indicate chord symbols above the staff.

6 Resolve each iiø7 chord to the best inversion of V7(b9). Indicate chord symbols above the staff.

7 Indicate whether each melody uses the natural minor or altered natural-minor scale for iiø7.

8 For each progression, write the harmonic-minor lick.

Turnaround to iv in Minor Keys

You learned in Book 2, Lesson 39, that jazz songs in major keys often tonicize the IV chord with a ii–V turnaround. The turnaround to iv is also typical for jazz tunes in minor keys. The iv chord for minor keys is itself a minor 7th chord.

The TURNAROUND TO iv IN MINOR is v⁰⁷–I7(♭9)–ivMI7, so alterations must be made to both the diatonic v and i chords. The diatonic v7 chord in minor keys is a MI7 chord, so the 5th is flatted for v⁰⁷ (ii/iv).

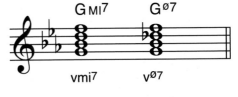

Of course, tonic chords in minor keys are minor. So, the diatonic 3rd must be raised to get a dominant I7 chord (V7/iv). The 9th of this chord is characteristically flatted, resulting in a dominant 7(♭9) chord.

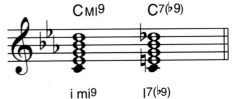

The ii⁰⁷–V7(♭9) turnaround to iv in C minor looks and sounds like ii–V–i in the key of F minor, although, in this case, the FMI7 is not altered to be a tonic.

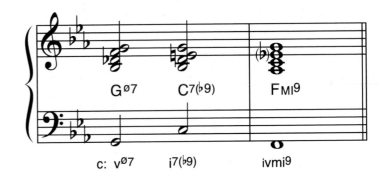

Melodies to the turnaround to iv should emphasize the non-diatonic pitches, for instance the 5th of v⁰⁷, which is a 1/2 step above tonic in the key (this same note is ♭9 of I7(♭9)). The other important chromatic note is the raised 3rd of I7. Both of these notes are in the harmonic minor of iv, so harmonic-minor language is very effective.

Exercises

1 For each minor key, indicate chord symbols for the turnaround to iv (v⁰⁷–I7(♭9)–ivMI9), and write closed voicings, with proper voice leading in the comping range.

2 Write a melody to the progression, using harmonic-minor language for the turnaround to iv.

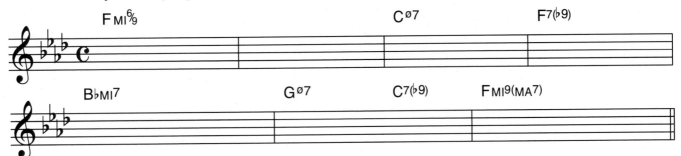

UNIT 15 Lesson 62

Minor Turnback, VI⁷–V⁷⁽♭⁹⁾–i Cadence

You learned with major keys that when a chorus ends on the tonic chord, a I–VI–ii–V turnback progression cycles back around to tonic for the next chorus. Jazz musicians similarly employ the MINOR TURNBACK for tunes in minor keys. The VI chord in the minor turnback is half-diminished, based on the raised 6th degree. So the entire progression is I–♯vi⁰⁷–ii⁰⁷–V⁷⁽♭⁹⁾. Notice that ♯vi⁰⁷ has all the same notes as imi⁶!

The minor turnback has been used by composers in various ways. For instance, Jerome Kern's composition "Yesterdays" begins with a minor turnback.

A variation on the minor turnback uses a dominant quality III⁷ chord in place of ♯vi⁰⁷.

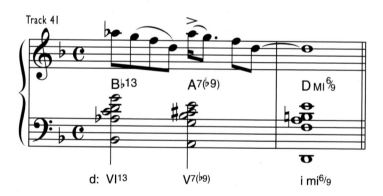

Another peculiarity of minor keys is that a dominant quality VI chord often substitutes for ii⁰⁷ in a turnaround progression. The VI⁷–V⁷⁽♭⁹⁾–i CADENCE creates a more "bluesy" sound. The diatonic VI chord in minor is a Major 7th (VIMA⁷), so the 7th must be flatted to create a dominant VI⁷ chord.

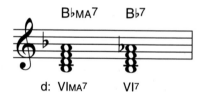

The natural 9th and 13th of VI⁷ are diatonic, so VI⁹ and VI¹³ chords are usual. A ♭9 extension of VI⁷ is avoided because that note implies a chord functioning as a dominant (V⁷), and in this context VI⁷ is substituting for ii. Additionally, ♯11ths are viable extensions. Notice that VI⁷ resolves to V⁷ in much the same way as ii does, with voices moving stepwise down. The notes of the VI⁷ chord cause solo ideas to sound naturally bluesy.

Exercises

1 For each minor key, write the chord symbols for the minor turnback progression and notate voicings, with proper voice leadings, in closed spacing in the comping range.

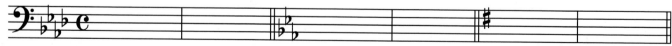

2 Write chord symbols and a solo melody to the progression.

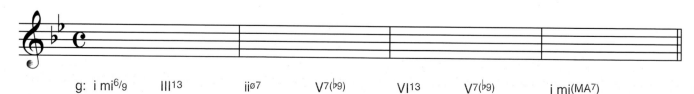

g: i mi⁶/⁹   III¹³   ii⁰⁷   V⁷⁽♭⁹⁾   VI¹³   V⁷⁽♭⁹⁾   i mi(MA⁷)

Blues Scale in Minor Keys, Minor Pentatonic & Pentatonic/Blues Scales

Melodies for minor turnbacks and turnarounds may be blues related, rather than focusing on each chord change. In Book 1, Lesson 25, you learned about the BLUES SCALE and it is exactly the same for parallel minor and major keys (e.g., C minor and C major). Of course, the notes that are ♭3 and ♭7 in major are diatonic in minor.

The MINOR PENTATONIC SCALE is the pentatonic scale from the relative major, so the D minor pentatonic scale has the same notes as the F major pentatonic scale. Minor pentatonic is a mildly bluesy sound, since all of the notes are also in the blues scale.

The notes of the blues scale for a minor key can be used in the relative major to create another blues sound. For instance, the notes of the E blues scale can be used in G major (the relative major of E minor). This scale is called the PENTATONIC/BLUES SCALE because it contains all the notes of major pentatonic, plus a flatted 3rd to the key (1, 2, ♭3, 3, 5, 6).

Dig it!—As with the blues scale, the pentatonic/blues scale isn't meant to *make the changes,* but rather create a bluesy pallet of sound. The scale tones 6, ♭3, and 1 are an appealing and often-used subset of the scale.

Exercises

1 Compose melodies to the turnbacks using blues and minor pentatonic scale materials.

2 Bracket the melody line that uses the pentatonic/blues scale and label the scale tones used.

UNIT 15   Ear Training for Lessons 61–63

1 You will hear four progressions in minor keys.
For each, indicate in which measure a turnaround to iv begins.

    a. measure ____   **b.** measure ____   **c.** measure ____   **d.** measure ____

2 You will hear four melodies to the progression $i\text{MI}^{6/9}$–$v^{ø7}$–$I7^{(\flat9)}$ –$iv\text{MI}7$.
In each turnaround to iv, indicated whether the melody uses the raised 3rd of $I7^{(\flat9)}$.

    a. yes / no   **b.** yes / no   **c.** yes / no   **d.** yes / no

3 Listen to the i–$\sharp vi^{ø7}$–$ii^{ø7}$–$V7^{(\flat9)}$ turnback and then a i–III^{13}–$ii^{ø7}$–$V7^{(\flat9)}$ turnback.
Identify whether each subsequent turnback uses $\sharp vi^{ø7}$ or III^{13}.

    a. $\sharp vi^{ø7}$ / III^{13} **b.** $\sharp vi^{ø7}$ / III^{13} **c.** $\sharp vi^{ø7}$ / III^{13} **d.** $\sharp vi^{ø7}$ / III^{13}

4 Listen to the blues scale and the minor pentatonic scale.
Indicate whether each melody uses blues or minor pentatonic.

    a. blues / minor pentatonic   **b.** blues / minor pentatonic

    c. blues / minor pentatonic   **d.** blues / minor pentatonic

5 Listen to the blues scale and the pentatonic blues scale (for major keys).
Indicate whether each melody uses the blues or pentatonic blues scale.

    a. blues / pentatonic blues   **b.** blues / pentatonic blues

    c. blues / pentatonic blues   **d.** blues / pentatonic blues

6 Listen to $ii^{ø7}$–$V7^{(\flat9)}$–$i\text{MI}^{6/9}$ and VI^{13}–$V7^{(\flat9)}$–$i\text{MI}^{6/9}$.
Write whether each subsequent turnaround uses $ii^{ø7}$ or VI^{13}.

    a. $ii^{ø7}$ / VI^{13} **b.** $ii^{ø7}$ / VI^{13} **c.** $ii^{ø7}$ / VI^{13} **d.** $ii^{ø7}$ / VI^{13}

7 Listen to the chord progression (played three times) and write the remaining chord symbols.

    $G\text{MI}^{6/9}$ _____ _____ _____ _____ _____ _____ _____

1   The turnaround to iv in minor keys uses the chords _____ – _____ – _____.

2   For a turnaround to iv in minor, the diatonic _____ of VMI7 must be flatted,

and the diatonic 3rd of iMI7 must be _____.

3   In the VI7–V7–i turnaround, the altered 9th is preferred for VI7.   **True / False**

4   The second chord of a minor turnback can be either _____ or _____.

5   For major keys, licks using the pentatonic blues scale often emphasize tones ____, ____, and ____.

6   Complete each turnaround to the iv progression and indicate chord symbols between the staves. On the top staff, write a melody for each progression.

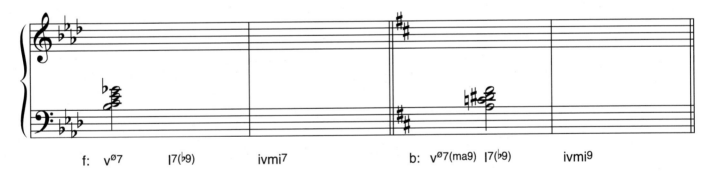

    f: v⌀7   I7(♭9)   ivmi7   b: v⌀7(ma9)   I7(♭9)   ivmi9

7   For each minor key, write voicings in the comping range to a VI13–V7(♭9)–IMI9(MA7) turnaround. Indicate the chord symbols above the staff.

8   For each major key, write the pentatonic blues scale.

Turnarounds to III and VI in Minor Keys

The major and minor seventh chords that are diatonic to major and minor keys serve as secondary tonics in jazz songs. A ii–V turnaround to any of these diatonic chords "tonicizes" that chord as a temporary new home. Minor keys have three major diatonic triads within them, over scale degrees 3, 6, and 7. Of those, the III and VI chords also have major 7ths.

Each diatonic major chord should have its own iimi7 chord (or iimi9), and dominant V9 chord (or V13). The TURNAROUND TO III in minor keys is entirely diatonic, ivmi9–VII13–IIImA7 (ii/III–V/III–III),

because III is the relative major in minor keys. So, the turnaround to III in C minor is the same as ii–V–I in Eb major, and this progression sounds like a temporarily modulation to the relative key.

The TURNAROUND TO VI requires some chromatic alteration. The turnaround to VI is VIImi7–III7–VImA7, and the same chromatic pitch (1/2 step above tonic) is the 3rd of VII and the 7th of III.

Dig it!—Check out this progression that turns around to VI and III before returning to the minor tonic. You can hear the music going to new major "homes." Notice how the melody *finds the chromatics*, emphasizing the non-diatonic tones.

Songs such as "Autumn Leaves," "Summertime," "Beautiful Love" and "What's New" all tonicize diatonic major chords in minor keys.

Exercises

1 Indicate chord symbols and write drop-two voicings for this progression.

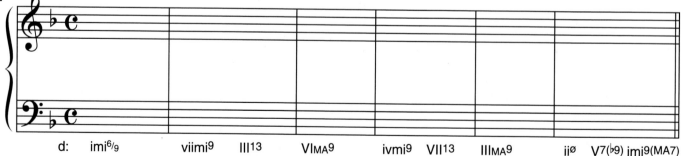

2 Write a solo that *finds the chromatics* to the progression.

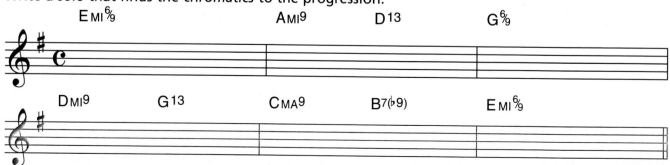

Minor 12-Bar Blues Progression

There is a 12-bar blues progression in minor, and songs such as "Mr. P.C." and "Coming Home Baby" are MINOR BLUES compositions. Wayne Shorter's "Footprints" is a variation of minor blues. The standard MINOR 12-BAR BLUES PROGRESSION is below. A review of the major 12-bar blues can be found in Book 2 (Lesson 50).

Measures 1–4: As with major blues, this phrase establishes tonic and moves towards subdominant. Unlike major blues, measure 2 of minor blues is less likely to feature the iv chord. But just as with major blues, ii–V to iv is often found in measure 4.

Measures 5–8: Just like major, this phrase begins on the iv chord, returns to tonic, and sets up a final turnaround. The unusual feature of minor blues is that it often features a ii-V back to tonic in measure 6. Measure 8 can be a turnaround to set up the VI chord.

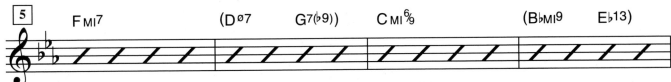

Measures 9–12: This phrase serves the same function as its counterpart in major, turnaround to tonic. However, minor blues most often uses the "bluesy" alternate cadence, VI7–V7–i. Of course, a turnback in the last two measures can set up additional choruses.

*Chords in parentheses are optional.

Track 54
Track 54 features the entire minor 12-bar blues progression.

Exercises

1 Notate the minor blues progression and compose a solo based on language you have learned.

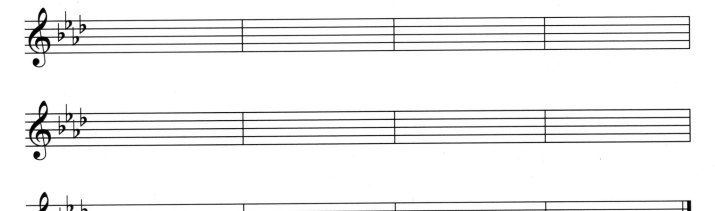

Lesson 66

Minor Turnarounds in Major Keys—to ii and vi

When a song in a minor key tonicizes a diatonic major chord (III or VI), a more hopeful energy is injected into the somber mood. Conversely, a song in major can become more reflective or melancholy when it tonicizes diatonic minor chords. Minor chords result over scale degrees 2, 3 and 6 in major keys and these chords can be tonicized with minor turnarounds.

Let's examine the two most popular minor turnarounds in jazz for major keys: the TURNAROUND TO ii and the TURNAROUND TO vi.

Turnarounds to the diatonic minor chords typically use half-diminished, secondary ii chords (iiø7), and secondary V chords with flat ninths (V7(b9))—chords that characterize minor turnarounds. The complete TURNAROUND TO iiMI7 progression is iiiø7–VI7(b9)–iiMI7 (ii/ii–V/ii–ii). The altered 5th of iiiø7 is the same note as the b9 of VI7(b9), which also needs a raised 3rd. Notice how the turnaround to ii in F major is the same as ii–V to tonic in G minor.

The song, "It Could Happen to You" by Johnny Burke and Jimmy Van Heusen begins with a tonic chord followed immediately by a turnaround to ii. Songs with the turnaround to ii progression often continue in the circle of fifths until reaching tonic, iii–VI–ii–V–I, and this progression ends many songs. The above example replaces iiiø7 with iiiMI7, which is common when the progression continues to tonic.

The TURNAROUND TO viMI7 is a tonicization of relative minor, and is so common that it appears in over 60% of the jazz standard songs! The entire turnaround to vi progression is viiø7–III7(b9)–viMI7, and requires the chromatic alteration of only one note (the 3rd of III7(b9)).

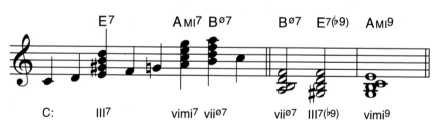

Dig it!—Do you hear a more somber tone when the melody turns around to vi in Track 56?

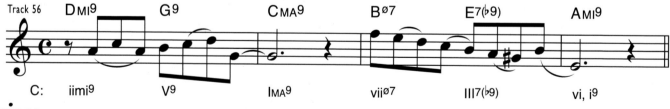

Exercises

1 Find two songs in a jazz fake book with turnarounds to both ii and vi.

2 Notate chord symbols to the progression and write a solo with characteristic jazz language.

Minor Turnaround in Major Keys—to iii, Deceptive Cadence (Backdoor Cadence)

While either a turnaround to ii or vi (or often both) can be found in almost every jazz standard song in a major key, tonicization of the diatonic iiiMI7 chord is less common. The relative rarity is due to the fact that for ii–V7 to iii, the secondary ii chord is based on a chromatic pitch a tritone away from tonic. So, the TURNAROUND TO iiiMI7 progression is less seamless than with other diatonic turnarounds. The entire turnaround to iii is #ivø7–VII7(b9)–iiiMI7. The turnaround to iii in C major is virtually the same as ii–V–i in E minor.

Turnarounds to iii are very expressive and beautiful, and found in tunes like "It Could Happen to You" by Johnny Burke and Jimmy Van Heusen and "There Will Never Be Another You" by Mack Gordon and Harry Warren. Notice how the 7th scale degree becomes more expressive when harmonized as the 11th of iiø7/iii.

Tunes that tonicize iii often continue in the circle of fifths to tonic. In fact, this progression represents the entire circle of fifths in a major key (#ivø7–VII7–iiiMI7–VI7–iiMI7–V7–IMA7)!

The notes of the iiiMI7 chord are all part of the IMA9 chord. It is called a DECEPTIVE CADENCE or BACKDOOR CADENCE when a ii–V progression to iii resolves to IMA7 instead. Notice that the 7th of VII7 (V7/iii) still resolves downward in a backdoor cadence.

Exercises

1 Write a melody to the progression and indicate the chord symbols above the staff.

2 For each major key, write the chord symbols for a deceptive cadence using the turnaround to iii. Then, notate chord voicings in closed spacing, with proper voice leading in the comping range.

Track 60

1 You will hear iMI$^{6/9}$ followed by the turnaround to III, then iMI$^{6/9}$ followed by turnaround to VI. For each subsequent example, indicate if the turnaround is to III or VI.

     a. III / VI   **b.** III / VI   **c.** III / VI   **d.** III / VI

Track 61

2 Listen to the progression and indicate in which measure the turnaround to VI begins.

     measure _____

Track 62

3 Listen to the solo to a minor blues progression.
Write whether the following harmonic and melodic devices are present.

Minor pentatonic	**yes / no**
Blues scale	**yes / no**
VI-V-I turnaround	**yes / no**
Turnback	**yes / no**
Harmonic-minor melody	**yes / no**
Turnaround to iv	**yes / no**

Track 63

4 You will hear IMA^9 followed by the turnaround to viMI^7, then IMA^9 followed by turnaround to iiMI^9. For each subsequent example, indicate if the turnaround is to vi or ii.

     a. vi / ii   **b.** vi / ii   **c.** vi / ii

Track 64

5 Listen to the turnaround to iiiMI^7, followed by the same progression deceptively resolving to IMA^9. Indicate whether each subsequent progression resolves to iii or I.

     a. iiiMI7 / IMA9   **b.** iiiMI7 / IMA9   **c.** iiiMI7 / IMA9   **d.** iiiMI7 / IMA9

Track 65

6 Listen to the solo and fill in the missing notes.

1 The three diatonic major chords in minor keys are built on scale degrees _____, _____, and _____.

2 A turnaround to III in minor sounds like a temporary modulation to _____ _____.

3 Turnarounds to minor chords in major keys should use _____ chords for secondary ii, and _____ chords for secondary V.

4 After a turnaround to ii, the next likely chord is _____.

5 More often than not, a standard song in major will contain a turnaround to vi. **True / False**

6 When a turnaround to iii resolves to _____ instead,
this is called a deceptive, or _____ cadence.

7 Write chord symbols and a solo melody to the progression.

f: ii⁰⁷   V7(♭9)   imi⁶ᐟ⁹   ivmi⁹   VII13   IIIMA⁹

8 Write the chord symbols for a minor blues progression in E minor.

| | | | | | | | | | | | ||

9 Write closed-spaced voicings, with proper voice leading in the comping range to the progression.

E♭: I⁶ᐟ⁹   vii⁰⁷   III7(♭9)   vimi⁷   iii⁰⁷   VI7(♭9)   iimi⁹

10 For each major key, write chord symbols and proper voicings for the turnaround to iiiMI7.

Altered Dominant Chords (V_{ALT})

Jazz musicians love to use a variety of chromatic pitches to alter dominant chords and almost always do so. After all, 10 of the 12 chromatic pitches are chord tones to any dominant chord!

The alterations to dominant chords that you already use include the 13th, #11th (typical for II7), and flatted 9th (minor turnarounds). Adding a SHARP 9TH (V7(#9)) is very bluesy and intense, because the note is enharmonically a blue note, and it is a 1/2 step below the chord 3rd. A three-note voicing of just the 3rd, 7th, and #9 is very effective. Musicians often misspell the #9 by writing that note as a ♭10 to show the bluesy quality. This chord was a favorite of guitarist, Jimi Hendrix.

Dig it!—The sharp 9th has no tendency to resolve down to the 5th of tonic, so melodies with this note can include the ♭9 to achieve resolution.

The FLAT 13TH (enharmonic to #5) is another preferred alteration of dominant harmony, and the note resolves downward to the 9th of the tonic chord. Dominant flat 13th chords (V(♭13)) always include altered (# or ♭) 9ths.

The ALTERED DOMINANT CHORD contains the ♭13th and *both* the flat and sharp 9ths (#11 is optional; otherwise there will be no 11th). The chord symbol is ALT (e.g., C ALT). In voicings, the chord 5th is omitted in favor of 3rd, 7th and altered notes. Also, one of the 9ths may be omitted to simplify a voicing.

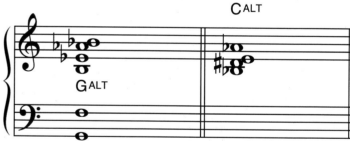

Exercises

1 Label and draw a line pointing to each altered tone in any voicing or melody from the examples in this lesson.

2 *Dig it!*—Dominant chords functioning in the circle of fifths can always use alterations for added color (such as V7(♭9), V7(#9), V13(♭9), V ALT, etc.). For the major keys below, write chord symbols and closed voicings for turnback progressions, using the indicated, colorful dominant chords.

Jazz Language—Diminished Scale for Dominant Chords & Altered Dominant Cell

With so many possibilities for colorful alteration, dominant chords are *where the fun is* for jazz improvisers and composers. For example, a $V^{7(\flat 9)}$ chord has a vii^{o7} contained in it . . .

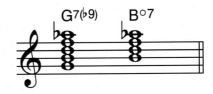

. . . so the diminished scale of vii^{o7} is effective for $V^{7(\flat 9)}$ (and $V^{7(\sharp 9)}$) chords. As an example, a rootless $G^{7(\flat 9)}$ is essentially B^{o7} (or $A\flat^{o7}$), so dominant chords use the DIMINISHED SCALE A HALF STEP UP. Every note in the scale is a chord tone to the dominant.

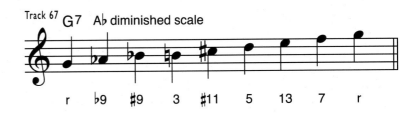

The diminished scale up a half step is also called the HALF-WHOLE DIMINISHED SCALE because, as you notice above, when you start the A♭ diminished scale on G, you are beginning with a 1/2 step, followed by a whole step, and then alternating 1/2 and whole steps.

The symmetrical licks from the diminished scale serve as great building blocks for melody to dominant chords. As presented in Book 2, Lesson 45, these motives are derived from using the 1/2 step below and the whole step above each diminished chord tone in sequential patterns.

The ALTERED DOMINANT CELL is composed of the notes from root to 3rd of a dominant chord, using the half-whole diminished scale. Lines constructed from the altered dominant cell often end with a 7–3 resolution to tonic.

Exercises

1   For each dominant chord, write the diminished scale up a half step (half-whole diminished scale), and circle the altered dominant cell within the scale.

2   Write a melody, using diminished language for the dominant chords.

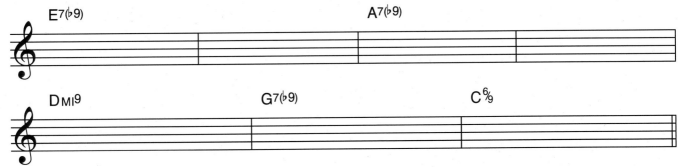

Jazz Language—Altered Dominant Lick and Scale

The ♭9th, 3rd, and ♭13th of the altered dominant chord combine to form a minor triad, up a 1/2 step. So, for instance, a G^ALT chord has an A♭ minor triad incorporated within.

The ALTERED DOMINANT LICK uses the minor triad (+ an added 9th) a half step above an altered dominant chord in a descending triplet arpeggio. These notes are the ♯9, ♭9, ♭13, and 3rd of the dominant chord, and ♭9 typically resolves to the 5th of tonic at the end of the lick.

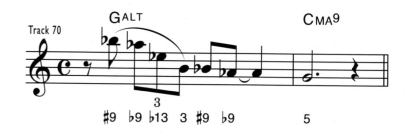

Jazz musicians love to create melodies from the altered dominant lick, which is also called the "Cry Me a River" lick, due to its similarity to the classic Arthur Hamilton song.

All the notes of a MELODIC-MINOR SCALE UP A HALF STEP are chord tones to the altered dominant chord (ALT).

This altered dominant scale has two other names, SUPER LOCRIAN and DIMINISHED/WHOLE TONE (because the bottom of the scale is the same as diminished and the top is all whole steps). It can be used to create a great variety of melodies.

Exercises

1 For each dominant chord, write the altered dominant lick.

2 For each dominant chord, write the melodic-minor scale up a half step.

3 Write a melody to the progression, using altered dominant language from this lesson.

B♭MI9   E♭ALT   A♭MA9   G^ALT   C MI⁶⁄9

Step-Down Progression

A delightful chord sequence that has been used too rarely in jazz songs is the step-down progression. The STEP-DOWN PROGRESSION tonicizes chords successively down whole steps, by altering tonics into ii chords. The great standards, "How High the Moon" by Nancy Hamilton and Morgan Lewis and "I'll Remember April" by Don Raye, Gene De Paul and Patricia Johnston both begin with step-down progressions.

A step-down sequence begins on IMA7. Lowering the 3rd and 7th of the chord results in iMI7, which sounds like iiMI7 of the major 7th chord a step below (subtonic - ♭VII). Next, a dominant IV7 becomes V of ♭VIIMA7 (V/♭VII). This progression is *borrowed* from the turnaround to VII in the parallel minor (i.e., FMA7 is ♭VII in G major, but diatonic VII in G minor).

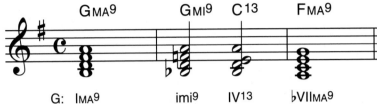

Next, the ♭VII chord is altered, lowering the 3rd and 7th to become iiMI7 of the ♭VI chord, one step below. ♭III7 is V of ♭VIMA7 (V/♭VI). This progression borrows from the turnaround to VI in the parallel minor (i.e., E♭MA7 is ♭VI in G major, but diatonic VI in G minor).

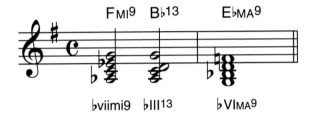

The dominant chords in the step-down progression usually have natural 13ths, and natural or ♭9ths, highlighting the warmth of the non-diatonic major chords to follow.

Dig it!—The appeal of the step-down progression is in the ironic sound of chords changing from MA7 to MI7. So, improvisers tend to emphasize the 3rds and 7ths, highlighting these shifts in chord quality. In fact, any melody to one of the major chords can be repeated, with 3rd and 7th lowered for the ensuing MI7 chord.

Track 72

Track 73

Once the step-down progression arrives at ♭VIMA7, it almost always proceeds directly to iiMI7 (almost the circle of fifths, a diminished 5th away), or to V7. Track 73 plays the step-down progression, followed by ii–V–I.

Exercises

1 Write the chord symbols for a step-down progression in the major key below. Also write closed voicings, with proper voice leading, in the comping range.

2 Write a melody to the step-down progression, emphasizing the changing 3rds and 7ths.

Track 74

1 Listen to the V7($\flat$9) chord and the V7($\sharp$9) chord.
Write whether each subsequent chord is V7($\flat$9) or V7($\sharp$9).

a. V7($\flat$9) / V7($\sharp$9)　　**b.** V7($\flat$9) / V7($\sharp$9)　　**c.** V7($\flat$9) / V7($\sharp$9)　　**d.** V7($\flat$9) / V7($\sharp$9)

Track 75

2 Listen to the diminished scale up a half step (half-whole) and the melodic-minor scale up a
half step for dominant harmony. Indicate whether each subsequent scale is diminished or
melodic minor.

a. diminished / melodic minor　　　　**b.** diminished / melodic minor

c. diminished / melodic minor　　　　**d.** diminished / melodic minor

Track 76

3 You will hear the altered dominant lick resolving $\flat$9–5 and then again,
resolving 7–3 into tonic. Write whether each subsequent melody resolves $\flat$9–5 or 7–3.

a. $\flat$9–5 / 7–3　　**b.** $\flat$9–5 / 7–3　　**c.** $\flat$9–5 / 7–3　　**d.** $\flat$9–5 / 7–3

Track 77

4 You will hear the altered dominant chord in closed spacing, and then in drop-two.
Write whether each subsequent chord is closed spaced or drop-two.

a. closed / drop-two　　　　**b.** closed / drop-two

c. closed / drop-two　　　　**d.** closed / drop-two

Track 78

5 Listen to the altered dominant cell, resolving 7–3 into tonic.
Write whether each melody uses the altered dominant cell.

a. yes / no　　**b.** yes / no　　**c.** yes / no　　**d.** yes / no

Track 79

6 You will hear two melodies to step-down progressions. Indicate whether each melody uses
the 3rd of each MA7 chord, changing to the lowered 3rd of the following MI7.

a. yes / no　　**b.** yes / no

1   A dominant chord with a ♭13th will also include an altered _____.

2   ♯9 is a tendency tone for a dominant chord, and resolves downward.   **True / False**

3   The altered dominant chord (V^{ALT}) contains these extensions: _____, _____ and _____.

4   A $V^{7(♭9)}$ chord can use a diminished scale _____ step up from the root, also called _____-_____ diminished.

5   More often than not, a major-key standard song will contain a turnaround to vi.   **True / False**

6   Super Locrian is another name for a _____ _____ scale, _____ step up from the root of a dominant chord.

7   The Step-Down Progression tonicizes chords down two successive _____ steps from tonic.

8   Write voicings, in the comping range for the indicated dominant chords.

C13(♭9)   F^{ALT} E♭^{ALT} B♭7(♯9)

9   For each V^7–I progression, write a melody using either the altered dominant lick or altered dominant cell, as indicated. Be sure that the melody resolves into tonic.

G^{ALT} C^{MA9} D^{ALT} G^{MA9} B♭^{ALT} E♭^{MA9}

lick   cell   lick

10   For each chord, write the half-whole diminished and super Locrian scales.

F^{ALT} D♭^{ALT} A^{ALT}

dim.   sup. loc.

11   For the major key below, write the chord symbols and a sequential melody to the step-down progression.

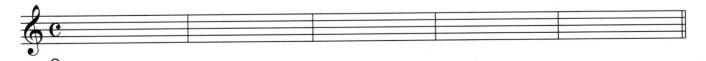

C:

IV-I (Plagal) Progressions, Backdoor Progressions

You learned in Book 1, Lesson 25, about the IV–I PLAGAL CADENCE, which evokes the "amen" at the close of a hymn. You learned in Book 2, Lesson 45, about a variation, the IV6–#iv°7–IMA7/V progression, in which the #iv°7 increases the tendency to resolve to tonic.

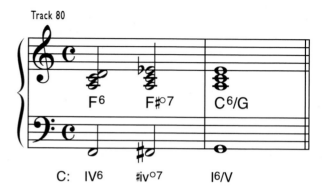

There are a number of interchangeable variations to the plagal resolution. Equally popular among composers is IVMA–ivMI–I, in which any of the chords can have a 6th or 7th, 9th, etc.

This resolution produces a melancholy feeling, or sense of resignation prior to tonic. It is effective when a melody to the IV–I progression establishes a motive with the IV chord that is altered to reflect the ensuing #iv°7 or ivMI.

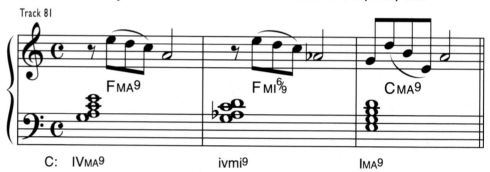

Since iiiMI7 is contained within IMA9, don't be surprised to find iii substituting for tonic in a IV–I progression. In these instances, the chord changes almost always continue in the circle of fifths toward tonic.

There is also a backdoor cadence used in some IV–I progressions. Here, the ivMI7, behaving like a secondary ii chord, resolves to ♭VII7 (this is a ii–V, up a minor 3rd from the key). ♭VII7 deceptively resolves to IMA7. So, ivMI7–♭VII7 in C major looks like ii–V in E♭ major, but is functioning as a backdoor cadence to tonic in this variation of the IV–I progression.

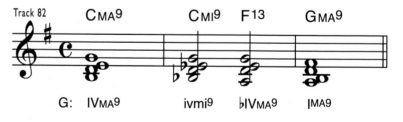

Exercises

1 Using a jazz fake book, find and name a song that contains a IV–I progression.

2 For each major key, write chord symbols for the indicated IV–I progression and compose a melody.

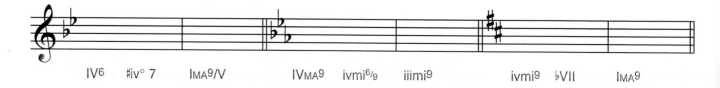

I–VI Progressions

You know that the "turnback" is I–VI⁷–iiMI⁷–V⁷, with each chord lasting two beats. The I–VI PROGRESSION ("one to six progression") is like a turnback, but the value of the tonic and VI⁷ chords are both doubled (one measure each). The value of the ensuing ii and V may or may not be doubled. The jazz standards "Doxy" by Sonny Rollins and "They Can't Take that Away from Me" by Ira and George Gershwin begin with this harmonic device.

In these four examples of the I–VI progression, varying chords are used to connect tonic and VI⁷. In the first instance, iiiMI⁷ in advance of VI adds a circle-of-fifth pull.

Secondly, a subdominant (IV) chord (major, minor, or dominant quality) may precede iii in I–VI progressions.

The supertonic chord (iiMI⁷) may also precede iii. In more elaborate instances, ♯iiº⁷ is a passing chord between ii and iii.

Last, an element of blues may be injected into the I–VI progression by using a series of dominant chords in descending 1/2 steps (I–VII⁷–♭VII⁷–VI⁷). In fact, a melody composed or improvised to this progression can be more "in the key," as opposed to clearly outlining the changes, highlighting the bluesy effect.

Dig It!—The I–VI progression is an example of the freedom of choice jazz improvisers enjoy. Not only are there a variety of interchangeable chord choices, but jazz musicians also get to choose, in the moment, from a palette of chord extensions (natural and altered 9ths and 13ths, and ♯11ths).

Exercises

1 Locate and name four jazz songs from fake books that employ I–VI progressions.

2 For each I–VI progression, write the chord symbols in between the staves, and notate the drop-two voicings.

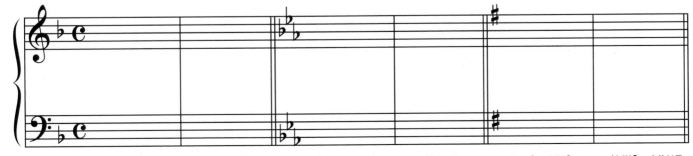

ABAC Standard Song Form

In Book 2, Lesson 47, you studied the AABA standard song form. Almost all 32-bar standard songs fall into either AABA or ABAC form. The ABAC STANDARD SONG FORM is organized into two, 16-bar halves, each beginning with an 8-measure 'A' phrase. The second phrase in each half is where variation occurs. However, some tunes have very similar B and C phrases and are more aptly described as ABAB' (the "prime" ['] denotes a similar, but slightly varied phrase from the original).

The progression to "There Will Never be Another You" by Mack Gordon and Harry Warren typifies the ABAC song form.

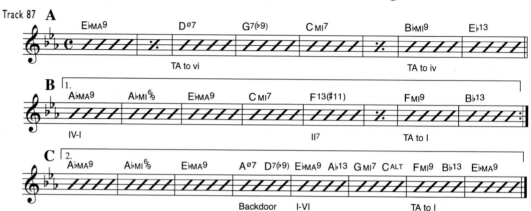

The "Another You" progression demonstrates how jazz songs are constructed; stringing together the language you've learned:

The 'A' Phrase —begins on tonic, and then has turnarounds to vi and IV.

The 'B' Phrase —logically uses a IV–I progression (IVMA–ivMI–I). Next is viMI[7] leading in turnback fashion to the dominant II[7] chord, which always goes to ii–V.

The 'C' (or B') Phrase —begins with the IV–I progression. Next is a backdoor turnaround to tonic (♯ivø7–VII7–IMA7), followed by a I–VI progression (IMA7–IV7–iiiMI7–VI7) which, of course, leads to ii–V–I.

Dig It!—ABAC compositions can be more expressive than AABA because in 16 measures there is more time to develop melodic ideas. Conversely, the melody to an AABA song begins again after eight bars.

Exercises

1 Analyze this solo melody to the second half of the "Another You" progression; identifying melodic devices, scales and note significant note choices.

2 Find and list four songs from a jazz fake book in the ABAC (or ABAB') form.

_____   _____

_____   _____

Slash Chords

"Slash chord" is an exotic name for a simple concept. A SLASH CHORD is a chord with a note other than the root in the bass. That note may be one of the other chord tones. Slash chords are notated with a diagonal line separating the chord symbol and bass note (i.e., GMA7/B). Since the root is not in the bass, it should be included in the chord voicing. Conversely, the bass note is often avoided in the voicing.

Using a slash chord can give a familiar chord a fresh sound. Slash chords also add interest and melodic contour to the bass line.

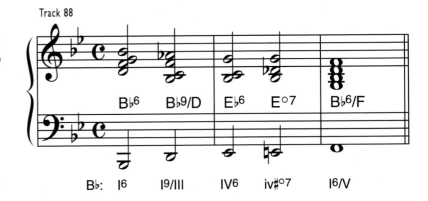

A triad over a different bass note can imply a new chord. For instance a major triad, over the note up a step (e.g., F/G) sounds like the sus7 chord of the bass (G7sus) with an added 9th. That same chord is also used in pop music as a substitute for V7 (i.e., F/G substitutes for G7).

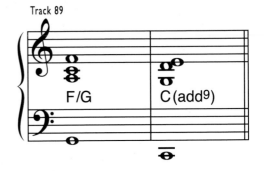

A triad over a bass note, up a 1/2 step, sounds diminished. The bass is the tone of the diminished chord, and the triad contains the other "juicy" notes from the diminished scale.

Exercises

1 Write in chord symbols for the slash chords.

UNIT 18   Ear Training for Lessons 72–75

Track 91

1 You will hear the progression IV6–$\sharp$iv°7–IMA9/V, followed by IVMA6–ivMI6–IIIMI7.
Write whether each subsequent progression uses $\sharp$iv°7 or ivMI6.

    a. $\sharp$iv°7 / ivMI6　　　**b.** $\sharp$iv°7 / ivMI6　　　**c.** $\sharp$iv°7 / ivMI6　　　**d.** $\sharp$iv°7 / ivMI6

Track 92

2 You will hear a $\sharp$iv°7–VII7($\flat$9)-IMA9 backdoor cadence, and then a ivMI7–$\flat$VII9–IMA9 backdoor cadence.
Indicate whether each subsequent progression starts with $\sharp$iv°7 or ivMI7.

    a. $\sharp$iv°7 / ivMI7　　　**b.** $\sharp$iv°7 / ivMI7　　　**c.** $\sharp$iv°7 / ivMI7　　　**d.** $\sharp$iv°7 / ivMI7

Track 93

3 Listen to IMA9–iiMII7–iiiMI7–vi7($\flat$9), and then IMA9–IV13–iiiMI7–vi7($\flat$9).
Write whether each subsequent progression uses iiMI7 or IV13.

    a. iiMI7 / IV13　　　**b.** iiMI7 / IV13　　　**c.** iiMI7 / IV13　　　**d.** iiMI7 / IV13

Track 94

4 CD track 94 begins with a I–VI progression, played twice.
Fill in the blanks, identifying which chords are used.

    IMA9 –_____ – _____– VI7($\flat$9)

Track 95

5 Listen to the 32-bar chord progression and indicate whether it is AABA or ABAC form.

    AABA / ABAC

Track 96

6 Listen to the solo to the "Another You" progression.
Indicate whether the following melody devices are used.

Sequence	**yes / no**
Altered dominant lick	**yes / no**
Harmonic minor	**yes / no**
Super Locrian	**yes / no**
Half-whole diminished	**yes / no**
Blues figures	**yes / no**

1 In a IV–I progression, a _____ chord can substitute for tonic.

2 The most bluesy I–VI progression has the chords I – _____ –_____ – VI⁷.

3 Most 32-bar standard songs are in either _____ or _____ form.

4 An E♭/F slash chord sounds much like _____⁷sus.

5 A slash chord with a major triad over the bass note up a 1/2 step sounds _____.

6 For this major key, write chord symbols and voicings for the indicated IV–I progressions.

IV⁶ᐟ⁹   ♯iv°⁷   IMA⁹/V   ivmi⁹ ♭VII¹³ IMA⁹   IV⁶ᐟ⁹ ivmi⁶ᐟ⁹ iiim⁷

7 Write chord symbols for each I–VI progression, as indicated by the melody.

8 Write chord symbols and a solo melody to the progression, using language you learned in this book.

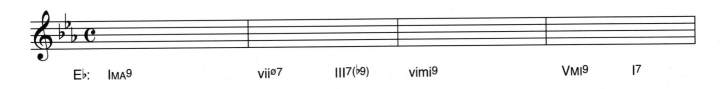

E♭: IMA⁹   vii⌀7   III7(♭9) vimi⁹   VMI⁹ I7

IVMA⁹   ♭VII⁹   IMA⁹

GLOSSARY & INDEX OF TERMS & SYMBOLS

Includes all the terms and symbols used in Book 3 and the page on which they are first introduced.

ABAC STANDARD SONG FORM: 32-bar song with two, 16-bar halves, each beginning with an 8-bar "A" phrase. The second "B" or "C" phrase in each half is where variation usually occurs (p. 116).

ALTERED DOMINANT CELL: notes from root to 3rd of a dominant chord, using the half-whole diminished scale. Motives constructed from the altered dominant cell often end with a 7–3 resolution to tonic (p. 109).

ALTERED DOMINANT CHORD (VALT): a dominant chord with extensions ♭13th and *both* ♭9 and ♯9. Extension ♯11 is optional, otherwise, no 11th. In voicings, chord 5th is omitted in favor of 3rd, 7th and altered notes (p. 108).

ALTERED DOMINANT LICK: descending triplet arpeggio using a minor triad plus an added 9th a 1/2 step above an altered dominant chord (♯9, ♭9, ♭13, and 3rd), and ♭9 typically resolves to the 5th of tonic at the end of the lick (p. 110).

BACKDOOR CADENCE: see deceptive cadence (p. 105).

CASCARA (KHAS-kah-rah): repetitive two-measure Afro-Cuban rhythmic pattern played in sync with clave. Named for playing on the "shell" or side of a drum (p. 85).

CLAVE (KLAH-vay):

repetitive two-measure Afro-Cuban rhythmic pattern, alternating 2 or 3 notes per bar (p. 84).

CLOSED VOICINGS: chord arrangements with consecutive chord tones (p. 86).

DECEPTIVE CADENCE: a ii–V progression resolving to a chord other than tonic, for example, ivmi7–VII7–IMA7; which also is called a backdoor cadence (p. 105).

DIMINISHED SCALE A HALF STEP UP: see half-whole diminished scale (p. 109).

DIMINISHED/WHOLE TONE SCALE: the bottom of the scale is the same as a diminished scale and the top is all whole steps; see melodic minor scale up a half step (p. 110)

DROP-TWO VOICING: taking the second note from the top of a closed voicing and dropping it one octave to create a more open or spacious sound (p. 86).

FAKE BOOK: large music book containing jazz standards in lead- sheet form (melody, chords and lyrics). Legal/licensed compilations pay royalties to composers for every song and are the most accurate (p. 104).

FLAT 13 (♭13): chord extension a flat 13th above the chord root of a V7 (enharmonic to ♯5) that resolves downward to the 9th of the tonic chord (p. 108).

FLAT 13 CHORD (V(♭13)): a dominant chord with extension ♭13 above the root; always includes ♯9 or ♭9 (p. 108).

HALF-DIMINISHED CHORD (ø7): similar to a MI7 chord but with the chord 5th flatted; also called a minor 7th flat five chord (p. 91).

HALF-WHOLE DIMINISHED SCALE: scale that begins with a 1/2 step, followed by a whole step, and then alternating half and whole steps (page 109).

HARMONIC-MINOR SCALE: the 5th mode of harmonic minor (harmonic minor of the tonic). The augmented second within the harmonic-minor scale is the 3rd and ♭9th of the V7 chord (p. 94).

HARMONIC-MINOR LICK: a motive based on the harmonic-minor scale that typically skips from 3rd up to ♭9th of V7(♭9), and then moves down the scale, resolving 7–3 into the tonic (p. 94).

JAZZ MINOR SCALE: ascending melodic minor scale used by jazz musicians to create melody to minor tonics. When the scale descends, the alterations remain, rather than reverting to the natural minor (p. 90).

MELODIC-MINOR SCALE UP A HALF STEP: a melodic minor scale a half step up from a dominant chord root, whereby the notes of the scale become chord tones to the altered dominant chord, V (alt). See also diminished whole-tone scale or super-Locrian scale (p. 110).

MELODIC SEQUENCE: repetition of an idea transposed by some interval (p. 83).

MINOR BLUES: a 12-bar chord progression analogous to jazz blues in major keys, but centered on a minor tonic (page 103).

MINOR 11th CHORD (MI11): a MI7 chord with added chord extension 11th (p. 87).

MINOR 6/9 CHORD (MI6/9): similar to the MI9 chord, with the chord 7th replaced by the 6th note of the ascending melodic minor scale (a m6 above the root) (p. 90).

MINOR MAJOR 7th CHORD: minor triad, with a major seventh above the root, see also minor tonic seventh chord (p. 90).

MINOR PENTATONIC SCALE: pentatonic scale from the relative major, e.g., D minor pentatonic has the same notes as F major pentatonic. A mildly bluesy sound (p. 99).

MINOR SEVEN FLAT FIVE CHORD (MI7(♭5)): see half diminished chord (p. 91).

MINOR TONIC SEVENTH CHORD: in jazz, a chromatically altered tonic minor chord based on the ascending melodic minor scale, e.g., using the raised 7th degree of melodic minor results in MI(MA7) (p. 90).

MINOR TURNBACK: chord progression I–♯vi°7–ii°7–V7(♭9) with each chord usually lasting two beats (p. 98).

MODAL JAZZ: jazz tunes based on a mode rather than a key (p. 87).

MONTUNO: triadic and syncopated Afro-Cuban comping figure, often played in octaves or 2 octaves apart. When tunes repeat a ii-V, the montuno often features common tones and 7-3 resolution (p. 85).

MELODIC SOLOING: basing musical phrases on simple ideas, which are repeated and varied (p. 83).

ONE-SIX PROGRESSION (I–VI): like a turnback (I–VI7–iiMI7–V7), but the value of the tonic and VI7 chords are both doubled (one measure each). The value of the ensuing ii and V may or may not be doubled (p. 115).

PENTATONIC/BLUES SCALE: contains all the notes of major pentatonic, plus a flatted 3rd to the key (1, 2, ♭3, 3, 5, 6) (p. 99).

QUARTAL HARMONY: chord arranged in Perfect 4ths (p. 87).

SECOND MODE OF NATURAL MINOR: a scale for half diminished chords (ø7) beginning on the second note of the natural minor scale, e.g., "a" natural minor, from B to B (p. 93).

SHARP 9 (♯9): chord extension ♯9 is bluesy and intense on a dominant chord because the note is enharmonically a blue note and it is a 1/2 step below the chord 3rd (p. 108).

SHARP 9 CHORD (V(♯9)): a dominant chord with extension ♯9 above the root. A three-note voicing of just 3rd, 7th, and ♯9 is very effective (p. 108).

SIX-FIVE-ONE MINOR CADENCE: The VI7–V7(♭9)–i cadence in a minor key substitutes a dominant quality VI chord for iiø7 in a turnaround progression which creates a more "bluesy" sound. The diatonic VI in minor is a Major 7th (VIMA7), so the 7th must be flatted to create a dominant VI7 chord (p. 98).

SLASH CHORD: chord with a note other than the root in the bass; may or may not be one of the other chord tones. Notated with a diagonal line separating the chord symbol and bass note (e.g., GMA7/B) (p. 117).

STEP-DOWN PROGRESSION: tonicizes chords successively down whole steps, by altering tonics into ii chords (p. 111).

SUPER LOCRIAN: see melodic minor scale up a 1/2 step (p. 110).

SUS CHORD (7sus): a chord that replaces (suspends) the chord 3rd with a 4th (p. 87).

TUMBAU (TOOM-bow): Afro-Cuban rhythm, played on a bass drum and by the bass player, that aligns with clave and features notes on the "and" of 2, and on beat 4 (p. 84).

TURNAROUND TO iiMI7: tonicization of ii using the chord progression iii°7–VI7(♭9)–iiMI7 (ii/ii–V/ii–ii). Songs with the turnaround to ii progression often continue in the circle of fifths until reaching tonic, iii–VI–ii–V–I, and this progression ends many songs (p. 104).

TURNAROUND TO iiiMI7: the progression ♯ivø7–VII7(♭9)–iiiMI7. Tunes that tonicize iii often continue in the circle of fifths to tonic. In fact, this progression represents the entire circle of fifths in a major key (♯ivø7–VII7–iiiMI7–VI7–iiMI7–V7–IMA7) (p. 105).

TURNAROUND TO viMI7: the tonicization of relative minor is achieved with a turnaround to vi progression (vii°7–III7(♭9)–viMI7). It requires the chromatic alteration of only one note (the 3rd of III7(♭9)) (p. 104).

MINOR 12-BAR BLUES PROGRESSION: see minor blues (p. 103).

Review of Basic Music Elements

Music is an intermingling of primary elements that include MELODY, HARMONY, and RHYTHM, and can be said to exist with the singular presence of any of the three. There are also secondary elements, chief among which are TEXTURE and FORM.

MELODY is that musical element that we sing alone. It is a succession of pitches, made memorable by contour and repetition. Melody is a linear (horizontal) musical element.

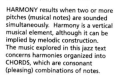

HARMONY results when two or more pitches (musical notes) are sounded simultaneously. Harmony is a vertical musical element, although it can be implied by melodic construction. The music explored in this jazz text concerns harmonies organized into CHORDS, which are consonant (pleasing) combinations of notes.

RHYTHM refers to the placement of notes in time, and their relationship to a beat (pulse). Rhythm is a linear element and is the propulsive engine of melody and harmony.

While melody, harmony and rhythm combine to give music its linear and vertical dimensions, it is TEXTURE that provides an aural dimension of "depth." Texture refers to how musical voices are combined into melodic and accompaniment components.

Among textures there is COUNTERPOINT, which is the simultaneous occurrence of two or more melodic voices. In jazz music, there typically exists a counterpoint between melody and bass.

FORM is the organization of musical statements and themes. Form is the "roadmap" of music, and it allows the listener to follow the journey.

Exercises

1 Listen to the three excerpts of CD Track 1 and describe the rhythm for each:

  a. Repeated / Varied   b. Driving / Calm   c. Syncopated (jerky) / Even

2 This excerpt has a form consisting of four musical statements. The first statement (phrase) is labeled "A" and the second is labeled "B." Label the third and fourth statements, using either the letter "A" or "C" for each.

Swing Feel & Swing Eighth Notes

The elements of music as we know them have been used in much the same way for the past four hundred years. So it is STYLE that gives any piece of music its unique imprint. Style refers to the characteristic usage of melodic, harmonic, rhythmic and textural building blocks. After all, Mozart and Dizzy Gillespie created music from virtually the same elements, yet their styles differ widely.

JAZZ is unique among Western art music styles, because it is both a composed and an improvised art. Jazz is an amalgam of elements thrown together in the "stew" of Americanism that existed at the turn of the 20th century which is why it is referred to as "America's only original musical art form." Jazz musicians developed their own harmonies, melodic gestures and rhythmic devices – even the basic subdivision of the beat is unique to jazz. Jazz is known for "blues" influences, syncopation, and most of all, swing.

SWING is an interpretation of eighth notes with a triplet subdivision, in which the first  Written as: eighth note of each beat has two-thirds of that beat's value. The second eighth note, although occupying only one third of the beat, is more often accentuated and articulated.

The example below shows a melody in typical notation, followed by the notation of how it would sound when interpreted by a jazz musician. For instance, wind players typically tongue the off-beat eighth note.

Written

Track 2
Played

* In swing feel, quarter notes are played short unless otherwise indicated.

Exercises

1 Play CD Track 2 and chant "doodle-DAH" and then "doo-DAH" underneath the melody.

2 Rewrite the following example as it would *sound* if played in swing style:

* = Accents are optional and can be varied.

Swing Groove

"It don't mean a thing, if it ain't got that swing!"—Duke Ellington

Another factor in achieving swing is GROOVE. Groove is a constant energy funneled into subdivision. In some way, all great performances "groove," whether Bach or Basie. The element of groove that produces swing is the concept of 2 AND 4.

In classical music in 4/4 time, the agogic (natural) accent almost always falls on beats 1 and 3.

In jazz, beats 1 and 3 are where harmonic changes typically occur, but the "feel" of the music has an infectious sense of FORWARD MOMENTUM derived from an underlying stress of BEATS 2 AND 4.

As a result, jazz musicians almost always snap their fingers or clap hands on 2 and 4. Also, most drummers play the hi-hat cymbal by stepping down on the pedal on 2 and 4. Jazz teachers often recommend practicing with the metronome beats indicating 2 and 4.

ENERGY is of equal importance, because this is the element that "casts the spell" of music. Swing style will feel subtly different if the energy is happy, excited, bluesy, or agitated. Swing music grooves when energy is channeled into the triplet. So, even if eighths are played evenly, the internal voice of the soloist is thinking the underlying triplet (and usually, so is the drummer!).

Track 3
In swing feel, eighth notes are played more evenly as tempo increases. At a quarter note value of 200 bpm, eighth notes are very uniform. In addition, many contemporary jazz musicians play eighth notes evenly at moderate tempos. In these instances, swing articulation, often initiated off the beat, enhances the swing feel of even eighth notes. Conversely, "The Mickey Mouse Club Theme" and Sousa's "Washington Post" have triplet subdivisions, but they are **not** in swing feel. CD Track 3 demonstrates a more even, yet still swinging interpretation of the melody from CD Track 2.

Exercises

1 *Dig it!*—Play the "2 & 4" melody above, first without a constant energy, and then with different kinds of constant energy. What do you notice?

2 *Dig it!*—Play one of the melody examples from Lesson 2 with the metronome indicating half notes on beats 1 and 3, then on 2 and 4. You should notice that having the metronomic emphasis on beats 2 and 4 promotes a swing feeling.

Mm. ♩ = 60

1   2   3   4

Jazz Melody & Improvisation—Syncopation, Bebop Style

IMPROVISATION, or spontaneous composition, is a signature element of jazz—in fact, improvisation is such an essential ingredient of jazz performance that without it, the music really isn't jazz. The jazz language for composed melody and improvised melody is basically the same, with composed melody naturally exhibiting a greater degree of organization. This text focuses principally on the melodic language of the improviser.

A constant virtue of jazz melody is the use of SYNCOPATION, which is an off-beat (second-half of a beat) accentuation. Syncopation in 4/4 time—standard for most jazz music—occurs when: 1) an eighth note is played on the second-half of a beat followed by a rest, 2) a note of a quarter note value or longer is played on the second-half of a beat, 3) two or more notes are played on successive off-beats.

Ragtime artists, the progenitors of jazz, created the earliest "jazzy" music with what they called "ragging" march or hymn tunes, in which they syncopated some of the rhythms.

Track 4

In the 1940s, BEBOP music (originated by Charlie Parker, Dizzy Gillespie, and others) literally burst onto the jazz scene, and its impact indelibly changed jazz melody. Since then, jazz soloists have exhibited great technical virtuosity. Now, improvised jazz melody in swing feel often moves in eighth notes, triplets, and sixteenth notes. Bebop melody is unpredictable. Phrases are unpredictable in length, as is the placement of accents, which often occur off the beat, offset by the occasional on-beat. Bebop melodies also feature frequent and sudden skips and changes of direction.

Exercises

1 Re-write this melody in a "rag" style, adding syncopation:

*This icon signifies that the students' answers will vary for this exercise.

Track 5
2 Listen to CD Track 5 as you read the following solo melody in a bebop-influenced style. What bebop characteristics do you notice?   *Syncopation, off-beat accents, unpredictable phrases, triplets, 16th notes, frequent stops, and direction changes.*

3 Circle the instances of syncopation in the melody above (CD Track 5).

4 Write a melody in the bebop style:

Lesson 5 — UNIT 1 — 7

Jazz Melody & Improvisation – Lick, Line and Melodic Soloing

A well conceived jazz SOLO (improvisation) balances the elements of lick, line and melodic soloing.
A LICK (*motive* in classical music) is a brief melodic cell, made memorable by repetition. Early arrangements of the Count Basie Orchestra and some of Duke Ellington's tunes are based on a lick (e.g., "In a Mellow Tone"). Licks lend unity and familiarity to a melody, and often evoke a feeling of blues (see Unit 6).

A lick can be repeated over different harmonies to build tension and excitement.

Track 6 C6   F7   D7   A13

A lick can also be varied to inject an element of surprise.

Track 7 C6   F7   D7   A13

In jazz soloing, a LINE is a melody of one measure or longer, and moving in eighth notes or faster values. Jazz lines exhibit a spectrum, from THROUGH-COMPOSED (never repeating an idea) to ORGANIC (building on small ideas).

Track 8 G6   GMI7   C7   FMA7

TENSION AND RELEASE play a vital role in the impact and emotion of music. A repeated lick, for instance, builds tension, and a sense of release is felt when the lick gives way to a more extended jazz line.

MELODIC SOLOING refers to playing phrases that sound more like a new song than a solo. These ideas move primarily in quarter notes or slower values. A melodic phrase is cohesive, with a short idea repeated and varied until it suggests the next idea. Poignant music results from this type of improvising, which is pure, spontaneous composition. This melodic solo is to the beginning of the chord progression from Billy Strayhorn's "Take the 'A' Train."

Track 9 C6   D7(♭5)   DMI7   G7   C6

Exercises

1 *Dig It!*—As you listen to the CD, sing the melody to "Take the 'A' Train." Is it complemented by the solo melody? Yes

2 Compose a lick.

3 Designate the lick, line, and melodic soloing passages in the spaces provided.

DMI7   G9   EMI7   A7
Melodic

D9   D♭9
Lick   Line

Review of Lessons 1–5 — UNIT 1 — 9

1 This melody is notated in a standard way. Re-write it as it would sound in jazz performance.

Note: Student may add articulation markings.

2 This melody is notated as it would sound in jazz. Re-write it in standard notation.

3 "Rag" the following melody with syncopation.

4 "Un-rag" the melody by removing syncopation.

5 Bebop melodies are characterized by __unpredictable__ phrase lengths and accents.

6 Off-beat accentuation is also called __syncopation__.

7 __Groove__ is a constant energy channeled into subdivision. The subdivision of swing is the __triplet__.

8 Compose two variations to this lick.

F6

9 Well-conceived jazz solos balance the elements of __lick__, __line__, and __melodic__ __soloing__.

---

8 — UNIT 1 — Ear Training for Lessons 1–5

Track 10
1 You will hear 4 melodies. Indicate for each whether it is played in "swing" or "non-swing" style.

a. swing / (non-swing)   b. swing / (non-swing)   c. (swing) / non-swing   d. (swing) / non-swing

Track 11
2 You will hear the same melody played correctly twice, but only once with a sense of groove. Identify which performance grooves, by circling the correct answer.

a.   (b.)

Track 12
3 The recording of the following melody is altered by the usage of syncopation. Notate the melody as altered on the recording.

Track 13
4 The recorded track is a melody in the bebop style. Count the number of a) phrases, b) sudden changes of direction, c) syncopated notes, and d) unpredictable accents.

a. __5-7__ phrases   b. __8__ direction changes

c. __11__ syncopations   d. __7__ unpredictable accents

Track 14
5 Listen to the lick on the recording. How many times is it played before it is varied?

__3__ times.

Track 15
6 Is the recorded excerpt exhibiting mostly "line" or "melodic soloing?"

Line / (melodic soloing)

---

10 — UNIT 2 — Lesson 6

Major Triad, Major Scale, Consonance

Virtually everyone knows the sound of a MAJOR CHORD. It is the "-men" at the end of "Amen" in hymns. It is the sound that ends nearly any "happy" song and it is the TONIC, or "home" chord of every major key. As a review, CHORDS are constructed by stacking notes a 3rd apart and occupy every other line or every other space on a staff. A 3-note chord is called a TRIAD.

A MAJOR TRIAD can be constructed using the 1st, 3rd and 5th notes of any major scale, and we call those tones the root, third and fifth of the chord, respectively. The intervals in major triad are a Major 3rd (M3) from root to third, a minor 3rd (m3) from third to fifth, and a perfect 5th (P5) from root to fifth.

C Major Scale   C
1   3   5   m3 / M3 / P5

The 1st and 2nd INVERSIONS of a major triad result from placing the 3rd and 5th of the chord respectively as the bottom note. By the way, when the root is on the bottom it is called ROOT POSITION.

F
Root position   1st inversion   2nd inversion

CONSONANCE is the occurrence of pleasing-sounding (consonant) notes throughout a melody. A consonant note is typically one that is found in the chord:

Track 16 E♭   D♭   E♭
R 5   5   R R 5   3   R 3 5   R   3 5 3 5

Exercises

1 Write the following major scales and triads (in root position and both inversions).

B♭   D
E♭   A

2 Circle the consonant tones in the following melody:

F   B♭

Lesson 7 UNIT 2 11

Major Seventh Chords (MA7, Δ7), *Chord Changes*

One of the distinctive features of the jazz language is the ubiquitous use of CHORD EXTENSIONS, such as 7ths, 9ths and beyond. Earlier musical genres used extended chords sparingly, and most often as unstable sounds, requiring resolution into triads. In jazz, chords with extensions are often considered to be consonant. They are staple harmonies that contribute to the exotic richness of jazz music.

The MAJOR SEVENTH CHORD adds the 7th note of the scale above the major triad. Since chords are a result of stacking 3rds, the chord 7th is the next 3rd in the chain, in this case a M3 above the fifth of the chord (also the interval of M7 above the root). Adding a 7th to a chord has a profound effect on the sound, which can be described as mellower, more emotional, or more exotic.

Major seventh chords have three inversions.

Root position   1st inversion   2nd inversion   3rd inversion

In jazz vernacular, the changes are the chords of the song. The "game" of being an improviser is to create a line that lands on a consonant chord tone each time the chord changes. So each new chord is referred to as a chord change, or change.

Cma7   Ebma7   Dma7   Dbma7   Cma7

Exercises

1 Construct the indicated scales and MA7 chords and their inversions.

2 *Dig it!*—CD Track 17 begins with an F major triad played by the pianist over a bass line and swing drum feel. After a few bars, the seventh is added to the chord. You can hear how much richer the sound becomes, and this is the richness of jazz! In what bar is the seventh added to the chord? ___5___

3 Notice how the melody below "makes the changes." Circle the chord tones and label each syncopated note with an "S."

Note: There are 6ths and 9ths in this excerpt, but they have not been addressed in this text.

UNIT 2 12 Lesson 8

Tonic Function, Scalar Melody, Passing & Neighboring Tones

Jazz musicians love to play STANDARDS – great songs from a lexicon of music created roughly between the 1920s and 1960s. Standard song forms are brief (usually 32 bars in length) and were often composed for Broadway musicals, or film. The harmonic language of jazz was codified in the standards, created by such composers as George Gershwin, Irving Berlin, Hoagy Carmichael, Harold Arlen and Cole Porter.

A chord built on the tonic (first) note of the scale is the TONIC CHORD, or ONE CHORD. Roman numerals are used to symbolize chords, so the symbol I MA7 is used for this "home" chord. Virtually all jazz standards in major keys end on the I MA7 chord (e.g., songs in the key of Bb major end on a Bbma7 chord).

For tonic chords, jazz musicians typically use the TONIC SCALE (major scale) to fill in other notes for melody or improvisation. Any SCALAR MELODY emphasizing the chord tones on most of the beats will be effectively consonant and will *make the changes*. Melody notes which are not part of the chord are called NON-HARMONIC TONES.

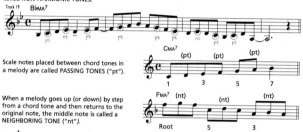

Scale notes placed between chord tones in a melody are called PASSING TONES ("pt").

When a melody goes up (or down) by step from a chord tone and then returns to the original note, the middle note is called a NEIGHBORING TONE ("nt").

Exercises

1 For the 4-bar melody above, circle and label the passing tones (pt) and neighboring tones (nt).

2 Compose a jazz melody to the tonic MA7 chord using chord tones, the tonic scale, and characteristic devices. Indicate the chord symbol above the staff.

FMA7

3 Analyze the following melody: label the chord tones, identify and circle passing and neighboring tones. Label syncopated notes (S), and also the beginnings of each phrase (phrase 1, phrase 2, etc.).

phrase 1 FMA7   phrase 2 BbMA7

phrase 3 FMA7

Lesson 9 UNIT 2 13

Dissonant 4th and Resolution

Beware the DISSONANT FOURTH! Except for one note, every note of the major scale sounds reasonably consonant over tonic harmony, because these pitches can be explained as chord tones or extensions. The offending, DISSONANT (non-consonant) tone is the fourth note of the scale. In fact, the note a perfect 4th (P4) above any major chord is very dissonant. When a melody emphasizes the dissonant 4th the result is extremely tense, and so the note must RESOLVE (release) by step—usually into the 3rd of the chord, 1/2 step below (CD Track 20). Skipping both into and out of the P4 above a major chord is not possible, because that is arpeggiating the wrong chord!

Track 20   BbMA7

Each 4th above is used as an APPOGGIATURA, which is a dissonant note on a strong beat. An appoggiatura (appog.) must be RESOLVED by stepwise motion into a chord tone (usually downward). As you can hear, the use of appoggiaturas is a wonderfully expressive device in music.

Exercises

1 *Dig It!*—Go back to CD Track 17, which features an FMA7 chord. Play the dissonant fourth along with the track. Next, play the 4th and resolve the dissonance by moving down a 1/2 step to the 3rd of the chord. You just experienced the power of appoggiatura and resolution!

2 Label each dissonant 4th (appog.) and circle each. Draw an arrow between each 4th and 3rd to show the resolution.

3 Compose jazz melodies to the following major seventh chords using 4th appoggiaturas and other characteristic devices. Can you use other notes as appoggiaturas?

UNIT 2 14 Ear Training for Lessons 6–9

1 Listen to the F major triad in root position and 1st inversion. Write whether each chord you hear is in root position or 1st inversion.

a. __root position__   b. __1st inversion__

c. __root position__   d. __1st inversion__

2 You will hear four major triads, followed by one of the notes in the triad. For each example, indicate if the note is root, 3rd or 5th of the chord.

a. __3rd__   b. __root__

c. __3rd__   d. __5th__

3 Listen to the Bb major triad and BbMA7 chord. Write whether each chord you hear is a major triad or MA7 chord.

a. __MA7__   b. __MA7__

c. __triad__   d. __MA7__

4 Listen to the GMA7 chord in root position, 1st, 2nd and 3rd inversion. Circle the correct answer for each subsequent chord you hear.

a. (root position) / 1st inversion   b. root position / (2nd inversion)

c. root position / (3rd inversion)   d. root position / (1st inversion)

5 For each melody you hear, write if it is primarily scalar or arpeggiated.

a. scalar / (arpeggiated)   b. (scalar) / arpeggiated

c. (scalar) / arpeggiated   d. scalar / (arpeggiated)

6 For each melody you hear, write if it contains an appoggiatura 4th.

a. yes / (no)   b. (yes) / no   c. (yes) / no   d. yes / (no)

Review of Lessons 6–9 UNIT 2 [15]

1 In 3rd inversion, the ___seventh___ of the chord is on the bottom.

2 Identify the following major triads and indicate root position or which inversion each is in.

Db — Root Position   E — 1st inversion   Ab — 1st inversion   D — 2nd inversion   F — root position

3 Each chord in jazz is referred to as a ___change (or chord change)___.

4 Notate the indicated MA7 chords in root position and all three inversions.

GMA7   EbMA7   AMA7   DbMA7

5 An ___appoggiatura___ is a dissonant note which resolves by step into a chord tone.

6 The most dissonant note over a tonic major chord is the ___4th___ note of the major scale.

7 Jazz musicians love to play ___standard___ songs, which were composed throughout the early to middle twentieth century.

8 Analyze this jazz melody by circling and identifying the chord tones and labeling appoggiaturas (appog.), passing tones (pt) and neighboring tones (nt), and syncopated notes (s). Also indicate the start of each phrase.

9 Compose melodies to the following major seventh chords, using the language studied so far.

FMA7

DMA7

CMA7

EbMA7

Subdominant Major Seventh Chords (IVMA7, IVΔ7)

As you know, chords are stacked 3rds, or "every other note" of a scale. Harmony in keys comes from creating chords over the various SCALE TONES (also called SCALE DEGREES). A chord built on the second note of the scale is the "ii" chord, over the third degree results in the "iii" chord, and so on. These are called the DIATONIC CHORDS (diatonic means "of the scale"). The diatonic chords have functions in the music. For instance, as you know, TONIC FUNCTION indicates the "home" chord of the key.

In every major key, the chord constructed of the 4th degree is also a Major 7th chord! This degree is called SUBDOMINANT and so the chord is the SUBDOMINANT SEVENTH CHORD (IVMA7). Here are the diatonic seventh chords in the key of G major, highlighting the two major seventh chords, IMA7 and IVMA7.

G: IMA7   IVMA7

Track 27
Take note that chord tones are referenced from the chord root and not from the key the chord is functioning in. So, although the IVMA7 chord is constructed of the 4th, 6th, 1st and 3rd notes of the scale, we still refer to its tones as root, third, fifth, and seventh of the chord.

The subdominant chord is used in at least 75% of jazz standards! SUBDOMINANT FUNCTION creates a feeling in the harmony that the music has gone to a temporary new home. But, since it is a diatonic chord, the IVMA7 chord progresses seamlessly back to

IMA7, as you hear in CD Track 27, which alternates between tonic and subdominant MA7 chords in the key of C major in two-bar increments. (Note: a set of chord changes is also called a CHORD PROGRESSION.)

Exercises

1 Notate the IVMA7 chords in root position and all three inversions for the indicated major keys. Write each chord symbol above the staff.

FMA7   GbMA7   BbMA7
C: Db: F:

EbMA7   AbMA7   GMA7
Bb: Eb: D:

2 For each note of the IVMA7 chord, write a note of the IMA7 that is a diatonic step away, or closer.

CMA7 GMA7   BbMA7   FMA7   GMA7   DMA7   EbMA7   BbMA7

G: IVMA7 IMA7   F: IVMA7 IMA7   D: IVMA7 IMA7   IVMA7 IMA7

Lesson 11 UNIT 3 [17]

Voice Leading Tonic & Subdominant Major Seventh Chords

The IMA7 and IVMA7 chords have two COMMON TONES: scale degrees 1 and 3 of the key are root and 3rd of the IMA7, and also 5th and 7th of the IVMA7.

CMA7   FMA7   Common Tones
C: IMA7   IMA7   IVMA7

If you play the IMA7 and IVMA7 chords successively in root position, every note skips up a 4th (or down a 5th), resulting in an awkward sound. The effect would be worse if four instruments, each playing a chord tone of the tonic chord, skipped up a 4th.

Proper and musical VOICE LEADING is achieved by placing one of the chords in inversion, so that each note of the first chord moves little or not at all into the next. The smoothest connection retains the common tones between the two chords. So, a IMA7 chord in root position smoothly leads to a IVMA7 in 2nd inversion.

Track 28 CMA7   FMA7
C: IMA7   IVMA7

CMA7   FMA7
C: IMA7   IVMA7

The 1st inversion IMA7 chord leads to a 3rd inversion IVMA7 chord.

CMA7   FMA7
C: IMA7   IVMA7

The second inversion IMA7 chord connects to root position IVMA7.

CMA7   FMA7
C: IMA7   IVMA7

And the 3rd inversion IMA7 chord connects to 1st inversion IVMA7.

CD Track 28 plays all of these progressions.

Exercises

Track 29
1 *Dig It!*—Listen to this melody to hear the sound of smooth voice leading. Write in the chord symbols.

AbMA7 EbMA7   EbMA7 AbMA7   AbMA7   EbMA7

2 For each IMA7 chord, notate the IVMA7 chord in that key, using inversion as necessary to achieve smooth voice leading. Indicate the chord symbols above the staff, and the chord inversions below the staff.

EbMA7 AbMA7   BMA7 EMA7   FMA7 BbMA7   AbMA7 DbMA7

Eb: 1st Inv. ___3rd inv.___   B: Root Pos. ___2nd inv.___   F: ___2nd inv.___ ___root pos.___   Ab: ___3rd inv.___ ___1st inv.___

3 Compose a characteristic melody to the following progression, using proper voice leading.

GMA7   CMA7   GMA7   GMA7   CMA7   GMA7   CMA7   GMA7

Modes, Lydian Scale

There has been ample confusion in jazz about the modes. In the medieval period, DIATONIC CHURCH MODES were used as the basis for MODAL compositions. In jazz we use the church mode *names* as a convenient way to refer to the scales we practice, even though standard songs are in *keys*, not modes.

Each MODE is a way of playing the major scale, starting and ending on one particular note. So, there are 7 modes of the major scale. The names of the consecutive diatonic church modes, beginning with the actual tonic major scale are *Ionian, Dorian, Phrygian, Lydian, Mixolydian, Aeolian,* and *Locrian*. A major scale starting and ending on degree 2 is called Dorian, etc.

C Major (Ionian) Scale   2nd Mode — D Dorian Scale   3rd Mode — E Phrygian Scale

The tonic scale is effective for creating melodies to IMA7 and IVMA7 chords, because the chord tones for both are within the scale. In fact, the tones of every diatonic chord are in the tonic scale, which is why musicians should practice the modes in eighth notes, from the root of each chord. Doing this places a chord tone on each beat.

The tonic scale in the fourth mode (from root to root of the IVMA7 chord) sounds like a major scale with a raised 4th degree. So, a C major scale from F-F sounds like an F major scale with raised 4. This mode is called LYDIAN, and the raised fourth note is the LYDIAN FOURTH.

In jazz, the Lydian (raised) 4th is consonant to any major chord, as opposed to the dissonant P4 above the root. So, jazz musicians typically use the Lydian 4th in improvising and composing on the IMA7 chord.

F Lydian Scale (Major, from 4-4)
C:

C Lydian Scale (Major, raised 4)
CMA7
C:

Exercises

Track 30
1 Listen to this jazz melody to IMA7 and IVMA7 chords which emphasizes chord tones, and employs the Lydian scales for both. Circle and identify chord tones (R, 3, 5, 7,) and draw a square around each Lydian 4th.

FMA7   BbMA7   FMA7

F: IMA7   IVMA7   IMA7

2 For each major key, write a Lydian scale in the fourth mode.

G Lydian   ___Bb Lydian___   ___Eb Lydian___   ___A Lydian___

3 Alter each major scale to become Lydian.

4 Compose a characteristic jazz melody to this progression, employing Lydian sounds.

EbMA7   AbMA7   EbMA7   AbMA7   EbMA7

Lesson 13 — UNIT 3 — 19

Hierarchy of 3rds and 7ths

Jazz is a contrapuntal music, which is to say that simultaneous melody and bass lines function together to obviate the harmony. Most often, each chord change begins with the bass line establishing the root, so the melody must clarify the chord in some other way. The two chord tones which "lock in" the sound of the chord against its root are the 3rd and 7th, and we place these notes at the top of the jazz melody hierarchy.

3rds and 7ths are at the top of the hierarchy because 5ths and chord extension 9ths (discussed in Unit 4), are the same for several different types of chords and are thus, far less effective in defining the harmony. As you study chord types, you'll find that CMA9, CMI9, and C9 all share the same 5th and 9th.

Jazz musicians must gain an "automatic" knowledge of 3rds and 7ths. The art of "making the changes" involves improvising a line (scalar, arpeggiated, or otherwise) which lands on the defining chord tone (3rd or 7th) just as the chord changes. If you analyze composed music from Bach, to Brahms, to Charlie Parker you find the same principle applies!

Exercises

1 (Track 31) Listen to this melody to MA7 chords, in which the 3rd and/or 7th of each chord clarifies the chord change against the root. Circle and identify chord 3rds and 7ths. Also analyze the use of other jazz melody devices, such as syncopation, licks, phrases, sudden direction shifts, etc.

2 Compose a jazz melody to this progression, emphasizing the 3rd and/or 7th as each chord changes. Use accidentals as needed!

---

20 — UNIT 3 — Ear Training for Lessons 10–13

1 (Track 32) Listen to the IMA7 followed by the IVMA7.
Write whether the chord in each example is a IMA7 or a IVMA7.

a. __IVMA7__   b. __IMA7__

c. __IMA7__   d. __IVMA7__

2 (Track 33) Listen to the IMA7 arpeggio in root position followed by the IVMA7 arpeggio in 2nd inversion. You will hear four examples of IMA7 followed by IVMA7. For each, write which position/inversion each chord is in.

a. IMA7 __root__ IVMA7 __2nd__   b. IMA7 __1st__ IVMA7 __3rd__

c. IMA7 __3rd__ IVMA7 __1st__   d. IMA7 __root__ IVMA7 __2nd__

3 (Track 34) Listen to the major scale followed by the Lydian scale. You will hear four scales. Write whether each is major or Lydian.

a. __major__   b. __Lydian__

c. __major__   d. __Lydian__

4 (Track 35) Listen to the 3rd and 7th of the MA7 chord. You will hear four MA7 chords. After each is played a 3rd or 7th will follow. Circle the correct answer for the chord tone you hear.

a. 3rd / (7th)   b. 3rd / (7th)   c. (3rd) / 7th   d. (3rd) / 7th

5 (Track 36) Listen to the melody. One of the notations below is correct. Circle A or B to indicate the correct melody :

(a.)   b.

6 (Track 37) Listen to the following progression of IMA7 and IVMA7 chords (bass plays the root for each and each chord lasts for one measure), write the progression.

IMA7 IMA7 IVMA7 IVMA7 IMA7 IVMA7 IMA7

Review of Lessons 10–13 — UNIT 3 — 21

1 The two major seventh chords found in a major key are __IMA7__ and __IVMA7__.

2 When chords are connected smoothly, it is referred to as proper __Voice leading__.

3 Jazz standard songs are in modes. True / (False)

4 There are __7__ modes of the major scale. The fourth mode is called __lydian__, and sounds like a major scale with the __4th__ note raised ½ step.

5 The most important notes for "making the changes" are the __3rd__ and __7th__ of a chord.

6 Notate the IVMA7 chord in the following keys, in root position and all three inversions.

GMA7   EbMA7   DMA7
D: Bb: A:

7 For each IMA7 chord, notate the IVMA7 in that key, using smooth voice leading.

FMA7 BbMA7 CMA7 FMA7 EbMA7 AbMA7 DMA7 GMA7

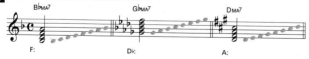

F: 3rd Inv. 1st inv.   C: 2nd Inv.   Eb: 1st inv. 3rd inv.   D: Root pos. 2nd inv.

8 For each IVMA7 chord, notate the IMA7 in that key, using smooth voice leading.

CMA7 GMA7 DbMA7 AbMA7 BbMA7 FMA7 GbMA7 DbMA7

G: 2nd Inv. root pos.   Ab: 3rd Inv. 1st inv.   F: root pos. 2nd inv.   Db: 1st inv. 3rd inv.

9 Notate the Lydian scales for the IV chords below.

BbMA7 GbMA7 DMA7
F: Db: A:

10 Compose a characteristic jazz solo melody to the following progression, using Lydian sounds, and 3rd and 7th emphasis.

FMA7 CMA7 FMA7 CMA7 FMA7 CMA7

---

22 — UNIT 4 — Lesson 14

Major 9th Chords (MA9, Δ9)

Jazz composers and soloists freely add ninth extensions to most chords. Adding a 9th to a MA7 chord results in a MAJOR NINTH CHORD. A 9th can be understood as the second note of a scale, repeated in the next octave.

C Major Scale

A note is called a 9th, and not a 2nd, because chords are stacked thirds, and the 9th is the next third over the chord 7th. The 9th of a MA9 chord is a major 9th (M9) above the root (a whole step, up an octave), and the proper symbol for the chord is MA9

Ninths can be considered consonant in jazz, and they add richness to the harmony.

Major ninth chords can be arpeggiated in 4-note groupings (in four inversions) omitting the root. Since jazz bass players almost always play the root, these ROOTLESS ARPEGGIOS are more interesting and complex. In jazz, 9th chords and 7th chords are interchangeable.

Ninths can also be heard as appoggiaturas, resolving down to the chord root.

(Track 38)

Exercises

1 *Dig it!*—Using CD Track 27, play the rootless CMA9 and FMA9 arpeggios from 3rd to 9th, lingering on each 9th to experience its consonance. Next, play the 9ths as appoggiaturas, and resolve downward to the chord roots. The chords change every two measures.

2 Construct the following IMA9 chords in all four rootless inversions.

BbMA9 GMA9 AbMA9 BMA9
Bb: G: Ab: B:

3 Construct the following IVMA9 chords in all four rootless inversions.

GMA9 BbMA9 DbMA9 AMA9
D: F: Ab: E:

4 Circle the chord 9ths and indicate whether each is consonant (C) or an appoggiatura (appog).

BbMA9 EbMA9 BbMA9

Lesson 15 — UNIT 4 — 23

Major 6/9 Chords (⁶/₉)

Interchangeable with MA7 or MA9 chords is the MAJOR 6/9 CHORD, which is designated as ⁶/₉ (e.g.: C⁶/₉, F⁶/₉ etc.). The ⁶/₉ chord is much the same as a MA9 chord, only with the chord 7th replaced by the 6th note of the scale (a Major 6th above the root).

Like MA9 chords, ⁶/₉ chords are typically arpeggiated without the root (which will be supplied by the bass player in jazz performance).

This sound of the ⁶/₉ chord is more stable than that of a major 7th chord, because the interval of a M6 above the root is more consonant than the M7. Compositionally, major ⁶/₉ chords should be used when the melody features the chord root. A major 7th in the harmony actually clashes with the root a ½ step away, while the 6th of the chord is harmonious against it. So, for example, the first two bars of "On Green Dolphin Street" or the first measure of "L-O-V-E" would best be harmonized by major ⁶/₉ chords. The following melody should employ a ⁶/₉ chord:

Track 39 C⁶/₉

Exercises

1 Track 39 — Dig it!—Play the melody above on the piano with your right hand, and a MA7 chord in root position in your left hand. Can you hear the 7th clashing against the root in the melody? Compare that to the sound of the melody using the ⁶/₉ chord.

2 Construct each ⁶/₉ chord, followed by the rootless arpeggios, in all four inversions.

Bb⁶/₉   Db⁶/₉   G⁶/₉

3 For this melody, indicate whether each chord should be ⁶/₉ or MA9.

Eb ⁶/₉   Ab MA9

Db ⁶/₉   Eb MA9   Ab ⁶/₉   Eb MA9

---

24 — UNIT 4 — Lesson 16

Major Pentatonic Scale (Pentatonic)

PENTATONIC means "five notes," so any scale of five notes can be called pentatonic. In jazz music, the scale referred to as pentatonic is actually a MAJOR PENTATONIC SCALE, which is analogous to notes 1, 2, 3, 5, and 6 of the major scale. These are exactly the notes found in the ⁶/₉ chord!

C⁶/₉ = Pentatonic Scale

Composed only of chord tones, the pentatonic scale is entirely consonant, and very useful for the corresponding MA9 and ⁶/₉ chords. There is no dissonant 4th in the pentatonic scale, so it is a great tool for both composition and improvisation. Some hymn tunes, such as "Amazing Grace" and "Swing Low, Sweet Chariot" (which have their basis in earlier Celtic music), are entirely pentatonic.

Although not named, there are modes of the pentatonic scale, and improvisers often take four-note groupings from the PENTATONIC MODES to use as MELODIC CELLS.

Track 40 G⁶/₉

Exercises

1 Construct the indicated pentatonic scales.

F Pentatonic   A Pentatonic   D Pentatonic   Gb Pentatonic

2 Notate the 4-note melodic cells from the modes of the pentatonic scales above.

F Pentatonic   A Pentatonic

D Pentatonic   Gb Pentatonic

3 Compose a characteristic jazz solo melody, using pentatonic scales.

C⁶/₉

D⁶/₉   Db⁶/₉   C⁶/₉

Lesson 17 — UNIT 4 — 25

Jazz Language - Grace Notes, Scoops & Turns

So far, this text has dealt with global aspects of jazz melody. GRACE NOTES, SCOOPS and TURNS represent more specific components of the jazz language.

Because jazz musicians value emotional impact over pristine clarity and perfection of line, GRACE NOTES are a frequent melodic embellishment. A grace note is an emphatic sound, which can add "heart" or "bluesyness" to the ensuing tone.

Grace notes can be diatonic...   or chromatic....(i.e., a 1/2 step away, even if that tone is non-diatonic).   or a few consecutive tones can "grace" a melody note.

A SCOOP into a note creates the same effect as using grace notes. "Scooping" is executed by beginning a note slightly flat, and sliding up to the pitch. Scoops are notated with the symbol (↙).

A TURN (mordent) is an embellishing melodic device, involving a tone quickly going to its neighbor (usually above) and back. The rhythm of a turn is typically an eighth-note triplet figure, or an eighth note followed by two sixteenths, or four sixteenth notes.

C⁶/₉   or   or

Turns can be written out or indicated with the symbol ∾. Often turns are followed with eighth-note movement by step or third in the opposite direction.

Eb⁶/₉

Turns have been around for hundreds of years, and are used liberally in jazz melody, especially in a bebop context. The hot bop styles of trumpeter, Lee Morgan and pianist, Oscar Peterson are characterized by the regular use of melodic turns.

Track 41 FMA9

Conversely, a stark characteristic of Miles Davis's "cool" playing was the eschewing of turns.

Exercises

1 Add grace notes, scoops, and turns to this melody.

DbMA7   AbMA9   Db⁶/₉   AbMA9

---

26 — UNIT 4 — Ear Training For Lessons 14–17

1 Track 42 — Listen to the MA7 arpeggio (r–7) and the MA9 arpeggio (3–9). Circle whether each arpeggio is MA7 or MA9.

a. (MA7) / MA9   b. MA7 / (MA9)

c. MA7 / (MA9)   d. (MA7) / MA9

2 Track 43 — Listen to the rootless MA9 arpeggio in all four inversions. Write which note is on the bottom of each arpeggio you hear.

a. _5th_ on bottom   b. _3rd_ on bottom

c. _9th_ on bottom   d. _7th_ on bottom

3 Track 44 — Listen to the MA9 arpeggio and the ⁶/₉ arpeggio (3–9). Circle whether each arpeggio is MA9 or ⁶/₉.

a. MA9 / (⁶/₉)   b. (MA9) / ⁶/₉

c. (MA9) / ⁶/₉   d. MA9 / (⁶/₉)

4 Track 45 — Is this melody accompanied by a MA9 chord or a ⁶/₉ chord?

MA9   (⁶/₉)

5 Track 46 — Listen to the major scale from 1–5 and the pentatonic scale. Circle whether each scale you hear is major (1–5) or pentatonic.

a. major / (pentatonic)   b. major / (pentatonic)

c. (major) / pentatonic   d. major / (pentatonic)

6 Track 47 — Listen to the melodic cells from the 1st (root on bottom), 3rd (3rd on bottom), and 4th (5th above root on bottom) modes of the pentatonic scale. Circle whether each example is the 1st, 3rd, or 4th mode cell.

a. 1st / (3rd) / 4th   b. (1st) / 3rd / 4th

c. 1st / (3rd) / 4th   d. 1st / 3rd / (4th)

7 Track 48 — Listen to the melody and count the number of jazz turns.

_7_ turns.

Review of Lessons 14–17 **UNIT 4** 27

1 Jazz musicians typically arpeggiate 9th chords without playing the _____root_____ .

2 _Pentatonic_ _____ means five notes.

3 Sliding into a note from below is called a _scoop_ .

4 A pentatonic scale is just another way of playing a ⁶⁄₉ chord. (True) / False

5 Another name for turn is _mordent_ .

6 Write the MA9 chords vertically (not arpeggiated) in all four rootless positions.

7 Notate the ⁶⁄₉ chords in rootless fashion (3rd on bottom), followed by the corresponding pentatonic scale.

8 Write the 4-note melodic cells from the modes of each of these pentatonic scales.

9 Compose a characteristic jazz solo melody, using pentatonic scales, grace notes and turns.

---

28 **UNIT 5** **Lesson 18**

Dominant 7th and 9th Chords (7, 9)

To understand the importance of DOMINANT SEVENTH CHORDS in music, sing a major scale from "do" to "ti." That overwhelming desire you feel to add the ensuing "do" is the tendency created by the existence of the dominant 7th chord. Dominant 7th chords are even more important in jazz because they can imply a sense of blues not found in earlier music. Advanced musicians find that dominant seventh chords offer a tapestry of melodic note choice, which is more varied than that of any other chord-type in jazz. The dominant chord is a favorite of jazz musicians for the richness of melodic options it invites.

DOMINANT 7TH AND DOMINANT 9TH CHORDS are analogous to major 7th and 9th chords, only with the chord seventh flatted a 1/2 step. The chord symbol for a dominant 7th or 9th chord is simply the number 7 or 9 (e.g.: C7, F9, etc.).

So, a dominant 7th chord contains a major triad and the interval of a *minor* 7th from root to seventh.
Track 49
The 1/2 step difference between major 7th and dominant 7th chords may seem insignificant, but in the way the chords *sound*, the difference is quite profound. CD Track 49 alternates between EbMA7 and Eb7 chords. The sound of the dominant 7th chord is more intense.

As is the case with MA9 chords, the ninth of a dominant 9th chord is a major ninth above the root. Of course, the dominant 9th chord can be written and played in four, rootless inversions.

Exercises

1 Construct the indicated dominant 7th chords in root position and the three inversions.

2 Construct the indicated dominant 9th chords in four rootless inversions.

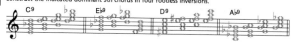

3 These MA7 and MA9 chords are in various inversions. For each, alter the chord so that it is a dominant 7th or 9th chord, and write in each chord symbol.

Lesson 19 **UNIT 5** 29

Dominant Function

The fifth degree of a major scale is called the DOMINANT PITCH, and a dominant 7th chord naturally results over that note. So, in major keys, we know the *quality* of the V7 chord will always be dominant 7th . . .

. . . and it is understood that the V9 chord in any major key is always a dominant 9th chord.

Notice that the V7 chord contains major scale tones 5, 7, 2, and 4, consecutively (although we still refer to these tones as root, 3rd, 5th, and 7th of the chord).

DOMINANT FUNCTION: In music of the past several hundred years, V7 chords have had a crucial role, because they don't

merely progress, but rather "resolve" to tonic chords. The sound of V7 feels like a musical tension, with a strong "tendency" to resolve to I.
Track 50
Dig it!—CD Track 50 alternates V7 and IMA7 chords in the key of Bb major. Can you feel a *pull* between these chords?

The resolution of V7 to I is called a CADENCE (authentic cadence in classical music), and the cadence is how virtually all jazz standards (and classical pieces, for that matter) end. Listening to CD Track 50, you notice how "final" it sounds each time V7 progresses to the tonic chord.

Exercises

1 For each major key below, construct the V7 chord in root position and all three inversions, and indicate the chord symbol.

2 For each major key below, construct the V9 chord in all four rootless positions, and indicate the chord symbol.

3 For each major key, indicate the chord symbols for the V7 to IMA7 cadence.

_Ab7_ _DbMA7_ _Bb7_ _EbMA7_ _C#7_ _F#MA7_ _Eb7_ _AbMA7_
Db: V7   IMA7   Eb: V7   IMA7   F#: V7   IMA7   Ab: V7   IMA7

---

30 **UNIT 5** **Lesson 20**

Resolution of V7 Chords, Tendency Tones and Tritone

As mentioned in Lesson 18, the 3rd of the V7 chord, which is the seventh scale degree, pulls towards the root of the tonic chord (7–8).

Scale Degrees: 7   8

Also, the chord 7th, (which is the fourth scale degree) has a strong tendency to resolve down by diatonic step into the 3rd of the tonic chord (4-3).

Scale Degrees: 4   3
Track 51
The 3rd and 7th of V7 chords are called TENDENCY TONES, because of their need to resolve. CD Track 51 performs the tendency tone resolutions (7-8, 4-3) over the V7-IMA7 progression. Listening to the track, you feel the satisfaction of tension and release with the tendency tones.

Dig It!—The interval between the 3rd and 7th of a dominant chord is a tritone (in other words A4 or d5). The tritone interval resolves either inward or outward, depending on which note is placed on top.

The 9th of a V9 chord is also a tendency tone, which resolves down by step into the 5th of the tonic chord.

Exercises
Track 52
1 Listen to this melody to hear the tendency-tone resolutions of V7-I. Find each tendency tone and draw an arrow from it to the resolving note. Write the chord-tone names of both notes.

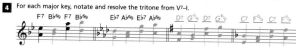

2 For each V7-I progression, write and resolve the tendency tones, chord 3rd and chord 7th.

3rd   R   7th   3rd   3rd   R   7th   3rd   3rd   R   7th   3rd

3 Notate and resolve the 9ths of the V9 chords.

9th   5th   9th   5th   9th   5th   9th   5th

4 For each major key, notate and resolve the tritone from V7-I.

_D7_ _G⁶⁄₉_ _D7_ _G⁶⁄₉_   _C7_ _F⁶⁄₉_ _C7_ _F⁶⁄₉_

Lesson 21 — UNIT 5 — 31

V7 – IMA7 Common Tones and Voice Leading

There are two common tones between the V7 and IMA7 chords. Most significantly, the 3rd of V7 is the same note as the 7th of IMA7!

In jazz, the 7th of a tonic chord is consonant. So rather than resolving the chord 3rd of V7, jazz musicians often hold it as a common tone to the most expressive note of the IMA7 chord.

Still, the resolution of the 7th of the V7 chord into the 3rd of the IMA7 chord is more significant.

In creating both melodies and harmonic accompaniments, jazz musicians use inversions for smooth voice leading between the V7 and IMA7 chords.

Rootless inversions of the V9 chord also smoothly connect to IMA9.

Exercises

1 *Dig It!*—This melody "makes the changes," with common tones, resolution, and voice leading. Notice the compelling sense of tension-and-release and musical emphasis. Label the tendency tones and the notes they resolve to, and draw straight lines to show the common tone connection from V7 to IMA7.

2 For each V7 and V9 chord, notate the closest inversion of a rootless IMA9. Draw straight lines between the common tones.

3 Compose a melody featuring tendency tones, resolution, common tone, and proper voice leading.

32 — UNIT 5 — Lesson 22

Dominant Scale (Mixolydian), Bebop Dominant Scale

As mentioned in Unit 3, all diatonic chords can use the scale from the tonic as a means for having other melody notes between the chord tones. So a G7 chord, functioning as V7 in C major, uses a C major scale from G to G. The major scale, when played in the fifth mode, sounds like a normal major scale, only with the seventh note flatted, and its church mode name is MIXOLYDIAN. When played in eighth notes, the ascending major scale from 5–5 (Mixolydian) places chord tones of the V7 on each beat, thus "making the change."

Jazz composers and soloists love the BEBOP DOMINANT SCALE, which is a descending major scale with *both* the major seventh and the flatted seventh. This scale, played in eighth notes, also places all the chord tones of the dominant seventh chord on the beats.

WHAT IS A SCALE? In jazz, a scale can be defined as "chord tones and notes in between." This is why both the major scale and major with raised 4 (Lydian) sound great for MA7 chords, and both the Mixolydian and bebop dominant scales are effective for dominant chords.

Here is a melody that makes the changes using both the Mixolydian and bebop dominant scales.

Exercises

1 For the jazz melody above, circle and label usage of the dominant and bebop dominant scales (note: the entire scale might not be used).

2 For each chord, write the dominant (Mixolydian) scale.

3 In each major key, write the bebop dominant scale for the V7 chord, and write the chord symbol above the staff.

Ear Training For Lessons 18–22 — UNIT 5 — 33

1 Listen to the MA7 chord and the dominant 7th chord. Indicate whether each chord is MA7 or dominant 7th (V7).

  a. MA7 /(V7)   b. (MA7)/ V7

  c. MA7 /(V7)   d. (MA7)/ V7

2 Listen to V9 and IMA9. Write whether each progression is V9-IMA9, or IMA9-V9.

  a. V9-IMA9   b. IMA9-V9

  c. IMA9-V9   d. V9-IMA9

3 Listen to the tendency tone resolution of V7-IMA7; 7th (to 3rd) and the common tone (3rd to 7th). Indicate which connection each melody uses.

  a. (7-3)/ 3-7   b. (7-3)/ 3-7

  c. (7-3)/ 3-7   d. 7-3 /(3-7)

4 Listen to 7th resolving to 3rd and 9th resolving to 5th as V7 progresses to IMA7. Indicate which resolution you hear.

  a. (7-3)/ 9-5   b. 7-3 /(9-5)

  c. (7-3)/ 9-5   d. 7-3 /(9-5)

5 Listen to the major scale and the dominant (Mixolydian) scale. Indicate whether each melody uses major or Mixolydian.

  a. major /(Mixolydian)   b. (major)/ Mixolydian

  c. (major)/ Mixolydian   d. major /(Mixolydian)

6 Listen to the descending dominant and bebop dominant scales. Indicate whether each melody uses dominant (Mixolydian) or bebop dominant.

  a. (Mixolydian)/ bebop   b. Mixolydian /(bebop)

  c. Mixolydian /(bebop)   d. (Mixolydian)/ bebop

34 — UNIT 5 — REVIEW OF LESSONS 18–22

1 A dominant 7th chord is like MA7 with the ____7th____ note flatted, and naturally occurs over the ____5th____ note of the major scale.

2 The V7-I progression is called a ____cadence____ .

3 Notes which require resolutions are called ____tendency____ ____tones____ .

4 The fifth mode of the major scale is called ____mixolydian____ .

5 Bebop dominant is a descending major scale with two ____sevenths____ .

6 For each major key, write a V7 chord, a V9 arpeggio (rootless) and the dominant scale.

7 For each V7 or V9 chord, write the best inversion of (rootless) IMA9 for smooth voice leading.

8 For each chord, write the bebop dominant scale.

9 Analyze the melody, indicating scales, arpeggios, resolution, common tone, non-harmonic tones and other characteristic jazz devices.

Lesson 23 | UNIT 6 | 35

"Bluesy" Dominant Chords

Blues music presents a true departure from the harmonies of classical music, because in a blues context dominant 7th chords can be stable. For instance, flatting the seventh of the IMA7 chord results in a dominant 7th chord which is a "bluesy" tonic (I7 instead of IMA7).

Bluesy subdominant chords with a dominant quality are also found in jazz.

Here is a melody to the dominant I9 and IV9 chords (interchangeable with dominant 7th chords).

Track 63

Track 64
How do you know whether a dominant 7th chord is functioning as V7 or as a bluesy tonic? You can tell by what happens next, because V7 chords are associated with the tonics they resolve to. For instance, a G7 chord progressing to CMA7 definitely is functioning as V7. CD Track 64 has the progression I7 – IV7 – V7 – IMA7, with each chord lasting two measures. You can hear the difference between the "bluesy" I7 and IV7 chords and the tension-and-release of V7 resolving to IMA7.

Exercises

1 *Dig It!*—Play the melody above. You should notice that the 7ths of the dominant I and IV chords don't feel like tendency tones, but rather as stable, bluesy sounds.

2 For each major key, notate the I7 and IV7 chords.

3 For each I7 chord, write the IV7 chord using inversion (if necessary) to create smooth voice leading.

4 Compose a melody to this progression, using a lick to unify the I7 and IV7 chords.

---

36 | UNIT 6 | Lesson 24

Blue Notes

Blue notes are a unique and important feature in the language of jazz. They are pitches that can be played in a key without "making the changes," creating a profound tension that must be resolved into chord tones.

The blue notes are the flatted 3rd, 5th, and 7th pitches of a key **or** chord, and are typically used over dominant 7th harmonies. Here are the blue notes in the key of F, and their usage over the I7, IV7 and V7 chords.

Track 65

Next, blue notes are separately constructed over bluesy tonic and subdominant chords. The subdominant chord seems more like a tonic when it has its own blue notes.

Track 66

*enharmonically spelled as ♯4

In our musical system the blue notes cannot be precisely notated, because they fall somewhere in the "cracks" between the actual pitches. Genuine performance of blue notes is predicated on an intensity of feeling in the "gut" of the performer.

Blue notes are ideal for usage in repeated licks, creating and escalating tension, followed by a release into a strong chord tone.

Track 67

3rd!

Exercises

1 *Dig It!*—As you listen to and play the excerpt above, concentrate on the intense feeling of the blue notes and also the feeling of resolution into the diatonic 3rd (tension/release).

2 For each major key, write the 3 blue notes.

3 For each major key, write the blue notes to the I7, IV7 and V7 chords.

4 Compose a lick-based melody to the progression, using the blue notes of the key.

5 Compose a lick-based melody to the progression, using separate blue notes for each chord.

Lesson 25 | UNIT 6 | 37

12-Bar Blues Progression, Blues Scale

The 12-BAR BLUES is the most often played chord progression in jazz. There are thousands of 12-bar blues tunes. Blues has its roots in "field hollers" from American slavery. The basic 12-bar blues contains the I7, IV7 and V7 chords, in three, 4-bar phrases.

Track 68
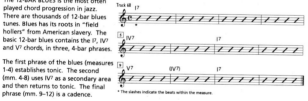
* The slashes indicate the beats within the measure.

The first phrase of the blues (measures 1-4) establishes tonic. The second (mm. 4-8) uses IV7 as a secondary area and then returns to tonic. The final phrase (mm. 9–12) is a cadence.

Without the parenthetical IV7 chord in measure 10 above, there is a V7-I authentic cadence. The IV7-I progression is called a PLAGAL CADENCE, which is the church ("amen") cadence.

Blues melodies can be in CALL-AND-RESPONSE form, also reminiscent of field hollers. The first phrase (call), is mimicked in the second (response). The third phrase is a summation. Once through a progression is called a CHORUS, so this is a one-chorus melody.

Track 69

Jazz musicians have developed a BLUES SCALE which contains the 3 blue notes of the key, and also scale degrees 4 and 5.

Bb Blues Scale

The blues scale is played in simple, repetitive licks, using a few of the tones in order. Because blue notes are dissonant, it is effective to resolve blues scale licks into chord tones.

Track 70

Exercises

1 Compose a chorus to the 12-bar blues, based on a lick and using call-response form.

2 Compose a chorus to the 12-bar blues, using few or no blue notes, and clearly "making the changes."

---

38 | UNIT 6 | EAR TRAINING FOR LESSONS 23–25

Track 71
1 Listen to the I7 and IV7 chords. Indicate whether each chord is I7 or IV7.

   a. (I7) / IV7   b. (I7) / IV7

   c. I7 / (IV7)   d. (I7) / IV7

Track 72
2 Listen to the blue notes ♭3, ♭5, ♭7. Indicate which blue note you are hearing.

   a. ♭3 / (♭5) / ♭7   b. ♭3 / ♭5 / (♭7)

   c. (♭3) / ♭5 / ♭7   d. (♭3) / ♭5 / ♭7

Track 73
3 For each melody, indicate whether the blue notes are in the key, or of each chord.

   a. (in the key) / each chord   b. in the key / (each chord)

   c. (in the key) / each chord   d. (in the key) / each chord

Track 74
4 Listen to the I7, IV7, and V7 chords. Write down the progression you hear (each chord lasts 2 bars).

   IV7 I7 IV7 I7 IV7 V7 I7 .

Track 75
5 Listen to the F blues scale. Write down the notes in the order you hear them.

F Blues Scale

Track 76
6 Listen to the V7-I7 authentic cadence and IV7-I7 plagal cadence. Write whether each cadence is authentic or plagal.

   a. (authentic) / plagal   b. authentic / (plagal)

   c. (authentic) / plagal   d. authentic / (plagal)

Track 77
7 Listen to a blues lick which resolves to the 3rd of the chord. Write whether each phrase resolves into the chord 3rd.

   a. (yes) / no   b. yes / (no)

   c. yes / (no)   d. (yes) / no

REVIEW OF LESSONS 23–25 — UNIT 6 — 39

1 When the 7th of IMA7 is flatted, the resulting chord is a ___I7___ .

This same alteration is also typical for the ___IV7___ chord in a key.

2 Dominant-quality I7 and IV chords are unstable. True / (False.)

3 The blue notes are the flatted _3rd_ , _5th_ and _7th_ of a chord or ___key___ .

4 Blue notes and the blues scale are best suited for (lick) / line / melody (circle one).

5 The 12-bar blues is based on the _I7_, _IV7_, and _V7_ chords, and is organized into _3_ phrases.

6 Blues melodies are often in a ___call___-and-_response_ form.

7 Blue notes "make the changes." True / (False.)

8 Above the staves, write out the basic 12-bar blues progression in the key of Bb.
Next, notate the rootless dominant ninth chords, using inversions for smooth voice leading.

*Note: Other inversions may be used.

9 Write out the blue notes for each key, followed by the blues scale.

Blue notes   Blues scale

*Enharmonic spelling OK.

10 Write a bluesy lick for the I7 chord, and transpose or alter it for IV7 and V7.

Lesson 26 — UNIT 7 — 43

Counterpoint—Bass and Melody

COUNTERPOINT is the simultaneous occurrence of two or more musical voices. The beauty of counterpoint lies in the interest created by the voices and the harmony that arises from them. Counterpoint between melody and bass has been an organizing principal of Western music for hundreds of years. In jazz, the bass voice establishes the harmony, which the melody clarifies and augments with "color" tones, such as 3rds and 7ths.

The joyful, forward momentum of swing music is due in large part to walking bass lines. WALKING BASS is a continual, quarter-note bass motion in which, more often than not, the chord root is on the downbeat of each measure. These lines typically are played in a register more than an octave below middle C, creating a polar counterpoint to the melody. String and electric basses have a range down to (at least) the E almost three octaves below middle C. (Note that bass sounds an octave lower than written.)

Track 2 demonstrates that walking bass is always played very legato; otherwise the feeling of swing is lost. Beats 1 and 3 are the *functional* beats, and are more apt to feature the chord root, 3rd, or 5th. Beats 2 and 4 are the *energy* beats. By energizing beats 2 and 4, and playing passing tones and other less structural pitches on these beats, the bass creates an energetic tendency to resolve to the next functional beat.

A TWO FEEL is created when the bass plays either half notes in each bar, or a dotted quarter, eighth-note pattern. This causes the music to feel in a 2-beat meter (cut time, 2/2), as opposed to 4/4. The bass plays almost exclusively an alternation of root and fifth.

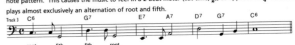

Exercises

1 Analyze these walking bass lines by circling and identifying the chord tones.
Label any passing (p.t.) or neighboring (n.t.) tones as well.

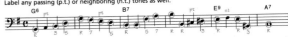

2 Compose a jazz melody to the bass line above. Remember that 3rds and 7ths (and even 9ths) complete the "picture" of counterpoint.

3 Compose a two-feel bass line to the progression.

UNIT 7 — Lesson 27 — 44

Walking Bass Lines

The most important things a bass line can do are: 1) reinforce the groove and momentum of swing, and 2) make the chord changes clear. The first element is a matter of performance (as discussed in Lesson 26), while the second is one of construction.

The two simplest ways for a walking bass to establish the chord progression are:

by playing roots and fifths. . .

or by arpeggiating the chords.

Passing and neighboring tones are also effective for walking bass construction. Typically, these tones are employed on the weak beats (2 and 4), and lead to structural (chord) tones on the strong beats (1 and 3).

One of the most appealing devices for walking bass lines is the usage of CHROMATIC APPROACH TONES (leading tones), which are notes a ½ step below or above the next chord tone. As with other non-harmonic tones, approach tones most often occur on the weak beats.

Exercises

1 Analyze this walking bass line by circling and identifying the chord tones.
Label any passing (p.t.), neighboring (n.t.), or chromatic approach tones (a.t.).

2 Compose a walking bass line to this progression.

Lesson 28 — UNIT 7 — 45

Walking Bass Lines in the Circle of Fifths, Two-Note Voicings

You know that the V7–I progression establishes a key. In Lesson 33 you will learn about the pervasive ii–V ("two-five") progression in jazz. Both are "circle-of-fifth" progressions, in which the bass moves by a perfect fifth interval from one chord to the next. Even the progression from I to IV is in the circle of fifths. Since these progressions are ubiquitous in jazz, standardized walking bass patterns have emerged.

The most common bass line for circle-of-fifth progressions is an ascending scale from one chord root to the next, using both major and minor third degrees. A variation on this line drops a 7th from the root.

The simplest bass line for the circle-of-fifth progression is a descending scale from one root to the next.

The combination of walking bass and melody creates a CONTRAPUNTAL TEXTURE (one using counterpoint). When ACCOMPANIMENT is added to the texture, such as one or more instruments playing chords, the texture is enhanced. Accompanimental chords can be played by a keyboard or guitar, or two or more instruments simultaneously sounding notes. These arrangements of chords are called voicings.

Simple, yet effective, TWO-NOTE VOICINGS are achieved by sounding just the chord 3rd and 7th, assuming the bass voice plays the root. These notes sound best in the "comping" range (see Lesson 29), which is approximately a sixth, either side of middle C.

Exercises

1 Compose a walking bass line to the melody and chord progression, employing typical, circle-of-fifth construction.

2 Notate two-note voicings, in the comping range, to the following chords:

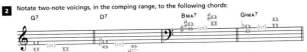

UNIT 7 Lesson 29

Comping & Comp Rhythms, Voice Leading

COMPING is a rhythmic accompaniment of chords, generally played by keyboard or guitar. Comping is the "glue" between the counterpoint of melody and bass, and can add to the tension and release in the music. Comping is reactive and interactive, like a listener in a conversation who says, "Mm-hmm," "Go on," or "Really!?" Comping is effective, as long as the music retains its clarity. If a comping instrument plays too loudly, or too often, the chords will clutter and obscure the beauty of the counterpoint.

COMP RHYTHMS are essential to the sense of groove. Voicings played on the occasional off-beat contribute to the propulsion of swing, and can be in short or long note values.

Jazz musicians often employ comp rhythms where chords are sounded one-and-a-half beats apart, e.g., beats "one" and the "and-of-two"; the "and-of-one" and "three", etc., in either long or short durations. So, just this one rhythmic device gives rise to 20 different comping figures! Chords played off a beat anticipate the next beat; so a chord played on the "and-of-four" anticipates the next measure.

Track 8

VOICE LEADING refers to chord voicings moving smoothly from one chord to the next. You know that when chords progress by a fifth (V–I, I–IV), the 7th of the first chord *resolves* down by a ½ step into the 3rd of the next, and, the 3rd of the first chord is a common tone with the 7th of the next. Applying these principles will result in appealing voice leading.

Track 9

Even when chords are not moving by fifth, voice leading should be as smooth as possible. The decision of whether the 3rd or 7th is on the bottom is determined by two factors: 1) placing the chord in the comping range, and 2) creating smooth voice leading.

Exercises

1 Use smooth voice leading to connect two-note voicings in the circle of fifths.

2 Create a comping texture using two-note voicings and a walking bass line.

Lesson 30 UNIT 7

Brazilian Bass Lines & Comping Patterns

Jazz music and swing feel developed together, and they are permanently intertwined. Other forms of popular music have incorporated jazz elements, and have also been subsumed into jazz. For example, Brazilian *bossa nova* and *samba* rhythms are very popular among jazz musicians and composers. The two grooves are almost identical, with bossa being in (4/4), while samba is faster and feels in cut time (2/2).

The prevalent Brazilian comping pattern is referred to as PARTITO ALTO, and is played by guitar and/or piano. In a traditional jazz group, the drummer will sometimes play all or part of the partito alto pattern using a cross stick on the snare drum.

Track 10

In Brazil, the samba drum sounds prominently in the middle of the measure, and an authentic Brazilian bass figure does the same, alternating root and 5th.

Track 11 C6

The Americanized version of bossa or samba bass uses a dotted quarter and eighth rhythm.

Track 12 CMA7

The partito alto has four permutations, including the one you learned above. The figure is two bars long, and can begin on either downbeat, or in the middle of either bar.

Track 13

Track 13 has a rhythm section playing each of the four partitio alto figures in eight-measure phrases. The bass may play the authentic figure you learned, or incorporate elements of the partito alto rhythm.

Exercises

1 Find a Brazilian jazz recording and analyze the rhythm. Is the bass playing Brazilian or American style? How many permutations of partito alto are used? Are other comping patterns incorporated?

2 For this chord progression, write a bossa bass line and also two-note voicings, in the comping range, employing partito alto rhythms.

UNIT 7 Ear Training for Lessons 26–30

Track 14
1 Listen to the walking bass line and fill in the missing notes below.

Track 15
2 Listen to the bass note and two-note voicing with the 3rd on the bottom. Next, listen to the same chord, inverted to place the 7th on the bottom. You will hear four additional chords. For each, indicate whether the 3rd or 7th is on the bottom of the voicing.

   a. (3rd) / 7th   **b.** 3rd / (7th)   **c.** (3rd) / 7th   **d.** 3rd / (7th)

Track 16
3 Listen to the bass note, followed by two-note voicings of MA7 and Dominant 7th. For the following four-chord voicings, indicate whether each is MA7 or 7.

   a. MA7 / (7)   **b.** MA7 / (7)   **c.** (MA7) / 7   **d.** (MA7) / 7

Track 17
4 Listen to this rhythm section with piano comping and indicate which example below correctly notates the comp rhythms.

Track 18
5 Listen to this rhythm section with piano comping and write the number of times that the comp rhythm is two chords one-and-a-half beats apart.

       3   comp rhythms one-and-a-half beats apart.

Track 19
6 Listen to the partito alto, and then the same rhythm beginning on the second measure. For each example, indicate whether the partito alto begins in the first or second measure.

   a. (measure 1) / measure 2   **b.** measure 1 / (measure 2)   **c.** (measure 1) / measure 2

Review of Lessons 26–30 UNIT 7

1 The simultaneous occurrence of two or more melodic voices is called ___counterpoint___, which often exists between melody and _bass_ in jazz.

2 _Walking bass_ is constructed of legato quarter notes in a range approximately two octaves below middle C.

3 When a jazz bass line seems to be in 2/2 time, this is called a _two_ feel.

4 Bass lines are made more colorful with _passing_ tones and _chromatic approach_ tones. (neighbor or)

5 A two-note _voicing_ is constructed of the chord 3rd and 7th.

6 _Comping_ is a rhythmic accompaniment by piano or guitar, and relies on smooth _voice leading_.

7 In Brazilian music the _bossa nova_ is in 4/4 time, while the _samba_ is in 2/2 (cut) time.

8 Brazilian bass lines typically alternate between _root_ and _fifth_, while the comping pattern is known as _partito alto_.

9 Notate a walking bass line using passing and approach tones, and also characteristic circle-of-fifth construction.

10 Write two-note, voicings in a partito alto rhythm, employing smooth voice leading, and a samba bass line to the following progression:

11 Write a walking bass line and voicings to the progression, employing characteristic comp rhythms.

Minor 7th and 9th Chords (MI⁷, MI⁹) & Inversions

When music is in a minor key there is a melancholy result. In jazz, however, the minor seventh chord is also the hopeful sound that propels the changes towards a major tonic.

A MINOR TRIAD is analogous to a major triad with the 3rd flatted a ½ step. This lowered 3rd accounts for the somber sound associated with minor. A MINOR SEVENTH CHORD is a minor triad with a minor 7th (m7) interval above the root, and is indicated by the chord symbol "MI⁷" (sometimes min⁷, m⁷ or –7).

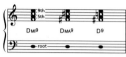

It is striking how similar major seventh, dominant seventh and minor seventh chords are, especially when you consider how different their sounds are. Flat the 7th of a MA⁷ chord and a dominant seventh chord results. A MI⁷ chord simply results from lowering the 3rd of a dominant seventh chord.

A MINOR NINTH CHORD is a MI⁷ chord with an added note a major 9th above the root. What's more, dominant 7, MI⁷, and MA⁷ chords all share the same ninth. In fact these three chords, built on a single root will share the same root, 5th, and 9th! This is precisely why 3rds and 7ths of chords are so important, because these tones establish chord *quality*.

Minor seventh chords, of course, can be arranged in root position and in three inversions, while MI⁹ chords can be practiced in four, rootless inversions. For jazz musicians, these rudimental inversions should be second nature.

Exercises

1 Construct the indicated MI⁷ chords in root position and all three inversions.

2 Construct the indicated MI⁹ chords in all four rootless inversions.

3 Below are MA⁷, MA⁹, and also dominant 7th and 9th chords in various positions. Alter each chord to be a MI⁷ or MI⁹, and indicate the chord symbol.

Supertonic Function—iiMI⁷ and iiMI⁹ Chords

You already know that constructing seventh chords above the tonic and subdominant notes (scale degrees 1 and 4) of major keys results in major seventh chords. Similarly, the chord constructed over the fifth degree is always a dominant seventh. Well, the diatonic chords over the 2nd, 3rd and 6th scale degrees are all minor seventh chords!

The SUPERTONIC SEVENTH CHORD (iiMI⁷ or iiMI⁹) is constructed with major scale degrees 2, 4, 6, and 8 (1). This chord is of great importance to jazz musicians because of its fifth relationship with V⁷ (see Unit 8, Lesson 33). Remember that chord tones are always referred to as root, 3rd, 5th and 7th, regardless of what scale degrees they represent.

Track 20 begins by alternating between IMA⁷ and iiMI⁷ chords in the key of E-flat major. Notice that, in this context, the minor seventh chord does not sound sad, but rather hopeful or perhaps, more mellow than the MA⁷ sound. Subsequently, the recording alternates between iiMI⁷ and V⁷ in that same key. You will notice a sense of tendency and resolution between these two chords.

When the major scale is played in eighth notes from scale degrees 2 to 2, all the tones of the supertonic seventh chord are on the beat, so the chord change is clearly established. This second mode of major is referred to as the DORIAN scale, and is practiced by jazz musicians over supertonic harmony. Notice that dorian sounds analogous to natural minor, but with the sixth note raised.

Exercises

1 Construct the iiMI⁷ and rootless iiMI⁹ chords in the indicated major keys. Also notate the dorian scales for each key.

2 For the iiMI⁷ and iiMI⁹ chords below, label all chord tones—root (r), 3rd, 5th, 7th, and 9th.

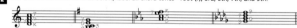

Resolution of iiMI⁷ to V⁷

You learned in Book 1, Lesson 20 that the V⁷ chord *resolves* to the tonic chord (I) because when chord roots are a fifth apart the tendency for resolution naturally occurs. You may have studied the circle of fifths, which is a sequential chain of all the chords with their roots a fifth apart. The ii chord is, after V⁷, the next removed from tonic in the circle of fifths.

Because of the circle of fifths, there is a strong tendency for resolution between iiMI⁷ and V⁷. Just like V⁷–IMA⁷, the 7th of iiMI⁷ is a tendency tone, which pulls downward by diatonic step into the 3rd of V⁷ (scale degrees 8–7), and the 3rd of the ii chord is a common tone to the 7th of the V⁷.

Analogous to V⁷–I is the fact that the 9th of the ii chord is another tendency tone, which resolves down by step to the 5th of V⁷.

The iiMI⁷ chord has two common tones with V⁷, and three with V⁹! So, appealing melodies can be made with use of the common tones and resolution between ii and V⁷.

Dig It!—Because the 7th of the iiMI⁷ chord is scale degree 8, a resolution of iiMI⁷–V⁷ is essentially "do-ti." Listen to the iiMI⁷–V⁷ progression in the second half of Track 20. Play "do" (E-flat—the 7th) for the iiMI⁷ chord, and resolve it to "ti" (D—the 3rd) for the V⁷ chord. These two pitches create the wonderful feeling of tension and release in the progression.

Exercises

1 Complete the indicated iiMI⁷ and rootless iiMI⁹ chords, followed by the V⁷ or V⁹ indicated. Use smooth voice leading. Draw straight lines to connect the common tones and arrows showing the resolutions.

2 Compose melodies to these ii–V progressions, using appropriate jazz language and making use of common tones and resolution.

The ii–V–I Turnaround Progression

Track 25 The circle-of-fifth "pull" of iiMI⁷ to V⁷ to IMA⁷ is how keys are established in jazz music. The iiMI⁷–V⁷–IMA⁷ progression is called THE TURNAROUND PROGRESSION, because the resolving tendencies of these chords "turn" the music back to tonic. Amazingly, approximately 75% of the chords in the standard jazz repertoire are ii–V or ii–V–I progressions! A ii–V sequence, without tonic, is enough to imply the key, and is also quite typical. Track 25 features the ii–V and ii–V–I turnaround in the key of F major.

The 3rd of the ii chord is also the 7th of V⁷, and the 7th of the ii chord resolves down by a ½ step to the 3rd of the V⁷. This is exactly how chord tones move in the V⁷–I progression. As a rule, there is this *swapping* of 3rds and 7ths in the circle of fifths.

The common tones and resolutions in the turnaround progression allow jazz musicians to smoothly arpeggiate between the chords.

Exercises

1 For each major key, indicate the chord symbols above the staff for iiMI⁷–V⁷–IMA⁷ and notate the chords, using inversion to create smooth voice leadings. Draw a line from each chord 3rd to the common tone 7th, and an arrow from 7ths to 3rds.

Note: Other inversions are possible.

2 For each major key, indicate the chord symbols for iiMI⁹–V⁹–IMA⁹ and notate the chords (rootless), using smooth voice leading. Draw a straight line from each chord 3rd to the common tone 7th, and an arrow from 7ths to 3rds.

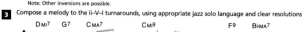

Note: Other inversions are possible.

3 Compose a melody to the ii–V–I turnarounds, using appropriate jazz solo language and clear resolutions.

UNIT 8 — Ear Training for Lessons 31–34

Track 27
1 Listen to the bass note, followed by two-note voicings of MA7 and MI7.
For the following four-chord voicings, indicate whether each is MA7 or MI7.

    a. MA7 /(MI7)   **b.**(MA7)/ MI7   **c.**(MA7)/ MI7   **d.** MA7 /(MI7)

Track 28
2 Listen to the sound of the MI7 chord, and then the MI9 chord.
Indicate whether each subsequent chord you hear is MI7 or MI9.

    a. MI7 /(MI9)   **b.**(MI7)/ MI9   **c.**(MI7)/ MI9   **d.** MI7 /(MI9)

Track 29
3 Listen to the MA9, dominant 9, and MI9 chords. Indicate the quality of each subsequent chord you hear.

    a. MA9 / 9 /(MI9)   **b.** MA9 /(9)/ MI9   **c.** MA9 / 9 /(MI9)   **d.**(MA9)/ 9 / MI9

Track 30
4 Listen to the major scale and the Dorian scale.
Indicate whether each subsequent scale is major or Dorian.

    a. major /(Dorian)   **b.** major /(Dorian)   **c.**(major)/ Dorian   **d.**(major)/ Dorian

Track 31
5 You will hear an eight-measure phrase played by the rhythm section.
Indicate whether the chord for each bar is IMA9 or iiMI9.

    IMA9 | _IMA9_ | _IIMI9_ | _IIMI9_ | _IMA9_ | _IIMI9_ | _IIMI9_ | _IMA9_ ‖

Track 32
6 Listen to the 7th of iiMI7 resolving to the 3rd of V7, then the 9th of iiMI9 resolving to the 5th of V9.
Write whether each resolution you hear is 7–3 or 9–5. You will hear each resolution TWICE.

    a.(7–3)/ 9–5   **b.** 7–3 /(9–5)   **c.**(7–3)/ 9–5   **d.** 7–3 /(9–5)

Track 33
7 Listen to smooth arpeggiation of iiMI7–V7, then iiMI9–V9.
Identify each example as indicated.

    a.(iiMI7–V7)/(iiMI9–V9)   **b.**(iiMI7–V7)/ iiMI9–V9

    c.(iiMI7–V7)/ iiMI9–V9   **d.** iiMI7–V7 /(iiMI9–V9)

Review of Lessons 31–34 — UNIT 8

1 The common tones of a dominant 9, MA9, and MI9 chord sharing the same root are __root__, __5th__, and __9th__.

2 In major keys, there are diatonic minor 7th chords on scale degrees __2__, __3__, and __6__.

3 The second mode of the major scale is called __dorian__, which sounds like a natural minor scale with the __6th__ note raised.

4 The __circle of fifths__ is a sequential chain of chords with roots a descending fifth apart.

5 The __7th__ of the iiMI7 chord resolves down by a ½ step to the __3rd__ of V7, while the __3rd__ of the iiMI7 chord is a common tone to the __7th__ of V7.

6 ii–V–I is called a __turnaround__ progression.

7 Alter the following MA7 and dominant 7th and 9th chords into MI7 and MI9 chords, indicating the new chord symbols above.

FMA7 FMI9   C9 CMI9   D♭MA7 D♭MI7   E♭MA7 E♭MI7   E9 EMI9

8 For each major key, notate the iiMI9 chord in all four, rootless inversions, followed by the major scale in the second (Dorian) mode.

AMI9   FMI9   BMI9

9 For each iiMI7–V7–IMA7 progression, notate 3rds and 7ths, showing the "swapping" that occurs.

CMI7 F7 B♭MA7   B♭MI7 E♭MI9 A♭MA7   GMI7 C7 FMA7

Note: These can be inverted.

UNIT 9 — Lesson 35

Jazz Language—Combined Scale/Arpeggio & "The ii–V Lick"

Consonance is the overriding factor in compelling melody. Since melody implies, and is constructed over chord changes, the chord tones must be primary. Using a scale in a melody without regard to the chord may not be consonant. Scalar melodies must emphasize the chord.

COMBINED SCALE/ARPEGGIO is a melodic fragment which is largely scalar, but also skips between successive chord tones. The example below shows combined scale/arpeggio for a iiMI7 chord, but these melodic figures are applicable to any type of harmony.

Track 34
DMI7

1 2 3 5   5 3 2 1   3 4 5 7   7 5 4 3   5 6 7 9   9 7 6 5   1 2 3 4 5 7   3 4 5 7 8 9

There is a scale/arpeggio figure so prevalent to jazz that it bears the name THE ii–V LICK:

Track 35
DMI7 7th 3rd G7

Notice that the 7th to 3rd resolution of ii–V is present in the ii–V lick, although in the example above it occurs early. The ii–V lick can be moved one beat later, placing the resolution on the proper downbeat.

Track 36 *[Track 35 region]*
DMI7   G7
    7th 3rd

Another permutation finds the ii–V lick extended up to the chord ninth, and resolving by descending scale into the V7.

Track 36
DMI9   G7
    9th 5th

Exercises

1 Use combined scale/arpeggio in creating a melody to this progression:

GMI7   C7   GMI9   C9   FMA9

2 Create melodies to these ii–V progressions, using various versions of the ii–V lick.

CMI7 F7   FMI9 B♭9   AMI9 D9

Lesson 36 — UNIT 9

Jazz Language—Triplet Arpeggio & "The Bebop Dominant Lick"

A language is distinguished, in part, by phrases associated with it. We hold together sentences with phrases like, "in other words," "as a matter of fact," and so on. The triplet arpeggio similarly propels the language of a jazz musician. Typically, a TRIPLET ARPEGGIO begins off the beat, a ½ step below the root or 3rd of a chord, and then arpeggiates up the chord with a triplet rhythm.

Track 37 CMA7   CMA9   DMI7   DMI9

Descending triplet arpeggio figures occur, but these typically begin on the 7th or 9th of a chord.

Track 38 B♭MA9 CMI7   CMI9 F9   B♭MA9

A variation of the triplet arpeggio uses 16th notes to encompass a wider range.

B♭MA9   B♭MA9   CMI9

In Book 1, Lesson 22 you learned that the bebop dominant scale is an important part of the jazz language for dominant 7th harmony. This descending scale is based on the major scale but begins with two ½ steps. The BEBOP DOMINANT LICK (and its variations) uses the first three notes of the bebop dominant scale, followed by a skip up to the chord 9th, and then another skip down to the 6th and then 5th of the chord. The bebop dominant lick often follows the ii–V lick, and any melody which makes use of the signature first three notes of bebop dominant scale is referred to as a bebop dominant idea.

Track 39 B♭7   FMI7 B♭7   E♭6

Exercises

1 For each chord, construct a triplet arpeggio figure, striving for variety.

DMA7   FMI9   E♭MI7   A♭MA9   D♭7

2 For each chord, notate the bebop dominant lick.

C7   G9   E♭7   B9

3 Compose a melody to the progression, using triplet arpeggio, the ii–V lick, and bebop dominant.

A♭MA7   B♭MI7 E♭9 CMI9 F9 B♭MI7   E♭9 A♭6

134

UNIT 9 — Lesson 37

Dominant 13th Chords (13) & ii–V–I Voicings

When a scale is followed to its second octave, the tones gain a value of seven (scale degree 2 becomes 9, degree 3 becomes 10, and so on.) By that formula, scale degree 6 becomes 13 in the second octave. The 13th also results by continuing to stack 3rds above the root.

The DOMINANT 13th CHORD is important in jazz, and is the same as a dominant 9th chord with a 13th added. (The 11th, which is the same as a 4th, is not consonant and so is not used.) A dominant 13th chord is called simply "13" (e.g., G13, Bb13, etc). A tone is called a 6th when it replaces a 7th, as in the 6/9 chord. When a chord has both a 6th and a 7th, the 6th is now called a 13th.

Track 40
Dig it!—Track 40 features a rhythm section playing dominant harmony. Every two measures the chord voicing switches from V9 to V13. The 13th chord is so much more colorful that jazz musicians don't consider the V9 to be very *hip* in comparison.

You know that when iiMi7 progresses to V9, only one note changes (the 7th of the iiMi7 resolves to the 3rd of V). The other tones of the iiMi7 are common to V9. When iiMi9 resolves, the same principle applies, and the result is a V13 (the 9th of iiMi9 is the 13th of V13). For iiMi9–V13 voicings, simply place the 3rd or 7th of iiMi9 on the bottom and add the remaining, consecutive chord tones. To get to V13, resolve the 7th of the ii and leave the other notes as common tones.

When V13 voicings connect to IMA9, an opposite procedure is used. The note that moved from ii–V (7 to 3) now is a common tone to I (3–7), and *all* the other notes of V13 are tendency tones and must move down by diatonic step into the IMA9 chord. So, 13ths are also tendency tones, and resolve to 9ths in the circle of fifths.

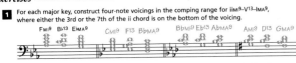

Exercises

1 For each major key, construct four-note voicings in the comping range for iiMi9–V13–IMA9, where either the 3rd or the 7th of the ii chord is on the bottom of the voicing.

2 For each major key, construct three-note voicings in the comping range for iiMi9–V13–IMA9, where the 3rd of the ii chord is on the bottom of the voicing (hint: omit the 5th of iiMi9).

UNIT 9 — Lesson 38

Passing Minor Major 7th Chord (MI(MA7)) & Progression

Music thrives on tension and release. Fulfilled and thwarted expectations are used alternatively to spark interest and convey emotion. The MINOR MAJOR 7th CHORD is a minor triad with the 7th raised a ½ step. The PASSING MINOR MAJOR 7th PROGRESSION consists of the chords ii–iiMi(MA7)–iiMi7–V7, and uses this raised 7th sound as an unexpected pleasure, which pulls towards the "expected" iiMi7 and increases the fulfillment of the resolution to V7.

Track 41
The iiMi(MA7) is called a PASSING CHORD, because the raised 7th is a passing tone that is not consonant for iiMi7 harmony, but that is precisely why the chord is expressive. In Track 41 you'll notice that the addition of the MI(MA7) chord *delays* the timing of V7 by two beats.

Melodies based on the passing iiMi(MA7) idiom often rely on repeated figures (motives), in which the only notes that change are the ones that highlight the idiom. These figures are typically based on arpeggio, which make the progression very clear.

Conversely, it is possible to form melodies in which the passing iiMi(MA7) idiom is more subtle.

Exercises

1 For each major key, notate the ii, iiMi(MA7), iiMi7, and V9 chords, as in the first example of this lesson.

2 Compose melodies to these ii-V-I progressions, using the passing MI(MA7) idiom based on a repeated figure.

3 Compose melodies to these ii-V-I progressions, using the passing MI(MA7) idiom in a more subtle way.

UNIT 9 — Ear Training for Lessons 35–38

Track 44
1 For each of the following four examples you will hear a chord followed by a combined scale/arpeggio to that chord. Circle the notation that is correct.

a. EMi7   b. AbMA7   c. FMA7   d. DMA9

Track 45
2 The recorded excerpts feature the ii-V lick. For each, indicate whether the 7th of the ii resolves to the 3rd of V early (before the chord changes), or on time (as the chord changes), or late.

a. early / **on time** / late   b. early / on time / **late**
c. **early** / on time / late   d. early / **on time** / late

Track 46
3 Count the number of triplet arpeggios in the recorded melody.

__5__ triplet arpeggios

Track 47
4 Indicate how many bebop dominant ideas you hear. Then, from those how many contain the exact bebop dominant lick.

__5__ bebop dominant ideas   __2__ bebop dominant licks

Track 48
5 You will hear the progression iiMi9–V13–IMA9, first with the 3rd of iiMi9 on the bottom, then with 7th of iiMi9 on the bottom. Indicate whether each iiMi9–V13–IMA9 progression begins with 3rd or 7th on bottom.

a. **3rd** / 7th   b. **3rd** / 7th   c. 3rd / **7th**   d. 3rd / **7th**

Track 49
6 You will hear the ii-V progression with four different two-note melodies in random order. These are resolution 7–3 and 9–5 and common tone 3–7 and 9–13. For each melody you hear (a, b, c, d), circle which of those connections it represents. You will hear each example TWICE.

a. **7–3** / 9–5 / 3–7 / 9–13   b. 7–3 / 9–5 / **3–7** / 9–13
c. 7–3 / 9–5 / 3–7 / **9–13**   d. 7–3 / **9–5** / 3–7 / 9–13

Track 50
7 For each melody using the passing MI(MA7), indicate whether a repeated figure, or a more subtle melody is used.

a. **repeated** / subtle   b. **repeated** / subtle   c. repeated / **subtle**

Review of Lessons 35–38 — UNIT 9

1 A scalar melody that skips between successive chord tones is called _combined scale / arpeggio_, and a favored figure using that device is the __ii__ __V__ lick.

2 Fill in the blanks and circle correct answers:
A ___triplet___ arpeggio begins:
on / **off** the beat,
a half step / whole step below a chord tone,
and then uses a ___triplet___ rhythm to arpeggiate the chord.

3 Any melody to dominant harmony, beginning on the root and descending two consecutive ½ steps can be called a _bebop_ _dominant_ figure.

4 When a chord contains both the 6th and 7th, the 6th is more properly referred to as _13th_.

5 When the 7th of iiMi9 is resolved, and the other voices stay stationary, the resulting chord is _V13_.

6 Supertonic chords sometimes are used with passing _major 7th_ tones, to add tension and tendency.

7 Compose a melody to the progression using combined scale/arpeggio and versions of the ii-V lick.

8 Compose a melody to the progression using triplet arpeggio and bebop dominant ideas.

9 For the progression below, write three-note voicings (in the comping range) in appropriate comp rhythms. On the upper staff, compose a jazz solo melody. Incorporate a passing MI(MA7) into your melody.

Lesson 39

Tonicisation of the IV Chord

In Lesson 34 it was noted that about 75% of the chords in standard jazz songs are in ii–V–I idioms. Quite simply, jazz standards almost always begin in the home key and tonicise other key areas with ii–Vs. Preceding any major or minor chord with its own V7, or ii and V chords, TONICISES it (makes it sound like its own key center).

In major keys, the most likely chord to be tonicised is the IV chord (IVMA7). The bass motion from I to IV is a descending perfect fifth, just like V–I. So, for instance, the I–IV progression in C major is identical to the V–I progression in F major:

By simply altering the IMA7 to a dominant quality (lowering the 7th a ½ step), it becomes the V7 chord of IV (e.g., C7 is V7 in F major). IV now sounds like a transitory tonic, and therefore has been *tonicised*.

Note: In classical music theory, a chord altered to serve this function is called a secondary dominant. I7 would be called "V7 of IV" and indicated with the symbol V7/IV.

Examining the keys of C and F major, you find that only one note is different: a B♮ in C major and a B♭ in F major. In fact, B♭ was the resulting, *new* note when we altered the CMA7 chord shown above. So in major keys, the flat 7th degree is the note that establishes the tonicization of the IV chord. Flat 7 is the 7th of the I7 chord, and it resolves to the 3rd of IVMA7, as is the case for any V7–I progression.

Exercises

1 Alter each tonic chord to become a dominant 7th (or 9th) of IV and write the chord symbols.

2 For each major key, notate a V7/IV in root position and a rootless V9/IV with the 3rd on the bottom.

3 For each major key, write the 7th of I7 (V7/IV) and resolve it to the 3rd of IVMA7. Write the chord symbols.

The ii–V Turnaround to IV

In early jazz music (up to around 1930) V7–I alone was often used to establish tonalities. As the music evolved and matured, ii chords became a staple sound. So, from the bebop period on, a fully tonicised IV is usually preceded by both its ii and V chords and called the TURNAROUND TO IV. Let's return to the key of C major to examine that progression.

- We know that in C major, FMA7 is IV, and an altered I chord (C7) is V7/IV.
- We also know that in the key of F major, GMI7 is ii.
- In C major, G7 is V, so we must alter that chord to a MI7 quality to realize the iiMI7 of IV.
- The complete turnaround to IV is VMI7–I7–IVMA7.

Remember that VMI7 is functioning as the ii chord to IV (ii/IV), and so its 7th resolves to the 3rd of the next chord, V7/IV (I7).

Dig it!—The great thing about tonicising IV is that it takes the music, tonally, to a temporary new home, a needed harmonic variety. And yet, since IV is diatonic to the key, it is never abrupt when the music returns to tonic.

After a turnaround to IV, the music can return to IMA7. . .

or the next chord might be ii, since IVMA7 is entirely contained in iiiMI9!

The turnaround to IV is found in a large cross section of jazz standards, including "Just Friends," "There Will Never Be Another You," "Take the 'A' Train," "My Romance," "Misty" and so on.

Exercises

1 Alter the following V7 (or V9) chords to become ii of IV (ii/IV, VMI).

2 Indicate the chord symbols for the turnaround progression to IV in the following major keys.

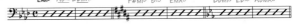

3 For each major key, notate the chord symbols for a turnaround to IV. Then, write and resolve each chord 7th to the following chord 3rd.

Lesson 41

Melody for the Turnaround to IV

Beethoven's "Eroica" Symphony begins with arpeggiation of the tonic triad altered in the fifth measure to V7/IV. A critic described this opening as a hero riding into battle. In the fifth measure, the hero pauses to think of the woman he left behind! Why this description? When a progression tonicises IV, a flat is temporarily added, or a sharp deleted. The result is that the music becomes warmer or darker.

The flat 7th is more than just a harmonic note. It is the expressive note in melodies that establishes the darker feeling of a turnaround to IV.

Bebop dominant ideas are very important to jazz melody in the turnaround to IV because they "tease" the listener with the major 7th before sounding the darker flat 7.

The ii–V lick is also a frequent component of melody for the turnaround to IV.

The turnaround to IV progression is a "borrowed" ii–V–I progression. For instance, in the key of C major, we are borrowing ii–V–I from F major. So naturally, the principals of voicing and voice leading you have learned for ii–V–I progressions will apply.

Exercises

1 Compose a melody to the progression using bebop dominant and resolution in the turnaround to IV.

2 For the following keys, indicate the chord symbols for the VMI7–I7–IVMA7 turnaround progression. On the staves, notate two-note voicings in the comping range.

3 For the following keys, indicate the chord symbols for the VMI7–I13–IVMA9 turnaround progression. On the following staff, notate four-note voicings in the comping range.

II Dominant Seventh Chords (II7)

After ii–V–I and the turnaround to IV, the next most common idiom in jazz harmony uses the II DOMINANT SEVENTH CHORD, a dominant chord built on ii. This chord is found in countless standards, including, "Take the 'A' Train," "There Will Never Be Another You," "Just Friends," "The Girl from Ipanema" and so on. Since the diatonic ii seventh chord is a minor 7th, simply raising the chord 3rd a ½ step results in a dominant II7.

The II7 chord is actually a secondary dominant, the V7 of V (V7/V). For instance, in the key of C major, DMI7 is ii and G7 is V. But, in the key of G, D7 is V!

Sometimes, II7 chords resolve to V, with the usual treatment of tendency tones. Notice, though, that the 3rd of II7 isn't a common tone to the 7th of V7, but rather is enharmonically a ½ step away.

While it is true that II7 chords move to V in some jazz tunes, more often they simply progress (or regress) to the diatonic iiiMI7. In this usage, the II7 chord is sort of "hanging around" and waiting for the iiiMI7–V–I cadence. The raised 3rd of II7 is a hopeful sound in melodies, and produces a pleasing sense of resolution into the natural 3rd of the following iiiMI7.

Exercises

1 For each major key, write a II7 chord in root position and also a rootless II9. Indicate chord symbols above the staff.

2 Resolve each II7 voicing into the indicated V chord. Label the 7th of II7 and draw an arrow to the 3rd of V. Draw a jagged line between the 3rd of II7 and the enharmonically different 7th of V7.

3 Compose a melody to the progression using resolution, jazz language, and highlighting the 3rds of both the II7 and iiiMI7 chords.

UNIT 10 — 66 — Lesson 43

II⁹⁽♯¹¹⁾ Chords, Lydian Dominant Scale, I Augmented Chord Extension (I+)

As mentioned in the previous lesson, the II7 chord sometimes resolves to V, but more often *dissolves* into the diatonic iiMi7. In the latter context, II7 isn't functioning as a secondary V7, but rather as a more stable sound. Jazz musicians typically extend this chord to a ♯11th, adding to its uniqueness in the progression, and call it the II⁹⁽♯¹¹⁾ CHORD.

Since ♯11 is the same note as ♯4, there is an inherent Lydian nature to the II⁹⁽♯¹¹⁾ chord. (You learned about the Lydian fourth in Book 1, Lesson 12.) A LYDIAN DOMINANT SCALE is the Mixolydian scale used for dominant harmony, altered by raising the 4th degree by a ½ step.

When a II7 melody features the ♯11, as it usually does, a sense of resolution is achieved by moving to the 5th of the ensuing iiMi7 chord.

The most effective melodies for II⁹⁽♯¹¹⁾ employ the I AUGMENTED CHORD (I+). The I+ chord is a tonic triad with the 5th raised chromatically. Notice that the I+ chord can also be explained as 7, 9 and ♯11 of II7! In fact, adding the major 7th (I+⁽ᴹᴬ⁷⁾) gives you the 13th of II7 (II¹³⁽♯¹¹⁾). So, any melody figure to IMA7 can be repeated, raising the 5th for II⁹⁽♯¹¹⁾.

The easiest way to create voicings for a II⁹⁽♯¹¹⁾ is to replace the chord 5th with the ♯11 (♯4) ½ step below.

Exercises

1 For each indicated II⁹⁽♯¹¹⁾, write the Lydian dominant scale and a rootless voicing in the comping range. In each case, circle the ♯11 (♯4) in the scale. Note: other voicings are possible.

Note: Other voicings are possible.

2 Compose a melody to the progression using I+ as extensions to II⁹⁽♯¹¹⁾ and achieving a sense of resolution into the iiMi7.

Ear Training for Lessons 39–43 — UNIT 10 — 67

Track 61
1 You will hear IMA⁹–IVMA⁹ followed by I⁹–IVMA⁹. For each example, write whether the first chord is IMA⁹ or I⁹.

a. (IMA⁹) / I⁹ b. IMA⁹ / (I⁹) c. IMA⁹ / (I⁹) d. (IMA⁹) / I⁹

Track 62
2 Listen to the melody with rhythm section. Indicate in which measure the turnaround to IV begins.

Measure _3_ .

Track 63
3 Listen to the demonstrated II7, iiMi7, and V7 chords. Indicate whether each following progression uses II7, iiMi7, or both.

a. II7 / (iiMi7) / both b. (II7) / iiMi7 / both c. II7 / iiMi7 / (both) d. II7 / (iiMi7) / both

Track 64
4 You will first hear a II⁹ chord and a II⁹⁽♯¹¹⁾ chord. Listen to the four chords following and indicate whether each chord you hear is II⁹ or II⁹⁽♯¹¹⁾.

a. II⁹ / (II⁹⁽♯¹¹⁾) b. (II⁹) / II⁹⁽♯¹¹⁾ c. II⁹ / (II⁹⁽♯¹¹⁾) d. II⁹ / (II⁹⁽♯¹¹⁾)

Track 65
5 Listen to the demonstrated dominant scale (Mixolydian) and the Lydian dominant scale. For the four scales following, circle whether each scale is Mixolydian or Lydian dominant.

a. (Mixolydian) / Lydian dominant b. Mixolydian / (Lydian dominant)

c. (Mixolydian) / Lydian dominant d. Mixolydian / (Lydian dominant)

Track 66
6 Transcribe the remaining notes of the melody you hear.

UNIT 10 — 68 — Review of Lessons 39–43

1 A chord is _tonicised_ by preceding it with its own ii and V.

2 Lowering the 7th of the _I7_ chord creates a dominant of IVMA7.

3 The complete turnaround to IV involves the chords _VMi7_, _I7_, and _IVMA7_

4 The turnaround to IV is seldom used in jazz standards. True / (False).

5 Most often the II7 chord progresses to _IIMi7_. It is typical to alter the II7 by adding _♯11_.

6 II⁹⁽♯¹¹⁾ melodies can use the _Lydian dominant_ scale. Also a _I+_ chord is really the upper extensions of II⁹⁽♯¹¹⁾.

7 Compose a melody to the progression using resolution and characteristic melody devices for the turnaround to IV. On the bass staff, write two-note voicings, in the comping range.

8 In the key of C major compose a melody to the progression II7–V7–IMA⁹, where we hear the 3rd of II7 moving chromatically into the 7th of V7, and also the 7th of V7 resolving into the 3rd of IMA⁹. Indicate the chord symbols above the staff.

9 Compose a melody to the progression using Lydian dominant and also the I+ extension for II⁹⁽♯¹¹⁾.

Lesson 44 — UNIT 11 — 69

Diminished 7th Chords (°7) & Diminished Scales

The DIMINISHED 7TH CHORD is one of the more fascinating and exotic sounds in music. It is mysterious and unstable, and in a jazz context, quite beautiful. Constructed of three minor thirds stacked on top of each other, it is indicated by the symbol °7 (also dim7). The chord is *symmetrical*, because no matter what note you put on the bottom, it is still the same arrangement of minor 3rds.

Notice that C♯°7, E°7, G°7, and A♯°7 are all the same chord! Consequently, there are only three different diminished 7th chords. Here are the two others.

The DIMINISHED SCALE contains all the notes of the diminished seventh chord, and is an alternation of whole and ½ steps. This scale is also known as OCTATONIC.

Because of the symmetry of diminished 7th chords, there are likewise only three diminished scales. To clarify, if you begin the C-sharp diminished scale (above) on E, G or B♭, you have E, G and B♭ diminished scales, alternating whole and ½ steps. On the contrary, a C major scale, starting on E is certainly *not* an E major scale! Here are the other two diminished (octatonic) scales.

Notes 1, 3, 5, and 7 of the diminished scale are the tones of the °7 chord. Notice that tones 2, 4, 6, and 8 combine to form a different °7 chord.

Exercises

1 Construct the indicated diminished seventh (°7) chords.

2 Construct the indicated diminished (octatonic) scales.

The vii°7 Chord, #iv°7 Chord, Diminished 7th Melody

In classical music, the diminished 7th chord functions as a dominant, just like V7. To clarify, a triad built on the 7th degree of a major scale is diminished, although a chromatic note is needed to form a diminished seventh chord (°7), and the diminished chord has three common tones to V7. So in classical music (and sometimes in jazz) THE vii°7 CHORD is a dominant function chord.

Often in jazz music, diminished seventh chords are NONFUNCTIONAL CHORDS, or embellishing sounds between two functional chords of a progression. Typically they connect chords with bass notes one step apart. THE #iv°7 CHORD is used in this manner in the progression IV6–#iv°7–IMA7/V (tonic chord with the 5th in the bass). Note: the IV6–#iv°7–IMA7/V idiom is found in "I Got Rhythm," "Paper Moon," and some versions of the 12-bar blues.

Ironically, the notes of the diminished chord are not very expressive for jazz melody, but rather sound old fashioned. The other notes of the diminished scale (2, 4, 6, 8) form the "juicy" notes. Jazz musicians often use the symmetry of diminished to fashion sequential motives, emphasizing these expressive notes, whole and ½ steps on either side of each chord tone. A melodic SEQUENCE repeats itself exactly, transposed by some interval. In the case of diminished, the sequence is by minor 3rd interval, as you would guess!

Dig it!—Track 71 has a rhythm section playing a C#°7 chord. Try playing (or singing) the notes of the chord. Now, play the other notes of the diminished scale, resolving each one up ½ step, or down 1 step. Hear the difference?

Exercises

1 For the indicated major keys, indicate the chord symbols for IV6–#iv°7–IMA7/V and write four-note voicings in the comping range, with smooth voice leading.

2 For each °7 chord, construct a sequential melody.

The Turnback Progression & The VI7 Chord

It is common to find phrases in jazz tunes ending with two measures of the tonic chord. In cases where the next phrase also begins on the IMA7, jazz musicians frequently employ a turnback progression to provide harmonic variety. A TURNBACK is the chords I–VI7–iimi7–V7, with each chord usually lasting two beats. And of course in jazz music, chordal extensions are encouraged!

You know that ii–V creates a pull towards IMA7. Similarly, a dominant VI chord pulls to ii, because VI precedes ii in the circle of fifths.

In major keys, the diatonic sixth chord is minor (vi), but in the turnback the 3rd is raised chromatically to make VI a dominant 7th. VI7 (or VI9) then, is the secondary dominant of ii (V7/ii). As you see below, D7 to Gmi is V–I in the key of G minor, but those same chords are V7/ii to ii in F major.

The VI7 chord provides a colorful new note for melody and soloing, because the 3rd of that chord is a ½ step above tonic in the key.

Exercises

1 For the indicated major keys, indicate the chord symbols for the turnback progression and notate keyboard voicings on the staff.

2 Construct jazz solo melodies to the turnback progressions emphasizing the 3rd of VI7 and jazz language you have learned so far.

AABA Standard Song Form—"Take the 'A' Train" Progression

Nearly a century of great jazz performance has been poured into a group of tunes (mostly in 32 bars) called "standards." At least half of these STANDARD SONGS are in AABA FORM, consisting of four, eight-bar phrases. The 'A' phrases are nearly identical in melody and harmony, while the 'B' phrase, or BRIDGE, is contrasting in both. Take a look at the harmonic progression to Billy Strayhorn's, "Take the 'A' Train:"

You can see that the 'A' phrases are almost identical, beginning with IMA7 and then II7 (Strayhorn's melody features #11). As expected, II7 goes to iimi7, which begins the inevitable ii–V–I turnaround. The first 'A' has an optional turnback to I (1st ending). The end of the second 'A' has a turnaround to IV, which begins the bridge (2nd ending). The final 'A' also has an optional turnback.

The Bridge ('B') provides contrast. Beginning with IVMA7, it creates a feeling that the music has gone to a new destination. The II7 signals that ii and V are on the way, so that the 'A' theme can return. This is a great example of how AABA standards are constructed.

Here is a solo to the "Take the 'A' Train" progression.

Exercise

1 Analyze the solo above, identifying characteristic jazz melodic devices, scales, resolutions, chord extensions, etc.

Track 76
1 Listen to the dominant 9th chord voicing and the diminished 7th chord. Write whether each chord is dominant 9th or diminished.

a. Dom 9 / °7   **b.** Dom 9 / °7   **c.** Dom 9 / °7   **d.** Dom 9 / °7

Track 77
2 Listen to the diminished scale and the Lydian dominant scale. Indicate whether each melody uses diminished or Lydian dominant.

a. diminished / Lydian dominant   **b.** diminished / Lydian dominant
c. diminished / Lydian dominant   **d.** diminished / Lydian dominant

Track 78
3 Listen to the progression, IV6–#iv°7–IMA7/V, demonstrated first. In the ensuing progression, at what bar does the IV–#iv°7–I/V progression begin?

Measure ___5___.

Track 79
4 Listen to the melody to a °7 chord, which employs both the diminished chord tones and the expressive, other notes of the scale. How many of the expressive notes are used?

___6___ expressive notes.

Track 80
5 Listen to the IMA9 and VI7 chords, the concurrent, two-note melody is the tonic note moving up ½ step to the 3rd of VI7. For each of the turnback melodies you hear next, indicate whether the 3rd of VI7 is used.

a. yes / no   **b.** yes / no   **c.** yes / no   **d.** yes / no

Track 81
6 Listen to the solo over the first half of the progression to "Take the 'A' Train." Indicate whether each of these melodic devices is employed.

7–3 resolution:	yes / no
Combined scale/arpeggio:	yes / no
The ii–V lick:	yes / no
Triplet arpeggio:	yes / no
Bebop dominant:	yes / no
Minor +7:	yes / no
Lydian dominant:	yes / no
I+ extension:	yes / no
3rd of the VI7 chord:	yes / no

UNIT 11 · 74 · Review of Lessons 44–47

1 The diminished 7th chord (°7) is __minor__ __third__ intervals stacked on each other. The chord is __symmetrical__ because any of its notes could be the root.

2 The diminished or __octatonic__ scale is an alternation of __whole__ and __half__ __steps__.

3 Diminished 7th chords (°7) in jazz are typically used to connect bass notes __1 step__ apart.

4 Notes 1, 3, 5, and 7 of the diminished scale are the most expressive tones. True / ~~False~~

5 A __sequential__ line features repetition of a melody, transposed by some interval.

6 The chords IMA7–VI7–iiMi7–V7 form a __turnback__ progression.

7 The __bridge__ is the 'B' section of an __AABA__ form.

8 In the key of G major compose a melody to the progression II7–V7–IMA9, where we hear the 3rd of II7 moving chromatically into the 7th of V7, and also the 7th of V7 resolving into the 3rd of IMA9. Indicate the chord symbols above the staff.

C: II7   V7   IMA9

9 Compose a melody to the first four bars of the "Take the 'A' Train" progression, using the I+ extension for II9(#11). Write the chord symbols above the staff.

10 Compose a melody to the last four bars of the bridge of the "Take the 'A' Train" progression, using Lydian dominant for II9(#11). Write the chord symbols above the staff.

Lesson 48 · UNIT 12 · 75

Jazz Language—Chromatic Leading & Passing Tones, Bebop Scales

Melodic chromaticism plays an important role in jazz melody. Chromatic notes which are not in the chord are used to great effect, because they create tension and tendency. A chord tone feels more satisfying when it arrives after chromatic embellishment. Classical musicians refer to these non-harmonic tones as *decorative chromaticism*.

A decorative LEADING TONE (l.t.) is a note a ½ step below a chord tone. Jazz melody often skips into chromatic leading tones

A good definition of "scale" is *chord tones and notes in between*. The scale below, entirely chord tones and leading tones, is actually "hipper" than the diatonic one.

Jazz musicians love to approach a chord tone from a step above, and then move by descending ½ steps into a CHROMATIC PASSING TONE and then the chord tone.

The bebop dominant scale is a result of this idea, approaching the chord 7th from a step above. So, it is possible to invent other bebop scales, by inserting a leading tone between chord tones.

Exercises

1 Analyze this melody by circling chromatic leading and passing tones, and labeling bebop scales. Do you notice how each decorative chromatic note *points* to the ensuing chord tone?

2 For each chord below, construct a bebop scale.

UNIT 12 · 76 · Lesson 49

Jazz Language—Auxiliary "Enclosure" Tones

There is one melodic gesture that sums up the language of the bebop era more than any other, and that is the use of multiple auxiliary, or enclosure tones. When a melody moves from a chord tone to a note a ½ or whole step away and back, the middle (decorative) note is called an auxiliary tone (also neighbor tone).

ENCLOSURE TONES are two or more auxiliary tones on both sides of the chord tone, sounded prior to the chord tone.

Most often, jazz musicians employ enclosure tones around the root, 3rd or 5th of a chord, but any chord tone can be embellished in this fashion. Here are a variety of enclosure tone figures around a chord root.

The note a ½ step away from a chord tone is always a viable enclosure tone, whether or not that note is consonant. A note one whole step away from a chord tone, which is outside of the consonant scale or key will not make a suitable enclosure tone. In that case, the dissonant note can be used, but it must move chromatically into the chord tone.

Bebop jazz melody often skips from one chord tone to enclosures of the next, even if the chord is going to change. This device provides the angularity that is a signature element of bebop style.

Exercises

1 For the melody above, circle the enclosure tones.

2 Compose a melody using only chord tones and enclosure tones.

Lesson 50 · UNIT 12 · 77

The Jazz Blues Progression, Finding the Chromatics

You learned a simple 12-bar blues progression in Book 1, Lesson 25. Now you have the tools to understand the blues as performed by more proficient jazz musicians. Here is the jazz blues progression in the key of F major (parenthetical chords are optional):

Notice that measure 4 can be a turnaround (ii–V) to the IV chord in measure 5. In measure 6, a #iv°7 chord creates a pull towards the return of I7 in measure 7. Likewise, the VI7 chord in measure 8 is V7 of the ii chord, which begins the last four measures. Finally a turnback is used in the last two measures, to repeat for more choruses.

Here is a solo melody to the jazz blues progression.

Jazz musicians know that chord tones (especially 3rds and 7ths), which are not in the key of the song, are very colorful and important to melody. Emphasizing those notes might be called FINDING THE CHROMATICS. In the solo above: the 7th of the IV chord is emphasized in measure 2, because it is a ½ step away from the 3rd of I7; the flat 7th of the key enables the turnaround to IV in measure 4; the iv°7 has a chromatic root and 7th; the 3rd of VI°7 is a ½ step above the tonic.

Exercises

1 *Dig it!*—When a musician finds the chromatics, you can hear the changes in the melody alone. In the solo above, locate and circle the chord tones that are chromatic to the key, then try playing the solo alone. Do you hear the progression?

2 Optional: on your own music manuscript paper, compose a solo to the jazz blues progression in E-flat major. Indicate the chord symbols above the staff.

UNIT 12 — Ear Training for Lessons 48–50

78

Track 90
1 In this jazz melody, how many chromatic leading tones are used?
How many enclosure tone figures are used?

__5__ chromatic leading tones   __2__ enclosure tone figures

Track 91
2 For this jazz melody, how many chord tones are approached chromatically from a step above?

__3__ chromatic approaches from above

Track 92
3 Listen to the bebop dominant and bebop major scales.
Indicate whether each scale is bebop dominant or bebop major.

a. bebop dominant / (bebop major)   b. bebop dominant / bebop major
c. bebop dominant / (bebop major)   d. bebop dominant / (bebop major)

Track 93
4 Listen to these bebop major and bebop minor scales.
Indicate whether each scale is bebop major or bebop minor.

a. bebop major / (bebop minor)   b. bebop major / (bebop minor)
c. (bebop major) / bebop minor   d. (bebop major) / bebop minor

Track 94
5 Listen to the solo to the 12-bar blues, which is written below.
Add accidentals so that the notation is correct.

Review of Lessons 48–50 — UNIT 12

79

1 Chromatic __leading__ tones and __passing__ tones add tension and tendency to a melody.

2 A scale can be defined as __chord__ tones and __notes__ in between.

3 Major, minor, and dominant chords can all have bebop scales. (True) / False

4 __Enclosure__ tones help create the angularity of bebop melody.

5 The important chromatic (non-diatonic) tones in the 12-bar blues are the 7th of __l7__ in measure 4, and the __3rd__ of VI7 in measure 9.

6 Write bebop scales to these chords:

7 Analyze this melody. Circle and identify instances of decorative chromaticism. Label bebop scales and any other scalar devices. Label resolutions and prominent functionally chromatic tones.

8 Compose a melody to the 12-bar jazz blues using leading tones, enclosure tones, bebop scales, and emphasizing important non-diatonic notes. Write the chord symbols above the staff.

Lesson 51 — UNIT 13

83

Jazz Language—Melodic Soloing & Melodic Sequence

If music is compared to painting, then melody represents the finest and most detailed brush strokes, and melodic devices are the paint colors. As introduced in Book 1, Lesson 5, MELODIC SOLOING (MOTIVIC SOLOING) is basing musical phrases on simple ideas, which are repeated and varied. It is actually composing a new melody to the chord structure. Using this device, a soloist may think of the original motive as a thought or emotion: repetition deepens or intensifies the emotion, while variation expands on it. Because the ideas are simple in melodic soloing, individual notes take on heightened significance. The example below demonstrates melodic soloing to the beginning of the "Take the 'A' Train" chord progression. Notice how the repetition is not exact, but altered to reflect the new color of the second chord.

Playing is said to be "organic" when the variation of a motive becomes the seed for the next variation.

MELODIC SEQUENCE is the repetition of an idea transposed by some interval. An idea may be sequenced once, or several consecutive times. An ascending sequence can be successively more soaring or thrilling…

…while a descending sequence can make a melody more somber or introspective.
Track 3 demonstrates both an ascending and descending melodic sequence.

Exercises

1 Continue the melody in the motivic style, using repetition and variation.

2 Continue the melody using sequence.

UNIT 13 — Lesson 52

84

Afro-Cuban Jazz: Clave & Tumbau

Thanks to trumpeter Dizzy Gillespie, a great jazz ambassador, Afro-Cuban influences were introduced into jazz in the 1940s when Gillespie traveled to Cuba and incorporated the vitality of the repetitive Cuban rhythms into the jazz mainstream.

The Afro-Cuban rhythms used in jazz are based on a figure called CLAVE (KLAH-vay), which is a two-measure rhythmic pattern, alternating two or three notes per bar. These figures can be clapped or played on claves, which are a pair of hardwood sticks struck together. There are variations of the rhythm pattern, but the two basic claves are either 3–2 CLAVE ("three-two clave"):

Or the opposite, 2–3 CLAVE:

Notice that when three notes are played in a measure, they occur on beat 1, the "and" of 2, and on beat 4. This clave is accentuated by another pattern, the tumbau (TOOM-bow). The TUMBAU rhythm, played on a bass drum and also by the bass player, features notes on the "and" of 2, and on beat 4.

In the tumbau, beat 1 is not accentuated at all, and often, beat 4 feels more like the downbeat. As a result of the lack of an accented beat 1, Afro-Cuban music feels very "circular" as the pattern endlessly repeats.

Bass lines based on tumbau feature chord roots and 5ths almost exclusively. They may or may not have a note on the downbeat of a bar, and the note on beat 4 may be tied into the next measure. Track 4 demonstrates the clave rhythms described above and then adds a tumbau bass line.

Exercises

1 Find a recording of an Afro-Cuban jazz song. Listen and determine if the clave is 2–3 or 3–2. Practice clapping along with the clave.

2 Compose a bass line to the progression below, based on tumbau.

Lesson 53 — UNIT 13 — 85

Afro-Cuban Jazz: Cascara & Montuno

You've probably noticed that Afro-Cuban rhythms are more effectively learned aurally than visually. The cascara rhythm is no exception. CASCARA (KHAS-kah-rah), or paila, is an Afro-Cuban rhythmic figure played in a two-measure pattern, which is based on, and embellishes the clave. Cascara is named for playing on the "shell" or side of a drum, but it is also played at times on the bell of a cymbal, cowbell, or with a rim knock on a snare drum.

Notice that the cascara has notes on beats 2 and 3 in one measure, and accentuates the "and" of 2 and beat 4 in the other, just the same as clave. So, the cascara should always be played in sync with the clave.

In Afro-Cuban jazz, pianists employ identifiable and repetitive comping patterns called montunos. A MONTUNO is a triadic and highly syncopated comping figure, often played in octaves, or two octaves apart. Some Afro-Cuban tunes repeat a ii–V progression, and in these instances the montuno often features common tones and the 7–3 resolution.

Another ii–V montuno uses the passing minor major 7th idiom (MI(MA7)).

A montuno to a single chord can emphasize two chord tones a step apart (often with a passing tone in between), such as 6th and 7th, 5th and 6th, etc. There are dozens of effective montuno patterns.

Exercises

1 Compose a montuno to the ii–V progression.

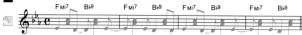

2 Compose a montuno to the Major 7th chord.

86 — UNIT 13 — Lesson 54

Drop-Two Voicings

You have learned that four-note voicings arise out of consecutive chord tones and usually omit the root. Chord arrangements with consecutive tones are called CLOSED VOICINGS, and you know that proper *voice leading* results from using common tones and resolutions.

DROP-TWO VOICINGS are derived directly from four-note, closed voicings. For a drop-two voicing, simply take the second note from the top of a closed voicing, and drop it one octave. The new, drop-two sound, is more open, or spacious than that of the closed voicing. Pianists use two hands for drop-two voicings, and drop-two voicings are effective when arranging for wind and string instruments.

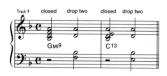

A drop-two voicing may also be achieved using an opposite procedure, which you might call "fly-two." In this instance, the second note from the bottom is raised one octave.

The principles of using common tones and resolution for smooth voice leading apply to drop-two chords.

Exercises

1 Convert the chords to drop-two or fly-two voicings as indicated.

2 Notate drop-two voicings for the progression, using smooth voicing leading.

Lesson 55 — UNIT 13 — 87

Minor 11th Chords (MI11) & Sus Chords (SUS, 7SUS)

As discussed in Book 1, Lesson 9, the note a perfect 4th (P4) above the root of any major triad is very dissonant. When the 4th is used in a melody to major or dominant chords, it creates tension, and must be resolved by step (usually downward).

Conversely, the P4 above the root of a minor triad is consonant and stable in jazz, and is known by its name up one octave, the 11th. A MINOR 11TH CHORD (MI11) is a MI7 chord with an added 11th. Voicings of the MI11 may omit the chord 5th, and may or may not include a 9th.

A MI11 chord functions the same as other minor chords in jazz, but may also serve as a modal tonic. In the 1960s MODAL JAZZ tunes, based on a mode rather than a key, came into fashion. The notes of the MI11 chord are in both the Dorian and Aeolian scales, so the chord is a mainstay of modal jazz. A modal jazz tune may stay on one chord for a long duration; for example, Miles Davis's hit, "So What."

A chord that functions similarly to a MI11 chord is the SUS CHORD (SUS or 7SUS). A sus chord replaces the chord 3rd with a 4th. Just as in jazz, classical composers of the 17th through 19th centuries considered the 4th dissonant, and called it a *suspension*, because it was suspended just above the 3rd. So, *sus* is jazz shorthand for *suspended*. Sus chords tend to use the 5th in the voicing, and the root also can be used. 7SUS chords have a minor 7th above the root.

Dig it!—The 7SUS chord may be arranged entirely in perfect 4ths, and modal jazz tunes and solos often favor the 4th interval. A chord arranged in perfect 4ths is called QUARTAL HARMONY.

Exercises

1 Write voicings to the MI11 and 7SUS chords, in closed spacing in the comping range.

2 Write a melody to the 7SUS chord, emphasizing 4ths.

3 What scale is used in the second example of this lesson? _____ D dorian _____

88 — UNIT 13 — Ear Training for Lessons 51–55

1 Track 12
You will hear four melodies.
For each, answer if the melody is motivic.

a. yes /(no)   b.(yes)/ no   c.(yes)/ no   d. yes /(no)

2 Track 13
You will hear four melodies.
For each, indicate if the melody is sequential.

a.(yes)/ no   b.(yes)/ no   c. yes /(no)   d.(yes)/ no

3 Track 14
You will hear four sequential melodies.
For each, write if the melody is sequenced up or down.

a.(up)/ down   b.(up)/ down   c.(up)/ down   d. up /(down)

4 Track 15
For each excerpt, indicate if the clave is 2–3 or 3–2.

a. 2–3 /(3–2)   b. 2–3 /(3–2)   c.(2–3)/ 3–2   d. 2–3 /(3–2)

5 Track 16
Write whether each montuno is to a ii–V, major chord, or minor chord.

a.(ii–V)/ MA / MI   b. ii–V /(MA)/ MI   c. ii–V /(MA)/ MI   d.(ii–V)/ MA / MI

6 Track 17
You will hear a closed voicing, then a drop-two voicing.
Write whether each following chord is closed or drop-two.

a. closed /(drop-two)   b.(closed)/ drop-two   c.(closed)/ drop-two   d. closed /(drop-two)

7 Track 18
Listen to the MI7 chord and the 7SUS.
Write whether each following chord is MI7 or 7SUS.

a. MI7 /(7SUS)   b. MI7 /(7SUS)   c.(MI7)/ 7SUS   d.(MI7)/ 7SUS

Review of Lessons 51–55   UNIT 13   89

1 The repetition of a melodic idea, transposed by an interval is called ___sequence___.

2 When three notes of clave are in one measure they fall on beat _1_, the "and" of _2_, and _4_.

3 In Afro-Cuban music, a bass/bass drum figure on the "and" of 2, and 4 is called ___tumbau___.

4 The Cascara pattern is based on clave.   (True) / False

5 ___Montuno___ is a highly syncopated Afro-Cuban piano pattern.

6 Convert the closed voicings into drop-two (or fly-two), staying close to the comping range.

7 Write drop-two voicings for the indicated chords.

8 Write chord symbols for these rootless voicings. Hint: each has a 3rd or 7th on the bottom.

9 Write voicings for the indicated chords, in closed spacing in the comping range.

---

90   UNIT 14   Lesson 56

Minor Tonic Chord (iMI(MA7), iMI6/9), Jazz Minor Scale

In jazz music, as in all other Western musical genres, sad or somber pieces are in minor keys. (For a review of minor keys see *Essentials of Music Theory, Book 3*) In classical music, a minor triad functions as the tonic chord. Jazz, on the other hand, features chord extensions of at least a 7th. Adding a diatonic 7th to the imi triad creates a minor seventh chord, a sound we associate with ii not tonic. So, jazz musicians chromatically raise the diatonic 7th to create a stable, tonic sound.

The raised 7th degree, which is from the melodic-minor scale, results in a minor major 7th chord, shown as MI(MA7) or MI9(MA7) (alternative chord symbols you may see include MI9(+7), MI9(♭7), or MI9(♮7)).

Another minor tonic is the MINOR 6/9 CHORD (MI6/9), using the raised 6th degree of melodic minor.

Dig it!—The sound of both minor tonics (iMI(MA7) and iMI6/9) are stable in jazz and the altered notes are the interesting, "juicy" notes that give the music its distinctive character.

Obviously, jazz musicians use the ascending melodic-minor scale to create melody to minor tonics. When the scale descends, the alterations remain, rather than reverting to the natural minor, and this is called the JAZZ MINOR SCALE.

Exercises

1 Notate the indicated rootless MI9(MA7) chords in all four positions.

2 Notate the indicated rootless MI6/9 chords on the treble staff, and then notate a drop-two voicing for each.

3 For each minor key, notate the jazz minor scale in ascending and descending direction.

Lesson 57   UNIT 14   91

Minor ii–V Turnaround, Half-Diminished Chord (ø7) & V7(♭9)) Chord

Keys are established by ii–V and ii–V–I turnaround progressions, and minor keys are no exception. The MINOR ii–V–i TURNAROUND uses the chords iiø7–V7(♭9) –imi(MA7) (or imi6/9). The diatonic ii7 chord in a minor key is the same as a minor 7th chord with the chord 5th flatted. This chord is called a HALF-DIMINISHED CHORD (ø7) or MINOR SEVEN FLAT FIVE CHORD (MI7♭5)).

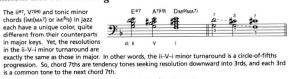

The diatonic 9th of ii in a minor key is a minor 9th above the root and is not a consonant note. So when a 9th is added to a half-diminished chord, it is typically a major 9th above the root (iiø7(MA7)).

As with MI7 chords, the 11th over ø7 harmony is consonant and can be included.

Just as with minor keys in classical music, V7 chords in jazz are altered by raising the chord 3rd, in order to have dominant 7th quality.

The diatonic 9th above V7 in minor keys is a minor 9th above the chord root. This note is great for V7 chords, and the resulting chord is called FIVE SEVEN FLAT NINE (V7(♭9)). The chord tones from 3rd to ♭9th of a V7(♭9) chord are a diminished 7th chord.

Exercises

1 Notate iiø7 and V7(♭9), in root position in the indicated keys, and write the chord symbols above the staff.

2 Write the indicated ø7 and 7(♭9) chords, in closed spacing in the comping range.

---

92   UNIT 14   Lesson 58

Resolutions and Voice Leading

The iiø7, V7(♭9) and tonic minor chords (iMI(MA7) or iMI6/9) in jazz each have a unique color, quite different from their counterparts in major keys. Yet, the resolutions in the ii–V–i minor turnaround are exactly the same as those in major. In other words, the ii–V–i minor turnaround is a circle-of-fifths progression. So, chord 7ths are tendency tones seeking resolution downward into 3rds, and each 3rd is a common tone to the next chord 7th.

It also holds true that 9ths resolve downward into 5ths, which are common tones to ensuing 9ths.

Dig it!—*Tension and release* is an important element in the drama of music, and it is the reason that melodies sound so good when tendency tones are used and resolved. When a tendency tone is a whole step above the resolving note, extra tension and release is achieved by passing through the chromatic half step, as with the natural 9th of iiø7 going to the 5th of V7(♭9) below.

Closed and drop-two voicings for iiø7–V7–i in minor are constructed as expected, using tendency tones and common tones for smooth voice leading. But, the root *is* a permissible note in a ø7 voicing, because it creates tension with the chord 5th, a tritone away.

Exercises

1 Compose melodies to the minor turnaround progressions, using tendency tones and resolution for tension and release.

2 Construct drop-two voicings to the indicated ii–V–i progressions. Indicate the chord symbols; draw arrows to show resolving tones, and straight lines for common tones.

Lesson 59 · UNIT 14 · 93

Jazz Language—Scales for the Half-diminished Chord (ᵒ⁷)

Jazz musicians practice scales as a tool for instrument mastery, and also as "raw material" for melodic ideas. There are two typical scales for ᵒ⁷ melody.

One is the SECOND MODE OF NATURAL MINOR. For instance, since Bᵒ⁷ is iiᵒ⁷ in A minor, that chord uses an A natural minor scale, from B to B.

The other scale for ᵒ⁷ is achieved by raising the second note of the scale shown above. The second note of any scale is the chord 9th, and in this case the raised second degree is the chord's major 9th, which is more consonant.

Dig it!—CD Track 24 has a rhythm section playing Aᵒ⁷ harmony. Try both ᵒ⁷ scales and listen for the subtle difference between them.

Melodies that use the natural minor scale for iiᵒ⁷ stay in a somber tone because the second scale degree is also the 3rd of the minor tonic chord.

The raised 2nd of the altered natural minor scale allows for more emphatic or, perhaps, hopeful melodies. That note resolves downward into the natural 3rd degree of the key.

Exercises

1 For each minor key, indicate the chord symbol for iiᵒ⁷ and construct both scales.

2 Write a melody using tones from the natural minor scale for iiᵒ⁷.

3 Write a melody using the tones from the altered natural minor scale for iiᵒ⁷.

94 · UNIT 14 · Lesson 60

Jazz Language—Harmonic-Minor Scale & Lick for V7(♭9)

A very effective and often-used scale for V7(♭9) is the 5TH MODE OF HARMONIC MINOR (in other words, harmonic minor of the tonic). A unique feature of harmonic minor is the augmented second contained within it. These two notes happen to be the 3rd and ♭9th of the V7(♭9) chord, so just playing the scale brings the chord alive.

The harmonic-minor scale is often played in descending order, and is very consonant when started on a beat, beginning with the 3rd, 5th, 7th, or ♭9th of the chord.

The HARMONIC-MINOR LICK is based on the harmonic-minor scale, and skips from the 3rd up to the ♭9th of V7(♭9), and then moves down the scale, resolving 7–3 into the tonic. This line is equally effective whether used over just the V7(♭9) harmony, or both the iiᵒ⁷ and V7(♭9).

The harmonic-minor lick works just as well with a descending skip from the 3rd to ♭9th.

A variation of the lick arpeggiates from the 3rd to ♭9th, and then resolves directly into the 5th of tonic.

Melodic ideas based on harmonic minor are very important for dominant harmony in jazz, and you will hear endless examples on great jazz recordings from all eras.

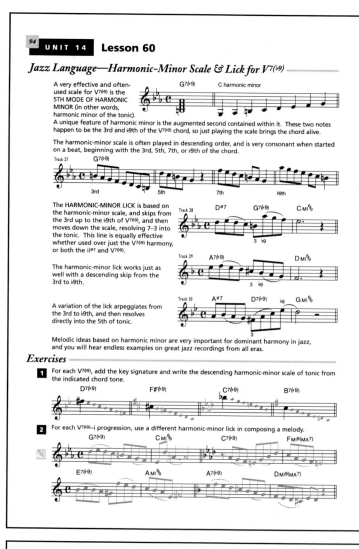

Exercises

1 For each V7(♭9), add the key signature and write the descending harmonic-minor scale of tonic from the indicated chord tone.

2 For each V7(♭9)–i progression, use a different harmonic-minor lick in composing a melody.

Ear Training for Lessons 56–60 · UNIT 14 · 95

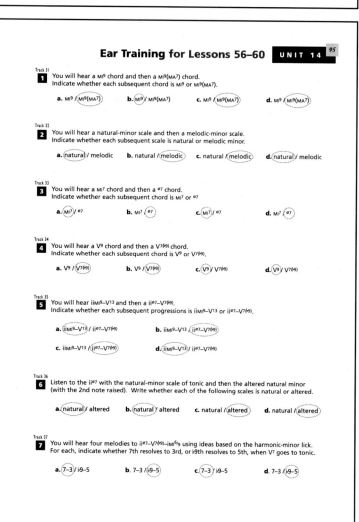

1 You will hear a MI⁹ chord and then a MI⁹(MA7) chord. Indicate whether each subsequent chord is MI⁹ or MI⁹(MA7).

a. MI⁹ / (MI⁹(MA7)) **b.** (MI⁹) / MI⁹(MA7) **c.** MI⁹ / (MI⁹(MA7)) **d.** MI⁹ / (MI⁹(MA7))

2 You will hear a natural-minor scale and then a melodic-minor scale. Indicate whether each subsequent scale is natural or melodic minor.

a. (natural) / melodic **b.** natural / (melodic) **c.** natural / (melodic) **d.** (natural) / melodic

3 You will hear a MI⁷ chord and then a ᵒ⁷ chord. Indicate whether each subsequent chord is MI⁷ or ᵒ⁷.

a. (MI⁷) / ᵒ⁷ **b.** MI⁷ / (ᵒ⁷) **c.** (MI⁷) / ᵒ⁷ **d.** MI⁷ / (ᵒ⁷)

4 You will hear a V⁹ chord and then a V7(♭9) chord. Indicate whether each subsequent chord is V⁹ or V7(♭9).

a. V⁹ / (V7(♭9)) **b.** V⁹ / (V7(♭9)) **c.** (V⁹) / V7(♭9) **d.** (V⁹) / V7(♭9)

5 You will hear iiMI⁹–V13 and then a iiᵒ⁷–V7(♭9). Indicate whether each subsequent progressions is iiMI⁹–V13 or iiᵒ⁷–V7(♭9).

a. (iiMI⁹–V13) / iiᵒ⁷–V7(♭9) **b.** iiMI⁹–V13 / (iiᵒ⁷–V7(♭9)) **c.** iiMI⁹–V13 / (iiᵒ⁷–V7(♭9)) **d.** (iiMI⁹–V13) / iiᵒ⁷–V7(♭9)

6 Listen to the iiᵒ⁷ with the natural-minor scale of tonic and then the altered natural minor (with the 2nd note raised). Write whether each of the following scales is natural or altered.

a. (natural) / altered **b.** (natural) / altered **c.** natural / (altered) **d.** natural / (altered)

7 You will hear four melodies to iiᵒ⁷–V7(♭9)–iMI⁶/₉ using ideas based on the harmonic-minor lick. For each, indicate whether 7th resolves to 3rd, or ♭9th resolves to 5th, when V⁷ goes to tonic.

a. (7–3) / ♭9–5 **b.** 7–3 / (♭9–5) **c.** (7–3) / ♭9–5 **d.** 7–3 / (♭9–5)

96 · UNIT 14 · Review of Lessons 56–60

1 The tonic chord for minor keys is MI⁷ or MI⁹.   True / (False)

2 The jazz minor scale uses the ascending form of ___melodic___ minor in both directions.

3 The ii chord for minor is ___iiᵒ⁷___ and the V⁷ chord is ___V7(♭9)___.

4 The natural minor scale of tonic, which is used for iiᵒ⁷ chords, can be altered by raising the ___2nd___ scale degree over the root of iiᵒ⁷.

5 For each minor key, write rootless iMI⁹(MA7) and iMI⁶/₉ chords with the 3rd on the bottom. Indicate chord symbols above the staff.

6 Resolve each iiᵒ⁷ chord to the best inversion of V7(♭9). Indicate chord symbols above the staff.

7 Indicate whether each melody uses the natural minor or altered natural-minor scale for iiᵒ⁷.

___altered___ ___natural___ ___natural___

8 For each progression, write the harmonic-minor lick.

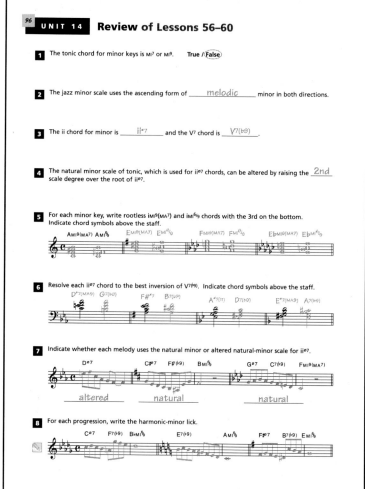

Lesson 61 — UNIT 15 — 97

Turnaround to iv in Minor Keys

You learned in Book 2, Lesson 39, that jazz songs in major keys often tonicize the IV chord with a ii–V turnaround. The turnaround to iv is also typical for jazz tunes in minor keys. The iv chord for minor keys is itself a minor 7th chord.

The TURNAROUND TO iv IN MINOR is vø7–I7(♭9)–ivMI7, so alterations must be made to both the diatonic v and i chords. The diatonic v7 chord in minor keys is a MI7 chord, so the 5th is flatted for vø7 (ii/iv).

Of course, tonic chords in minor keys are minor. So, the diatonic 3rd must be raised to get a dominant I7 chord (V7/iv). The 9th of this chord is characteristically flatted, resulting in a dominant 7(♭9) chord.

The iiø7–V7(♭9) turnaround to iv in C minor looks and sounds like ii–V–i in the key of F minor, although, in this case, the FMI7 is not altered to be a tonic.

Melodies to the turnaround to iv should emphasize the non-diatonic pitches, for instance the 5th of vø7, which is a 1/2 step above tonic in the key (this same note is ♭9 of I7(♭9)). The other important chromatic note is the raised 3rd of I7. Both of these notes are in the harmonic minor of iv, so harmonic-minor language is very effective.

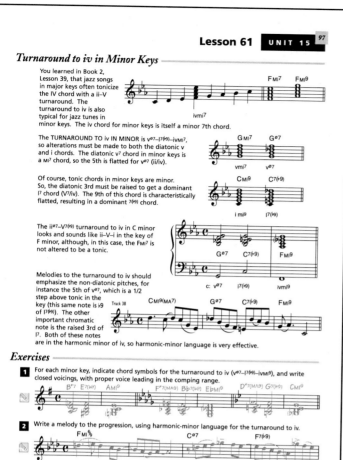

Exercises

1 For each minor key, indicate chord symbols for the turnaround to iv (vø7–I7(♭9)–ivMI9), and write closed voicings, with proper voice leading in the comping range.

2 Write a melody to the progression, using harmonic-minor language for the turnaround to iv.

---

98 — UNIT 15 — Lesson 62

Minor Turnback, VI7–V7(♭9)–i Cadence

You learned with major keys that when a chorus ends on the tonic chord, a I–VI–ii–V turnaround progression cycles back around to tonic for the next chorus. Jazz musicians similarly employ the MINOR TURNBACK for tunes in minor keys. The VI chord in the minor turnback is half-diminished, based on the raised 6th degree. So the entire progression is i–#viø7–iiø7–V7(♭9). Notice that #viø7 has all the same notes as iMI6!

The minor turnback has been used by composers in various ways. For instance, Jerome Kern's composition "Yesterdays" begins with a minor turnback.

A variation on the minor turnback uses a dominant quality III7 chord in place of #viø7.

Another peculiarity of minor keys is that a dominant quality VI chord often substitutes for iiø7 in a turnaround progression. The VI7–V7(♭9)–i CADENCE creates a more "bluesy" sound. The diatonic VI chord in minor is a Major 7th (VIMA7), so the 7th must be flatted to create a dominant VI7 chord.

The natural 9th and 13th of VI7 are diatonic, so VI9 and VI13 chords are usual. A ♭9 extension of VI7 is avoided because that note implies a chord functioning as a dominant (V7), and in this context VI7 is substituting for ii. Additionally, #11ths are viable extensions. Notice that VI7 resolves to V7 in much the same way as ii does, with voices moving stepwise down. The notes of the VI7 chord cause solo ideas to sound naturally bluesy.

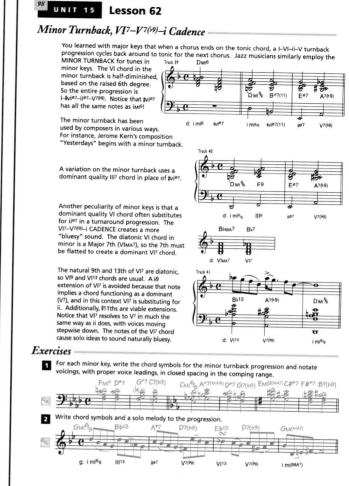

Exercises

1 For each minor key, write the chord symbols for the minor turnback progression and notate voicings, with proper voice leadings, in closed spacing in the comping range.

2 Write chord symbols and a solo melody to the progression.

Lesson 63 — UNIT 15 — 99

Blues Scale in Minor Keys, Minor Pentatonic & Pentatonic/Blues Scales

Melodies for minor turnbacks and turnarounds may be blues related, rather than focusing on each chord change. In Book 1, Lesson 25, you learned about the BLUES SCALE and it is exactly the same for parallel minor and major keys (e.g., C minor and C major). Of course, the notes that are ♭3 and ♭7 in major are diatonic in minor.

The MINOR PENTATONIC SCALE is the pentatonic scale from the relative major, so the D minor pentatonic scale has the same notes as the F major pentatonic scale. Minor pentatonic is a mildly bluesy sound, since all of the notes are also in the blues scale.

The notes of the blues scale for a minor key can be used in the relative major to create another blues sound. For instance, the notes of the E blues scale can be used in G major (the relative major of E minor). This scale is called the PENTATONIC/BLUES SCALE because it contains all the notes of major pentatonic, plus a flatted 3rd to the key (1, 2, ♭3, 3, 5, 6).

Dig it!—As with the blues scale, the pentatonic/blues scale isn't meant to *make the changes*, but rather create a bluesy pallet of sound. The scale tones 6, ♭3, and 1 are an appealing and often-used subset of the scale.

Exercises

1 Compose melodies to the turnbacks using blues and minor pentatonic scale materials.

2 Bracket the melody line that uses the pentatonic/blues scale and label the scale tones used.

---

100 — UNIT 15 — Ear Training for Lessons 61–63

Track 45
1 You will hear four progressions in minor keys.
For each, indicate in which measure a turnaround to iv begins.

   a. measure _3_   **b.** measure _3_   **c.** measure _4_   **d.** measure _2_

Track 46
2 You will hear four melodies to the progression iMI6/9–vø7–I7(♭9)–ivMI7.
In each turnaround to iv, indicated whether the melody uses the raised 3rd of I7(♭9).

   a. yes /(no)   **b.**(yes)/ no   **c.**(yes)/ no   **d.** yes /(no)

Track 47
3 Listen to the i–#viø7–iiø7–V7(♭9) turnback and then a i–III13–iiø7–V7(♭9) turnback.
Identify whether each subsequent turnback uses #viø7 or III13.

   a. #viø7 /(III13)   **b.**(#viø7)/ III13   **c.**(#viø7)/ III13   **d.** #viø7 /(III13)

Track 48
4 Listen to the blues scale and the minor pentatonic scale.
Indicate whether each melody uses blues or minor pentatonic.

   a.(blues)/ minor pentatonic   **b.** blues /(minor pentatonic)

   c. blues /(minor pentatonic)   **d.**(blues)/ minor pentatonic

Track 49
5 Listen to the blues scale and the pentatonic blues scale (for major keys).
Indicate whether each melody uses the blues or pentatonic blues scale.

   a. blues /(pentatonic blues)   **b.** blues /(pentatonic blues)

   c.(blues)/ pentatonic blues   **d.** blues /(pentatonic blues)

Track 50
6 Listen to iiø7–V7(♭9)–iMI6/9 and VI13–V7(♭9)–iMI6/9.
Write whether each subsequent turnaround uses iiø7 or VI13.

   a. iiø7 /(VI13)   **b.** iiø7 /(VI13)   **c.**(iiø7)/ VI13   **d.** iiø7 /(VI13)

Track 51
7 Listen to the chord progression (played three times) and write the remaining chord symbols.

   GMI6/9   _E#7_   _A#7_   _D7(♭9)_   _DMI6/9_   _D#7_   _G7(♭9)_   _CMI9_

Review of Lessons 61–63 UNIT 15 101

1 The turnaround to iv in minor keys uses the chords ___V⁰⁷___ - ___I⁷(♭⁹)___ - ___IVMI⁷___

2 For a turnaround to iv in minor, the diatonic ___5th___ of vMI⁷ must be flatted, and the diatonic 3rd of iMI⁷ must be ___raised___.

3 In the VI⁷–V⁷–i turnaround, the altered 9th is preferred for VI⁷.   True /(False)

4 The second chord of a minor turnback can be either ___#vi⁰⁷___ or ___III⁷___.

5 For major keys, licks using the pentatonic blues scale often emphasize tones ___6___, ___♭3___, and ___1___.

6 Complete each turnaround to the iv progression and indicate chord symbols between the staves. On the top staff, write a melody for each progression.

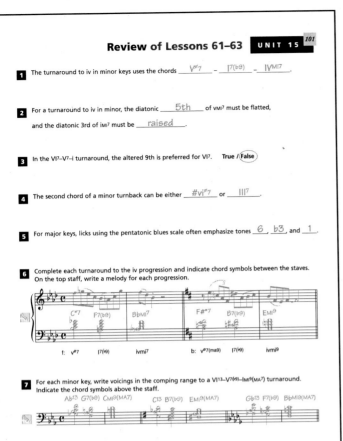

f: V⁰⁷   I⁷(♭⁹)   ivMI⁷   b: V⁰⁷(ma9)   I⁷(♭⁹)   ivMI⁹

7 For each minor key, write voicings in the comping range to a VI13–V7♭9–IMI⁷(MA7) turnaround. Indicate the chord symbols above the staff.

Ab13 G7(♭9) CMI9(MA7)   C13 B7(♭9) EMI9(MA7)   G♭13 F7(♭9) B♭MI9(MA7)

8 For each major key, write the pentatonic blues scale.

Turnarounds to III and VI in Minor Keys

The major and minor seventh chords that are diatonic to major and minor keys serve as secondary tonics in jazz songs. A ii–V turnaround to any of these diatonic chords "tonicizes" that chord as a temporary new home. Minor keys have three major diatonic triads within them, over scale degrees 3, 6, and 7. Of those, the III and VI chords also have major 7ths.

E♭MA7   A♭MA7   A7
c: IIIMA7   VIMA7

Each diatonic major chord should have its own iiMI⁷ chord (or iiMI⁹), and dominant V⁹ chord (or V13). The TURNAROUND TO III in minor keys is entirely diatonic, ivMI⁹–VII13–IIIMA7 (ii/III–V/III–III), because III is the relative major in minor keys. So, the turnaround to III in C minor is the same as ii–V–I in E♭ major, and this progression sounds like a temporarily modulation to the relative key.

Track 52
FMI⁹ B♭13 E♭MA⁹
c: IIIMI⁷ ivMA⁷   VII⁷   IIIMA⁹

The TURNAROUND TO VI requires some chromatic alteration. The turnaround to VI is VIIMI⁷–III⁷–VIMA⁷, and the same chromatic pitch (1/2 step above tonic) is the 3rd of VII and the 7th of III.

Track 53
B♭MI⁹ E♭13 A♭MA⁹
c: III⁷ VIMA⁷ viiMI⁷   viiMI⁷ III13 VIMA⁹

Dig it!—Check out this progression that turns around to VI and III before returning to the minor tonic. You can hear the music going to new major "homes." Notice how the melody *finds the chromatics*, emphasizing the non-diatonic tones.

GMI⁹ FMI⁷ B♭⁷ E♭MA⁹   CMI⁹ F13 B♭MA⁹   A⁰⁷ D7♭⁹ GMI⁶⁄₉
g: iiMI⁹   IV(MI⁷)   VII⁷   IIIMA⁹   IVMI⁹   VII⁷   IIIMA⁹   iiⁱ⁰⁷   V7♭⁹   imi⁶⁄₉

Songs such as "Autumn Leaves," "Summertime," "Beautiful Love" and "What's New" all tonicize diatonic major chords in minor keys.

Exercises

1 Indicate chord symbols and write drop-two voicings for this progression.

DMI⁶⁄₉   CMI⁹   F13   B♭MA⁹   GMI⁹ C15 FMA⁹   E⁰⁷ A7(♭9) DMI⁹(MA7)
d: iMI⁶⁄₉   viiMI⁹   III13   VIMA⁹   ivMI⁹ VII13 IIIMA⁹   iiⁱ⁰⁷ V7(♭9) imi⁹(MA7)

2 Write a solo that *finds the chromatics* to the progression.

EMI⁶⁄₉   AMI⁹   D13   G⁶⁄₉
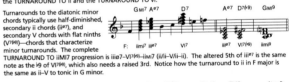
DMI⁹   G13   CMA⁹   B7(♭9)   EMI⁶⁄₉

Minor 12-Bar Blues Progression UNIT 16 103

There is a 12-bar blues progression in minor, and songs such as "Mr. P.C." and "Coming Home Baby" ARE MINOR BLUES compositions. Wayne Shorter's "Footprints" is a variation of minor blues. The standard MINOR 12-BAR BLUES PROGRESSION is below. A review of the major 12-bar blues can be found in Book 2 (Lesson 50).

Measures 1–4: As with major blues, this phrase establishes tonic and moves towards subdominant. Unlike major blues, measure 2 of minor blues is less likely to feature the iv chord. But just as with major blues, ii–V to iv is often found in measure 4.

CMI⁶⁄₉   (FMI⁷)*   CMI⁶⁄₉   (G⁰⁷   C7(♭9)

Measures 5–8: Just like major, this phrase begins on the iv chord, returns to tonic, and sets up a final turnaround. The unusual feature of minor blues is that it often features a ii–V back to tonic in measure 6. Measure 8 can be a turnaround to set up the VI chord.

5 FMI⁷   (D⁰⁷   G7(♭9)   CMI⁶⁄₉   (B♭MI⁹   E♭13)

Measures 9–12: This phrase serves the same function as its counterpart in major, turnaround to tonic. However, minor blues most often uses the "bluesy" alternate cadence, VI⁷–V⁷–i. Of course, a turnback in the last two measures can set up additional choruses.

9 A♭13   G7(♭9)   CMI⁶⁄₉   (E♭⁹   D⁰⁷   G7(♭9))

*Chords in parentheses are optional.

Track 54
Track 54 features the entire minor 12-bar blues progression.

Exercises

1 Notate the minor blues progression and compose a solo based on language you have learned.

FMI⁶⁄₉   C⁰⁷   F7(♭9)

B♭MI⁷   G⁰⁷   C7(♭9)   FMI⁶⁄₉   E♭MI⁷   A♭13
D♭13   C7(♭9)   FMI⁶⁄₉   D⁰⁷   G⁰⁷   C7(♭9)

Minor Turnarounds in Major Keys—to ii and vi

When a song in a minor key tonicizes a diatonic major chord (III or VI), a more hopeful energy is injected into the somber mood. Conversely, a song in major can become more reflective or melancholy when it tonicizes diatonic minor chords. Minor chords result over scale degrees 2, 3 and 6 in major keys and these chords can be tonicized with minor turnarounds.

GMI⁷ AMI⁷ DMI⁷
F: iiMI⁷ iiiMI⁷   viMI⁷

Let's examine the two most popular minor turnarounds in jazz for major keys: the TURNAROUND TO ii and the TURNAROUND TO vi.

Turnarounds to the diatonic minor chords typically use half-diminished, secondary ii chords (iiⁱ⁰⁷), and secondary V chords with flat ninths (V7♭9)—chords that characterize minor turnarounds. The complete TURNAROUND TO iiMI⁷ progression is iiiⁱ⁰⁷–VI7♭9–iiMI⁷ (ii/ii–V/ii–ii). The altered 5th of iiⁱ⁰⁷ is the same note as the ♭9 of VI7♭9, which also needs a raised 3rd. Notice how the turnaround to ii in F major is the same as ii–V to tonic in G minor.

GMI⁷ Aⁱ⁰⁷   D7   Aⁱ⁰⁷ D7(♭9) GMI⁹
F: iiMI⁷ iiiⁱ⁰⁷   VI⁷   iiⁱ⁰⁷ VI7(♭9) iiMI⁹

The song, "It Could Happen to You" by Johnny Burke and Jimmy Van Heusen begins with a tonic chord followed immediately by a turnaround to ii. Songs with the turnaround to ii progression often continue in the circle of fifths until reaching tonic, iii–VI–ii–V–I, and this progression ends many songs. The above example replaces iii⁰⁷ with iiiMI⁷, which is common when the progression continues to tonic.

Track 55
CMI⁹   F7(♭9)   B♭MI⁹   E♭13   A♭MA⁹
A♭:   iiMI⁹   VI7(♭9)   iiMI⁹   V13   IMA⁹

The TURNAROUND TO viMI⁷ is a tonicization of relative minor, and is so common that it appears in over 60% of the jazz standard songs! The entire turnaround to vi progression is viiⁱ⁰⁷–III7♭9–viMI⁷, and requires the chromatic alteration of only one note (the 3rd of III7♭9).

E7   AMI⁷ B⁰⁷   B⁰⁷ E7(♭9)   AMI⁹
C: III⁷   viMI⁷ viiⁱ⁰⁷   viiⁱ⁰⁷ III7(♭9)   viMI⁹

Dig it!—Do you hear a more somber tone when the melody turns around to vi in Track 56?

Track 56
DMI⁹   G9   CMA⁹   B⁰⁷   E7(♭9)   AMI⁹
C: iiMI⁹   V9   IMA⁹   viiⁱ⁰⁷   III7(♭9)   vi, i⁹

Exercises

1 Find two songs in a jazz fake book with turnarounds to both ii and vi.
It Could Happen to You & Darn That Dream

2 Notate chord symbols to the progression and write a solo with characteristic jazz language.

GMI⁹   C13   FMA⁹   A⁰⁷   D7(♭9)   GMI⁹   E7   A7(♭9)   DMI⁹
F: iiMI⁹   V13   IMA⁹   iiiⁱ⁰⁷   VI7(♭9)   iiMI⁹   VII⁷   III7(♭9)   viMI⁹

Lesson 67 UNIT 16 105

Minor Turnaround in Major Keys—to iii,
Deceptive Cadence (Backdoor Cadence)

While either a turnaround to ii or vi (or often both) can be found in almost every jazz standard song in a major key, tonicization of the diatonic iiimi7 chord is less common. The relative rarity is due to the fact that for ii–V7 to iii, the secondary ii chord is based on a chromatic pitch a tritone away from tonic. So, the TURNAROUND TO iiimi7 progression is less seamless than with other diatonic turnarounds. The entire turnaround to iii is ♯ivø7–VII7(♭9)–iiimi7. The turnaround to iii in C major is virtually the same as ii–V–i in E minor.

Turnarounds to iii are very expressive and beautiful, and found in tunes like "It Could Happen to You" by Johnny Burke and Jimmy Van Heusen and "There Will Never Be Another You" by Mack Gordon and Harry Warren. Notice how the 7th scale degree becomes more expressive when harmonized as the 11th of iiø7/iii.

Tunes that tonicize iii often continue in the circle of fifths to tonic. In fact, this progression represents the entire circle of fifths in a major key (♯ivø7–VII7–iiimi7–VI7–iimi7–V7–Ima7)!

The notes of the iiimi7 chord are all part of the Ima9 chord. It is called a DECEPTIVE CADENCE or BACKDOOR CADENCE when a ii–V progression to iii resolves to Ima7 instead. Notice that the 7th of VII7 (V7/iii) still resolves downward in a backdoor cadence.

Exercises

1 Write a melody to the progression and indicate the chord symbols above the staff.

2 For each major key, write the chord symbols for a deceptive cadence using the turnaround to iii. Then, notate chord voicings in closed spacing, with proper voice leading in the comping range.

---

106 UNIT 16 **Ear Training for Lessons 64–67**

Track 60
1 You will hear imi6/9 followed by the turnaround to III, then imi6/9 followed by turnaround to VI. For each subsequent example, indicate if the turnaround is to III or VI.

  a. III (VI)   **b.** III (VI)   **c.** (III) VI   **d.** (III) VI

Track 61
2 Listen to the progression and indicate in which measure the turnaround to VI begins.

  measure __4__

Track 62
3 Listen to the solo to a minor blues progression. Write whether the following harmonic and melodic devices are present.

  Minor pentatonic .... (yes) / no
  Blues scale .... (yes) / no
  VI-V-I turnaround .... yes / (no)
  Turnback .... (yes) / no
  Harmonic-minor melody ... (yes) / no
  Turnaround to iv .... yes / (no)

Track 63
4 You will hear Ima9 followed by the turnaround to vimi7, then Ima9 followed by turnaround to iimi9. For each subsequent example, indicate if the turnaround is to vi or ii.

  a. vi (ii)   **b.** (vi) ii   **c.** vi (ii)   **d.** (vi) ii

Track 64
5 Listen to the turnaround to iiimi7, followed by the same progression deceptively resolving to Ima9. Indicate whether each subsequent progression resolves to iii or I.

  a. (iiimi7) / Ima9   **b.** iiimi7 / (Ima9)   **c.** iiimi7 / (Ima9)   **d.** (iiimi7) / Ima9

Track 65
6 Listen to the solo and fill in the missing notes.

Review of Lessons 64–67 UNIT 16 107

1 The three diatonic major chords in minor keys are built on scale degrees __III__, __VI__, and __VII__.

2 A turnaround to III in minor sounds like a temporary modulation to __relative major__.

3 Turnarounds to minor chords in major keys should use __♯7__ chords for secondary ii, and __7(♭9)__ chords for secondary V.

4 After a turnaround to ii, the next likely chord is __V__.

5 More often than not, a standard song in major will contain a turnaround to vi. (True) / False

6 When a turnaround to iii resolves to __I__ instead, this is called a deceptive, or __back door__ cadence.

7 Write chord symbols and a solo melody to the progression.

8 Write the chord symbols for a minor blues progression in E minor.

9 Write closed-spaced voicings, with proper voice leading in the comping range to the progression.

10 For each major key, write chord symbols and proper voicings for the turnaround to iiimi7.

---

108 UNIT 17 **Lesson 68**

Altered Dominant Chords (Valt)

Jazz musicians love to use a variety of chromatic pitches to alter dominant chords and almost always do so. After all, 10 of the 12 chromatic pitches are chord tones to any dominant chord!

The alterations to dominant chords that you already use include the 13th, ♯11th (typical for II7), and flatted 9th (minor turnarounds). Adding a SHARP 9TH (V7(♯9)) is very bluesy and intense, because the note is enharmonically a blue note, and it is a 1/2 step below the chord 3rd. A three-note voicing of just the 3rd, 7th, and ♯9 is very effective. Musicians often misspell the ♯9 by writing that note as a ♭10 to show the bluesy quality. This chord was a favorite of guitarist, Jimi Hendrix.

Dig it!—The sharp 9th has no tendency to resolve down to the 5th of tonic, so melodies with this note can include the ♭9 to achieve resolution.

The FLAT 13TH (enharmonic to ♯5) is another preferred alteration of dominant harmony, and the note resolves downward to the 9th of the tonic chord. Dominant flat 13th chords (V♭13) always include altered (♯ or ♭) 9ths.

The ALTERED DOMINANT CHORD contains the ♭13th and *both* the flat and sharp 9ths (♯11 is optional; otherwise there will be no 11th). The chord symbol is ALT (e.g., Calt). In voicings, the chord 5th is omitted in favor of 3rd, 7th and altered notes. Also, one of the 9ths may be omitted to simplify a voicing.

Exercises

1 Label and draw a line pointing to each altered tone in any voicing or melody from the examples in this lesson.

2 *Dig it!*—Dominant chords functioning in the circle of fifths can always use alterations for added color (such as V7(♭9), V7(♯9), V13(♭9), Valt, etc.). For the major keys below, write chord symbols and closed voicings for turnback progressions, using the indicated, colorful dominant chords.

Lesson 69 · UNIT 17 · 109

Jazz Language—Diminished Scale for Dominant Chords & Altered Dominant Cell

With so many possibilities for colorful alteration, dominant chords are *where the fun is* for jazz improvisers and composers. For example, a V7(♭9) chord has a vii°7 contained in it . . .

. . . so the diminished scale of vii°7 is effective for V7(♭9) (and V7(♭9)) chords. As an example, a rootless G7(♭9) is essentially B°7 (or A♭°7), so dominant chords use the DIMINISHED SCALE A HALF STEP UP. Every note in the scale is a chord tone to the dominant.

Track 67 G7 A♭ diminished scale

The diminished scale up a half step is also called the HALF-WHOLE DIMINISHED SCALE because, as you notice above, when you start the A♭ diminished scale on G, you are beginning with a 1/2 step, followed by a whole step, and then alternating 1/2 and whole steps.

The symmetrical licks from the diminished scale serve as great building blocks for melody to dominant chords. As presented in Book 2, Lesson 45, these motives are derived from using the 1/2 step below and the whole step above each diminished chord tone in sequential patterns.

Track 68 G7(♭9)(A♭°7)

The ALTERED DOMINANT CELL is composed of the notes from root to 3rd of a dominant chord, using the half-whole diminished scale. Lines constructed from the altered dominant cell often end with a 7–3 resolution to tonic.

Track 69 G7(♭9)

Exercises

1 For each dominant chord, write the diminished scale up a half step (half-whole diminished scale), and circle the altered dominant cell within the scale.

2 Write a melody, using diminished language for the dominant chords.

---

110 · UNIT 17 · Lesson 70

Jazz Language—Altered Dominant Lick and Scale

The ♭9th, 3rd, and ♭13th of the altered dominant chord combine to form a minor triad, up a 1/2 step. So, for instance, a G^ALT chord has an A♭ minor triad incorporated within.

The ALTERED DOMINANT LICK uses the minor triad a half step above an altered dominant chord in a descending triplet arpeggio. These notes are the ♭9, ♭9, ♭13, and 3rd of the dominant chord, and ♭9 typically resolves to the 5th of tonic at the end of the lick.

Track 70 G^ALT C^MA9

Jazz musicians love to create melodies from the altered dominant lick, which is also called the "Cry Me a River" lick, due to its similarity to the classic Arthur Hamilton song.

F^ALT B♭^MA9

All the notes of a MELODIC-MINOR SCALE UP A HALF STEP are chord tones to the altered dominant chord (ALT).

Track 71 G^ALT A♭ melodic minor

This altered dominant scale has two other names, SUPER LOCRIAN and DIMINISHED/WHOLE TONE (because the bottom of the scale is the same as diminished and the top is all whole steps). It can be used to create a great variety of melodies.

Exercises

1 For each dominant chord, write the altered dominant lick.

2 For each dominant chord, write the melodic-minor scale up a half step.

Note: Other note spellings may be used.

3 Write a melody to the progression, using altered dominant language from this lesson.

Lesson 71 · UNIT 17 · 111

Step-Down Progression

A delightful chord sequence that has been used too rarely in jazz songs is the step-down progression. The STEP-DOWN PROGRESSION tonicizes chords successively down whole steps, by altering tonics into ii chords. The great standards, "How High the Moon" by Nancy Hamilton and Morgan Lewis and "I'll Remember April" by Don Raye, Gene De Paul and Patricia Johnston both begin with step-down progressions.

A step-down sequence begins on IMA7. Lowering the 3rd and 7th of the chord results in iMI7, which sounds like iiMI7 of the major 7th chord a step below (subtonic - ♭VII). Next, a dominant IV7 becomes V of ♭VIIMA7 (V/♭VII). This progression is *borrowed* from the turnaround to VII in the parallel minor (i.e., FMA7 is ♭VII in G major, but diatonic VII in G minor).

G: IMA9 imi9 IV13 ♭VIIMA9

Next, the ♭VII chord is altered, lowering the 3rd and 7th to become iiMI7 of the ♭VI chord, one step below. ♭III7 is V of ♭VIMA7 (V/♭VI). This progression borrows from the turnaround to VI in the parallel minor (i.e., E♭MA7 is ♭VI in G major, but diatonic VI in G minor).

♭viimi9 ♭III13 ♭VIMA9

The dominant chords in the step-down progression usually have natural 13ths, and natural or ♭9ths, highlighting the warmth of the non-diatonic major chords to follow.

Dig it!—The appeal of the step-down progression is in the ironic sound of chords changing from MA7 to MI7. So, improvisers tend to emphasize the 3rds and 7ths, highlighting these shifts in chord quality. In fact, any melody to one of the major chords can be repeated, with 3rd and 7th lowered for the ensuing MI7 chord.

Track 72 GMA9 GMI9 C13 FMA9 FMI9 B♭13(♭9) E♭MA9

Track 73 Once the step-down progression arrives at ♭VIMA7, it almost always proceeds directly to iiMI7 (almost the circle of fifths, a diminished 5th away), or to V7. Track 73 plays the step-down progression, followed by ii–V–I.

Exercises

1 Write the chord symbols for a step-down progression in the major key below. Also write closed voicings, with proper voice leading, in the comping range.

B♭MA9 B♭MI9 E♭13 A♭MA9 A♭MI9 D♭13 G♭MA9

2 Write a melody to the step-down progression, emphasizing the changing 3rds and 7ths.

FMA9 FMI9 B♭13 E♭MA9 E♭MI9 A♭13(♭9) D♭MA9

---

112 · UNIT 17 · Ear Training for Lessons 68–71

Track 74
1 Listen to the V7(♭9) chord and the V7(♯9) chord. Write whether each subsequent chord is V7(♭9) or V7(♯9).

a. V7(♭9) / **V7(♯9)** b. **V7(♭9)** / V7(♯9) c. V7(♭9) / **V7(♯9)** d. V7(♭9) / **V7(♯9)**

Track 75
2 Listen to the diminished scale up a half step (half-whole) and the melodic-minor scale up a half step for dominant harmony. Indicate whether each subsequent scale is diminished or melodic minor.

a. diminished / **melodic minor** b. **diminished** / melodic minor

c. **diminished** / melodic minor d. diminished / **melodic minor**

Track 76
3 You will hear the altered dominant lick resolving ♭9–5 and then again, resolving 7–3 into tonic. Write whether each subsequent melody resolves ♭9–5 or 7–3.

a. **♭9–5** / 7–3 b. ♭9–5 / **7–3** c. **♭9–5** / 7–3 d. ♭9–5 / **7–3**

Track 77
4 You will hear the altered dominant chord in drop-two, and then in closed spacing. Write whether each subsequent chord is closed spaced or drop-two.

a. **closed** / drop-two b. closed / **drop-two**

c. **closed** / drop-two d. closed / **drop-two**

Track 78
5 Listen to the altered dominant cell, resolving 7–3 into tonic. Write whether each melody uses the altered dominant cell.

a. yes / **no** b. yes / **no** c. **yes** / no d. **yes** / no

Track 79
6 You will hear two melodies to step-down progressions. Indicate whether each melody uses the 3rd of each MA7 chord, changing to the lowered 3rd of the following MI7.

a. yes / **no** b. **yes** / no

Review of Lessons 68–71 UNIT 17 [113]

1 A dominant chord with a ♭13th will also include an altered __9th__ .

2 #9 is a tendency tone for a dominant chord, and resolves downward. True / (False)

3 The altered dominant chord (V^ALT) contains these extensions: __♭9__ , __#9__ and __♭13__ .

4 A V7(♭9) chord can use a diminished scale __1/2__ step up from the root, also called __half__ - __whole__ diminished.

5 More often than not, a major-key standard song will contain a turnaround to vi. (True) / False

6 Super Locrian is another name for a __melodic__ __minor__ scale, __1/2__ step up from the root of a dominant chord.

7 The Step-Down Progression tonicizes chords down two successive __whole__ steps from tonic.

8 Write voicings, in the comping range for the indicated dominant chords.

C13(♭9)   F^ALT   E♭^ALT   B♭7(#9)

9 For each V7–I progression, write a melody using either the altered dominant lick or altered dominant cell, as indicated. Be sure that the melody resolves into tonic.

G^ALT   C^MA9   D^ALT   G^MA9   B^ALT   E♭^MA9
lick   cell   lick

10 For each chord, write the half-whole diminished and super Locrian scales.

F^ALT   D♭^ALT   A^ALT
dim.   sup. loc.

11 For the major key below, write the chord symbols and a sequential melody to the step-down progression.

C^MA7   C^MI9   F13   B♭^MA9   B♭^MI9   E♭13   A♭^MA9
C:

---

[114] UNIT 18 Lesson 72

IV–I (Plagal) Progressions, Backdoor Progressions

You learned in Book 1, Lesson 25, about the IV–I PLAGAL CADENCE, which evokes the "amen" at the close of a hymn. You learned in Book 2, Lesson 45, about a variation, the IV6–#iv°7–IMA7/V progression, in which the #iv°7 increases the tendency to resolve to tonic.

Track 80
F6   F#°7   C6/G
C: IV6   #iv°7   I6/V

There are a number of interchangeable variations to the plagal resolution. Equally popular among composers is IVMA–ivMI–I, in which any of the chords can have a 6th or 7th, 9th, etc. This resolution produces a melancholy feeling, or sense of resignation prior to tonic. It is effective when a melody to the IV–I progression establishes a motive with the IV chord that is altered to reflect the ensuing #iv°7 or ivMI.

Track 81
F^MA9   F^MI9   C^MA9
C: IVMA9   ivmi9   IMA9

Since iiiMI7 is contained within IMA9, don't be surprised to find iii substituting for tonic in a IV–I progression. In these instances, the chord changes almost always continue in the circle of fifths toward tonic.

F^MA9   A^MI7   B♭^MA9   B♭^MI9   A^MI7   D7(♭9)
F: IMA9   iiimi7   IVMA9   ivmi9   iiimi7   VI7(♭9)

There is also a backdoor cadence used in some IV–I progressions. Here, the ivMI7, behaving like a secondary ii chord, resolves to ♭VII7 (this is a ii–V, up a minor 3rd from the key). ♭VII7 deceptively resolves to IMA7. So, ivMI7–♭VII7 in C major looks like ii–V in E♭ major, but is functioning as a backdoor cadence to tonic in this variation of the IV–I progression.

Track 82
C^MA9   C^MI9   F13   G^MA9
G: IVMA9   ivmi9   ♭IVMA9   IMA9

Exercises

1 Using a jazz fake book, find and name a song that contains a IV–I progression.
__There Will Never Be Another You / Just Friends / All of Me__

2 For each major key, write chord symbols for the indicated IV–I progression and compose a melody.

E♭6   E°7   B♭MA9/F   A♭MA9   A♭MI6/9   G^MI9   G^MI9   C7   F^MA9
IV6   #iv°7   IMA9/V   IVMA9   ivmi6/9   iiimi9   ivmi9   ♭VII   IMA9

---

[115] UNIT 18 Lesson 73

I–VI Progressions

You know that the "turnback" is I–VI7–iiMI7–V7, with each chord lasting two beats. The I–VI PROGRESSION ("one to six progression") is like a turnback, but the value of the tonic and VI7 chords are both doubled (one measure each). The value of the ensuing ii and V may or may not be doubled. The jazz standards "Doxy" by Sonny Rollins and "They Can't Take that Away from Me" by Ira and George Gershwin begin with this harmonic device.

In these four examples of the I–VI progression, varying chords are used to connect tonic and VI7. In the first instance, iiiMI7 in advance of VI adds a circle-of-fifth pull.

Track 83
F^MA9   A^MI9   D7(♭9)   G^MI9   C13
F: IMA9   iiimi9   VI7(♭9)   iimi9   V13

Secondly, a subdominant (IV) chord (major, minor, or dominant quality) may precede iii in I–VI progressions.

Track 84
F6/9   B♭13   A^MI7   D^ALT   F6/9   B♭MI6/F   A^MI7   D^ALT
F: I6/9   IV13   iiimi7   VIALT   I6/9   ivmi6/9   iiimi7   VIALT

The supertonic chord (iiMI7) may also precede iii. In more elaborate instances, #ii°7 is a passing chord between ii and iii.

Track 85
F^MA9   G^MI7   A^MI7   D^ALT   F^MA9   G^MI7   G#°7   A^MI7   D^ALT
F: IMA9   iimi7   iiimi7   VIALT   IMA9   iimi7   #ii°7   iiimi7   VIALT

Last, an element of blues may be injected into the I–VI progression by using a series of dominant chords in descending 1/2 steps (I–VI7–♭VI7–V7). In fact, a melody composed or improvised to this progression can be more "in the key," as opposed to clearly outlining the changes, highlighting the bluesy effect.

Track 86
F6   E9   E♭9   D7(#9)
F:

Dig It!—The I–VI progression is an example of the freedom of choice jazz improvisers enjoy. Not only are there a variety of interchangeable chord choices, but jazz musicians also get to choose, in the moment, from a palette of chord extensions (natural and altered 9ths and 13ths, and #11ths).

Exercises

1 Locate and name four jazz songs from fake books that employ I–VI progressions.
__Love is Here to Stay__   __There is No Greater Love__
__It Could Happen to You__   __My Romance__

2 For each I–VI progression, write the chord symbols in between the staves, and notate the drop-two voicings.
F^MA9   B♭13   A^MI7   D^ALT   E♭6   F^MI7   F#°7   G^MI7   C^ALT   G^MA9   F#9   F9   E^ALT
IMA9   IV13   iiimi7   VIALT   I6/9   iimi7   #ii°7   iiimi7   VIALT   IMA9   VII7   ♭VII9   VIALT

---

[116] UNIT 18 Lesson 74

ABAC Standard Song Form

In Book 2, Lesson 47, you studied the AABA standard song form. Almost all 32-bar standard songs fall into either AABA or ABAC form. The ABAC STANDARD SONG FORM is organized into two, 16-bar halves, each beginning with an 8-measure 'A' phrase. The second phrase in each half is where variation occurs. However, some tunes have very similar B and C phrases and are more aptly described as ABAB' (the 'prime' ['] denotes a similar, but slightly varied phrase from the original).

The progression to "There Will Never be Another You" by Mack Gordon and Harry Warren typifies the ABAC song form.

The "Another You" progression demonstrates how jazz songs are constructed; stringing together the language you've learned:

The 'A' Phrase—begins on tonic, and then has turnarounds to vi and IV.

The 'B' Phrase—logically uses a IV–I progression (IVMA–ivMI–I). Next is viMI7 leading in turnback fashion to the dominant II7 chord, which always goes to ii–V.

The 'C' (or B') Phrase—begins with the IV–I progression. Next is a backdoor turnaround to tonic (#iv°7–iiiMI7–IMA7), followed by a I–VI progression (IMA7–IV7–iiiMI7–VI7) which, of course, leads to ii–V.

Dig It!—ABAC compositions can be more expressive than AABA because in 16 measures there is more time to develop melodic ideas. Conversely, the melody to an AABA song begins again after eight bars.

Exercises

1 Analyze this solo melody to the second half of the "Another You" progression; identifying melodic devices, scales and significant note choices.

2 Find and list four songs from a jazz fake book in the ABAC (or ABAB) form.
__Just Friends__   __My Romance__
__Here's That Rainy Day__   __It Could Happen to You__

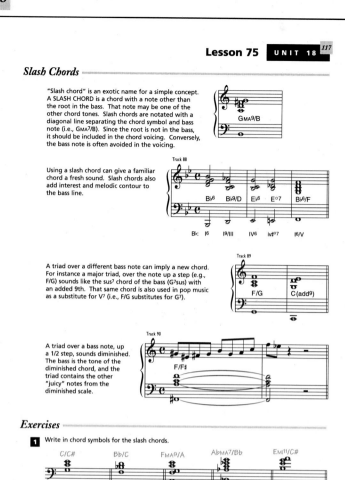

Lesson 75 — UNIT 18 — 117

Slash Chords

"Slash chord" is an exotic name for a simple concept. A SLASH CHORD is a chord with a note other than the root in the bass. That note may be one of the other chord tones. Slash chords are notated with a diagonal line separating the chord symbol and bass note (i.e., GMA7/B). Since the root is not in the bass, it should be included in the chord voicing. Conversely, the bass note is often avoided in the voicing.

Using a slash chord can give a familiar chord a fresh sound. Slash chords also add interest and melodic contour to the bass line.

A triad over a different bass note can imply a new chord. For instance a major triad, over the note up a step (e.g., F/G) sounds like the sus7 chord of the bass (G7sus) with an added 9th. That same chord is also used in pop music as a substitute for V7 (i.e., F/G substitutes for G7).

A triad over a bass note, up a 1/2 step, sounds diminished. The bass is the tone of the diminished chord, and the triad contains the other "juicy" notes from the diminished scale.

Exercises

1 Write in chord symbols for the slash chords.

C/C#   Bb/C   FMA9/A   AbMA7/Bb   EMi11/C#

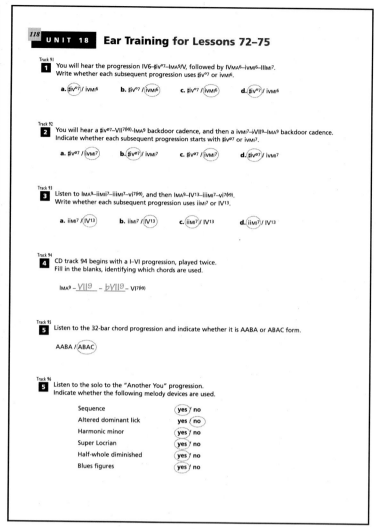

118 — UNIT 18 — Ear Training for Lessons 72–75

Track 91

1 You will hear the progression IV6–#ivº7–IMA9/V, followed by IVMA6–ivMi6–IIIMi7. Write whether each subsequent progression uses #ivº7 or ivMi6.

a. (#ivº7) / ivMi6   b. #ivº7 /(ivMi6)   c. #ivº7 /(ivMi6)   d. (#ivº7) / ivMi6

Track 92

2 You will hear a #ivº7–VII7(b9)–IMA9 backdoor cadence, and then a ivMi7–bVII9–IMA9 backdoor cadence. Indicate whether each subsequent progression starts with #ivº7 or ivMi7.

a. #ivº7 /(ivMi7)   b. (#ivº7) / ivMi7   c. #ivº7 /(ivMi7)   d. (#ivº7) / ivMi7

Track 93

3 Listen to IMA9–iiMi7–iiiMi7–vi7(b9), and then IMA9–IV13–iiiMi7–vi7(b9). Write whether each subsequent progression uses iiMi7 or IV13.

a. iiMi7 /(IV13)   b. iiMi7 /(IV13)   c. (iiMi7)/ IV13   d. (iiMi7)/ IV13

Track 94

4 CD track 94 begins with a I–VI progression, played twice. Fill in the blanks, identifying which chords are used.

IMA9 – _VII9_ – _bVII9_ – VI7(b9)

Track 95

5 Listen to the 32-bar chord progression and indicate whether it is AABA or ABAC form.

AABA /(ABAC)

Track 96

5 Listen to the solo to the "Another You" progression. Indicate whether the following melody devices are used.

Sequence	(yes) / no
Altered dominant lick	yes /(no)
Harmonic minor	(yes)/ no
Super Locrian	(yes)/ no
Half-whole diminished	(yes)/ no
Blues figures	(yes)/ no

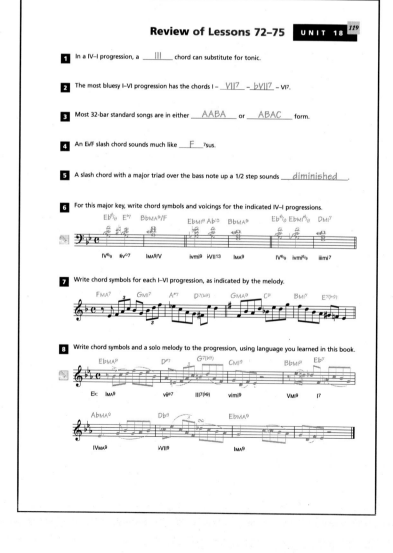

Review of Lessons 72–75 — UNIT 18 — 119

1 In a IV–I progression, a ___III___ chord can substitute for tonic.

2 The most bluesy I–VI progression has the chords I – _VII7_ – _bVII7_ – VI7.

3 Most 32-bar standard songs are in either ___AABA___ or ___ABAC___ form.

4 An Eb/F slash chord sounds much like ___F___ 7sus.

5 A slash chord with a major triad over the bass note up a 1/2 step sounds ___diminished___.

6 For this major key, write chord symbols and voicings for the indicated IV–I progressions.

Eb6/9 Eº7   BbMA9/F   EbMi9 Ab13   BbMA9   Eb6/9 EbMi6/9 DMi7

IV6/9   #ivº7   IMA9/V   ivMj9 bVII13   IMA9   IV6/9   ivMi6/9   iiiMi7

7 Write chord symbols for each I–VI progression, as indicated by the melody.

FMA7   GMi7   A#7   D7(b9)   GMA9   C#   BMi7   E7(b9)

8 Write chord symbols and a solo melody to the progression, using language you learned in this book.

EbMA9   Dº7   G7(b9)   CMi9   BbMi9   Eb7

Eb: IMA9   viiº7   III7(b9)   vimi9   VMi9   I7

AbMA9   Db9   EbMA9

IVMA9   bVII9   IMA9